# DOMESTIC VIOLENCE

## AND
## PROTECTION FROM HARASSMENT

## THE NEW LAW

### SECOND EDITION

# DOMESTIC VIOLENCE

## AND
## PROTECTION FROM HARASSMENT

## THE NEW LAW

### SECOND EDITION

## District Judge Roger Bird LLB

**𝑓𝑗 Family Law**

1997

Published by Family Law
a publishing imprint of
Jordan Publishing Limited
21 St Thomas Street
Bristol BS1 6JS

**British Library Cataloguing-in-Publication Data**

A catalogue record for this book is available
from the British Library.

ISBN 0 85308 450 5

Photoset by Mendip Communications Ltd, Frome, Somerset
Printed and bound in Great Britain by MPG Books Ltd, Bodmin, Cornwall

# PREFACE

In the preface to the first edition of this book, I remarked that it seemed that under Part IV of the Family Law Act 1996 all applications for occupation and non-molestation orders, except those made in the course of existing proceedings, would have to be commenced in Family Proceedings courts. This gave rise to apprehension in some practitioners, not because of any feeling that magistrates were not competent to deal with such matters (there is no reason to think this), but rather because restricting jurisdiction in that way could have led to unnecessary delay. In the event, there is to be a free choice of venue which demonstrates at least that the Lord Chancellor was prepared to listen to and take heed of all points of view.

What was not foreseen at that time was that Parliament would legislate to provide a parallel and overlapping set of remedies in the shape of the Protection from Harassment Act 1997, and that this would be in force earlier than Part IV of the Family Law Act 1996. One presumes that Parliament was aware of the existence of Part IV (although some might regard that view as unduly charitable); whether or not that is so, the representations made as to the possible confusion which might arise were certainly not heeded. It will be interesting to observe the consequences of the overlap between the two statutes.

What is clear is that Part IV is a considerable improvement on what went before. It will now be for all concerned in the family justice system to ensure that the hopes of its proponents are fulfilled.

The law is stated as at 1 October 1997.

Roger Bird
Wells
*5 September 1997*

# CONTENTS

## CHAPTER THREE – OCCUPATION ORDERS

## CHAPTER FOUR – NON-MOLESTATION ORDERS

## CHAPTER FIVE – ARREST AND ENFORCEMENT

## CHAPTER SIX – AMENDMENTS TO THE CHILDREN ACT

## CHAPTER SEVEN – THE EFFECT ON THIRD PARTIES

## CHAPTER EIGHT – TRANSFER OF TENANCIES

## CHAPTER NINE – PROCEDURE

## CHAPTER TEN – THE PROTECTION FROM HARASSMENT ACT 1997

# TABLE OF CASES

**References in the right-hand column are to paragraph numbers.**

# TABLE OF STATUTES

References in the right-hand column are to paragraph numbers.

# TABLE OF STATUTORY INSTRUMENTS

**References in the right-hand column are to paragraph numbers.**

# TABLE OF ABBREVIATIONS

CCR     County Court Rules 1981

DPMCA     Domestic Proceedings and Magistrates' Courts Act 1978

DVMPA     Domestic Violence and Matrimonial Proceedings Act 1976

FPR     Family Proceedings Rules 1991

MCA     Matrimonial Causes Act 1973

MHA     Matrimonial Homes Act 1983

PRFD     Principal Registry of the Family Division

RSC     Rules of the Supreme Court 1965

# CHAPTER ONE

# The Background and Aims of Part IV of the Family Law Act 1996

## Introduction

**1.1**  In May 1992, The Law Commission published a report entitled 'Domestic violence and occupation of the family home' (Law Com No 207; hereafter referred to as 'Law Com'). This was designed to deal with what the report described as:

> 'two distinct but inseparable problems: providing protection for one member of a family against molestation or violence by another and regulating the occupation of the family home where the relationship has broken down whether temporarily or permanently.' (Law Com para 1.1)

It was said that the existing remedies were 'complex, confusing' and that they 'lack integration' (Law Com para 1.2). The report contained a draft Bill which was intended to provide a unified body of law dealing with civil remedies for molestation, violence and occupation of the family home between family members.

In February 1995, the Government published the Bill which became the Family Homes and Domestic Violence Bill, and which adopted, almost entirely, the recommendations in The Law Commission report including the format of the draft Bill in its Appendix A. As will be seen later in this chapter, the 1995 Bill encountered unexpected difficulties at the end of its Parliamentary progress, and was abandoned at the end of 1995, only to reappear as part of the Family Law Bill; in this form, it became Part IV of the Family Law Act 1996. In setting out the background to the Act, it will be necessary to consider the pre-existing law, since the 1995 Act incorporates, in part, quite large sections of previous statutes; as a guide to the issues involved, it will also be necessary to quote extensively from the report to show the reasoning which lay behind many of the changes.

## What is domestic violence?

**1.2**  As the report pointed out (Law Com para 2.3), domestic violence can take many forms:

> 'The term "violence" itself is often used in two senses. In its narrower meaning it describes the use of threat of physical force against a victim in

the form of an assault or battery. But in the context of the family, there is also a wider meaning which extends to abuse beyond the more typical instances of physical assaults to include any form of physical, sexual or psychological molestation or harassment which has a serious detrimental effect upon the health and well-being of the victim, albeit that there is no "violence" involved in the sense of physical force.'

The report goes on to give common examples of such 'non-violent harassment or molestation', covering a very wide range of behaviour. These include pestering, shouting, denigration, installing a mistress in the family home, nuisance phone calls, anonymous letters and filling car locks with superglue; human ingenuity in such matters knows no limits.

'The degree of severity of such behaviour depends less upon its intrinsic nature than upon it being part of a pattern and upon its effect on the victim. Acts of molestation often follow upon previous behaviour which has been violent or otherwise offensive. Calling at the applicant's house on one occasion may not be objectionable. Calling frequently and unexpectedly at unsocial hours when the victim is known to be afraid certainly is.' (Law Com para 2.3)

## The law before the 1995 Bill

**1.3**   The High Court has always had inherent jurisdiction to grant injunctions where it was just and expedient to do so (see Supreme Court Act 1981, s 37(1); this was declaratory of the existing law). By statute (County Court Act 1984, s 38(1)), the county courts have acquired the same powers. Before 1967, this was the sole basis of the court's jurisdiction, although the court was prepared to make quite drastic orders for the protection of spouses and children (see eg *Gurasz v Gurasz* [1970] P 11).

In 1967, the Matrimonial Homes Act 1967 gave wives rights of occupation which could be registered and enforced against third parties, and also gave the courts powers to regulate occupation of the matrimonial home; these provisions were repeated and extended by the Matrimonial Homes Act 1983 (MHA). In 1976, the Domestic Violence and Matrimonial Proceedings Act (DVMPA) empowered courts to grant non-molestation injunctions and to exclude one party from the home; these powers extended to unmarried couples as well as to spouses. Similar powers were conferred on magistrates' courts by the Domestic Proceedings and Magistrates' Courts Act 1978. Under both these Acts, a valuable new power in the form of a power of arrest was available.

Each of these statutes will now be examined in turn, briefly, since the new law will not be completely intelligible without this background knowledge.

At the same time, it should not be forgotten that the inherent jurisdiction of the court has not been, and will not be, lost. It is hoped that the rationalisation of the law which has now taken place will make it unnecessary, and even more unusual than has been the case, to fall back on that somewhat archaic source of jurisprudence. It would seem that the inherent jurisdiction could only be invoked by someone who fell completely outside the scope of legislation. Given its broad terms, and the even broader terms of the Protection from Harassment Act 1997, it would be difficult to establish in any foreseeable situation to which the term 'domestic violence' applied that there was no statutory protection.

### The Domestic Violence and Matrimonial Proceedings Act 1976

**1.4**　Section 1(1) of the DVMPA provided that a county court could, on the application of a party to a marriage, grant an injunction containing one or more of certain provisions; these could restrain the other party from molesting the applicant or any child, exclude the other party from the home or from a specified area in which the home was included, and require the other party to permit the applicant to enter and remain in the home.

By s 2(1), where a judge granted an injunction restraining one party from using violence to the other or to a child, or excluding that party from the home or a specified area, he could, if satisfied that that party had caused actual bodily harm to the applicant or child and was likely to do so again, attach a power of arrest to the injunction. The result of this was that where a power of arrest was attached, a constable could arrest without warrant a person when he had reasonable cause to suspect that person of being in breach of one of the terms of the injunction to which the power attached, and bring him before the judge.

Section 2(2) extended the protection of the Act to 'a man and woman who are living with each other in the same household as husband and wife'.

The DVMPA contained no specific guidelines as to how the court should exercise its jurisdiction, although, as will be seen below, some case-law developed.

### The Matrimonial Homes Act 1983

**1.5**　It should be noted that neither the MHA nor the DVMPA excluded the other; they were intended to co-exist alongside each other.

Section 1 of the MHA dealt with the position where one spouse was entitled to occupy a dwelling-house by virtue of some beneficial estate, or interest, or contract, or by virtue of any enactment giving him the right to remain in occupation, and the other spouse was not so entitled. In such circumstances, the 'non-entitled spouse' had the right, if in occupation, not to be evicted or excluded by the other spouse except by order of the court, and, if not in occupation, the right with leave of the court to enter into and occupy the dwelling-house. These rights were called 'rights of occupation'.

By s 2, as long as one spouse had rights of occupation, either spouse might apply to the court for an order:

(a)　declaring, enforcing, restricting or terminating those rights; or

(b)　prohibiting, suspending or restricting the exercise by either spouse of the right to occupy the dwelling-house; or

(c)   requiring either spouse to permit the exercise by the other of that right.

These were the rights of occupation conferred by the Act. Much of the remainder of the MHA dealt with what might be called the consequential provisions, that is to say the provisions which were necessary to give efficacy to the occupation rights. These included such matters as the right of a person with occupation rights to make or tender payments of rent or mortgage instalments to third parties, and the registration of occupation rights as land charges. Since these have been carried over into the new legislation, they will not be considered in detail here. The MHA also contained provisions as to the transfer of tenancies, which have been enlarged and incorporated into the 1996 Act.

**1.6**   The MHA differed from the DVMPA in the important respect that it contained specific directives to courts as to how they should exercise their discretion to make, or not to make, as the case might be, orders. Section 1(3) directed the court to:

> 'make such order as it thinks just and reasonable having regard to the conduct of the spouses in relation to each other and otherwise, to their respective needs and financial resources, to the needs of any children and to all the circumstances of the case. . . . '

It will be remembered that these instructions applied only to cases to which the MHA applied. It will also be observed that the MHA applied only where the parties were married. As will be seen below, the precise guidelines of the MHA were largely ignored until they came to be considered by the House of Lords in *Richards v Richards* [1984] AC 174.

### The Domestic Proceedings and Magistrates' Courts Act 1978

**1.7**   This Act conferred on magistrates' courts powers similar to, but not absolutely identical with, those contained in the DVMPA. Where the court was satisfied that the respondent had used or threatened violence against the person of the applicant or a child, it could make an order that the respondent should not use or threaten such violence. Where, in addition, it was satisfied that the applicant or child was in danger of being physically injured by the respondent, it could make an order requiring him to leave the matrimonial home or prohibiting him from entering the home. A power of arrest could be attached. An essential difference between the magistrates' court and county court was that a magistrates' court had no power to commit to prison for breach of an undertaking, with the result that there was little point in accepting undertakings.

### Other remedies

**1.8**   The inherent jurisdiction of the court has already been mentioned. In addition, potential applicants who fell outside the various statutory criteria, for example because they were not married, or had never cohabited with the violent party, had to fall back on applications in the course of actions for trespass to the person or to land. It had to be remembered in all such cases that the power of arrest, regarded by many as the most useful protection, was available only when the applicant qualified under the DVMPA.

### The effect of case-law

**1.9** Not surprisingly, applications for orders under the MHA and, even more frequently, the DVMPA, became a regular source of business for the courts, and resulted in quite a wide divergence of approach. Appellate courts therefore found it necessary to set guidelines as to how the discretion of the court should be exercised. Most of this is now of little interest, but mention must be made of two particular developments which have had some effect on the thinking behind the new legislation.

The first of these was the decision of the House of Lords in *Richards v Richards* [1984] AC 174. The facts are unimportant, save that the wife, who had been granted an injunction by the county court ousting the husband from the matrimonial home, had on any reckoning a weak case; the judge had found nothing to criticise in the husband's conduct, but felt obliged to make the order to take account of the needs and welfare of the children and to provide them (and the wife) with a home apart from the husband. In his speech, Lord Hailsham LC said that many of the reported cases had erred in principle. It was strange that in none of them was the statutory basis of the jurisdiction to grant ouster injunctions properly discussed or investigated. The effect of the MHA had been to codify and spell out the jurisdiction of the court in ouster injunctions, and the criteria to be used were those referred to in s 1 (3) (see para **1.6** above) and not any other criteria sometimes treated as paramount by reported decisions of the courts.

In his speech, Lord Brandon said that it was of the utmost importance to appreciate that none of the s 1 (3) factors was necessarily of more weight than the others. All four factors were to be regarded, and the weight to be given to any of them must depend on the facts of the case. Conduct of the applicant was not necessarily, and in all cases, decisive. However, it was an important factor to be weighed in the scales, and, in many cases, it might lead the court to think that it would not be just or reasonable to grant the application.

It is fair to say that, after *Richards*, the courts could no longer approach these cases as a kind of social engineering.

**1.10** The second set of judicial developments dealt with the question of whether, and in what circumstances, an order should be made ex parte, that is to say, not on notice to all parties affected by it. The basic principle is, of course, that no order should be made without giving all parties likely to be affected by it the chance to be heard; this is an elementary principle of justice. In injunctions not involving a domestic element this has always been clear: 'ex parte applications are for cases of real urgency where there has been a true impossibility of giving notice' (*Bates v Lord Hailsham* [1972] 1 WLR 1373). As long ago as 1978, in *Practice Note (Injunction: Ex parte Applications)* [1978] 1 WLR 925, the President stated that:

> 'an ex parte injunction should not be made, or granted, unless there is real immediate danger of serious injury or irreparable damage.'

This guidance was not always heeded, with the result that the issue had to be considered more than once by the Court of Appeal, notably in *G v G (Ouster: Ex parte Application)* [1990] 1 FLR 395, and the County Court Rules were amended to provide that, where an ex parte application was made, the affidavit in support must state why notice should not be given (see CCR Ord 13, r 6(3A)).

Even so, the prevailing practice has been to apply for non-molestation injunctions ex parte more often than not and, as will be seen in the chapters dealing with occupation orders and non-molestation orders, this is an issue which it has been thought right to govern by statute in the new legislation.

## The Law Commission report

**1.11**   The Law Commission report (Law Com) has already been mentioned in para **1.1**, above. It came about because of the practical and other problems arising out of some of the matters already set out in this chapter. These problems were: the fact that the law was contained in three statutes, not all of which were identical, and in the inherent jurisdiction of the court; three separate tiers of court might have jurisdiction; there was uncertainty about the correct way to exercise a discretionary jurisdiction; the two separate problems of occupation and molestation co-existed somewhat uneasily; some potential applicants appeared to fall outside the net altogether, with the grant of decree absolute in divorce proceedings causing great problems; and finally, unmarried couples appeared to be at a disadvantage compared with married couples.

The Law Commission's aims were threefold. The first was to remove the gaps, anomalies and inconsistencies in the existing remedies, with a view to synthesising them into a clear, simple and comprehensive code. Secondly, it was taken for granted that any reform should not reduce the level of protection currently available, and might wish to improve it. Thirdly, it was desirable, where possible, to avoid exacerbating hostilities between the adults involved (Law Com para 1.2).

The major proposal was that there should be a single, consistent set of remedies which would be available in all courts.

The Commission therefore made the proposals for a unified body of law dealing with civil remedies for molestation, violence and occupation of the family home between family members which were incorporated in the draft Bill appended to its Report, and which were adopted by the Government in the 1995 Bill. The content, and implications, of this measure will be the subject of the remainder of this book, after brief consideration of the legislative progress of that Bill and its successor.

## The Parliamentary history of the Family and Domestic Violence Bill

**1.12** The 1995 Bill was introduced in February 1995. It was recognised from the outset as a valuable and welcome measure, and attracted all-party support. Nevertheless, there were clear divisions of opinion about some important matters of detail. These related in particular to the classes of potential applicants; The Law Commission had proposed wider categories than those adopted by the Government. This gave rise to quite lengthy debate, as a result of which the Lord Chancellor was persuaded to change his mind on at least one important issue, namely the inclusion in the list of potential applicants of persons who have made an agreement to marry. Another recommendation of The Law Commission, that the police should have the power to pursue civil remedies on behalf of an aggrieved party, was also rejected by the Government and, despite various efforts, was not included in the 1995 Bill.

The Bill was dealt with in the House of Lords under the Special Public Committee procedure, pursuant to the recommendations of a committee headed by Lord Jellicoe. This procedure allows the Committee to admit written and oral evidence, and is a 'streamlined' procedure for Bills such as those emanating from The Law Commission which are of a non-controversial nature. The detailed evidence which the Committee received was of an expert nature and this enabled the Committee to amend the Bill in certain important and practical respects. It was generally accepted that the proposed legislation which emerged from this procedure was a significant improvement on the original Bill.

It was, therefore, somewhat of a surprise to many when, in October 1995, it emerged that the Bill was 'controversial' and, it seemed, a threat to 'family values'. At the eleventh hour, after the Bill had completed its Parliamentary passage, but before it had received Royal Assent, certain back-bench Members of Parliament had noticed the Bill's provisions for the first time (notwithstanding the exceptionally thorough examination it had received in the Special Public Committee), and had decided that it should be challenged. Faced with the impossibility of dealing with these amendments within the time available the Government decided to abandon the Bill.

What had been the 1995 Bill then emerged as part of the Family Law Bill. The original intention of that measure had been to reform the law of divorce, but it was seen as an obvious vehicle on which to load the 1995 Bill. In the meantime, certain amendments, of a more or less cosmetic nature, had been made to ensure that the parts of the 1995 Bill which had given offence were less likely to do so again. In the event, there was little detailed discussion of these provisions during their second journey through Parliament, and they have emerged as Part IV of the Family Law Act 1996, which received Royal Assent on 4 July 1996.

# A brief outline of Part IV of the 1996 Act

**1.13**   The remedies which Part IV of the Act provides are called 'non-molestation orders' and 'occupation orders'. These are available in all courts exercising jurisdiction in family matters, although, as will be seen, the Lord Chancellor may, by order, direct the level of court in which certain classes of case are to be heard.

Some people have, or may be granted, 'matrimonial home rights'. Eligibility to apply for the remedies is based on a concept of 'associated persons', defined at some length.

A spouse who is not entitled to occupy a dwelling-house but who is in occupation is protected from eviction, and, where not in occupation, he or she may occupy with leave of the court. The court may make orders to regulate the occupation of a dwelling-house, and the Act specifies the factors to be taken into account. A distinction is made between a person entitled to occupy and one not so entitled.

Provision is made for the registration of rights of occupation as land charges. Occupation orders may provide for ancillary matters such as payment of outgoings or repairs.

The Act confers the power to make non-molestation orders, and enlarges the range of persons eligible to apply for such orders from those entitled under the previous law. The circumstances in which an ex parte order may be made are defined. The power to attach a power of arrest is extended and harmonised as between courts, and the procedure to be followed on arrest is modified.

The Children Act 1989 is amended to enable the court to oust an abuser when making an emergency protection order or interim care order.

Earlier provisions as to transfer of tenancies are repeated and enlarged, and extended to cohabitants.

**1.14**   The immediate differences from the previous law which the practitioner will notice are as follows:

(1)   The class of potential applicants is larger; the significant term is 'associated persons'.
(2)   The court in which the application must be issued is determined by the rules, and jurisdiction must therefore be checked before issue.
(3)   The law and practice of the various tiers of court will be identical.
(4)   The law governing ex parte applications has been relaxed. This is no longer the exceptional procedure it was.
(5)   Detailed guidelines now exist to direct the court in the exercise of its jurisdiction. A 'balance of harm' test has been established where violence has been proved.

(6)  The court is obliged to attach a power of arrest where violence has been proved, unless the court is satisfied that the applicant will be protected without it. This does not apply to ex parte orders, but the previous discouragement from attaching a power of arrest to an ex parte order has gone and this is now entirely within the discretion of the court.

(7)  Where a power of arrest has not been attached, an order may still be enforced by the new procedure of the issue of a warrant for arrest. This is designed to take the place of the application for committal. The wrongdoer will be brought before 'the relevant judicial authority', who may be a judge, district judge or magistrates' court who will be able either to deal with the matter there and then or remand in custody or on bail; medical reports may be ordered.

## The Protection from Harassment Act 1997

**1.15**   This brief survey of legislative history would not be complete without a mention of the Protection from Harassment Act 1997. The Bill which was eventually enacted, and which is considered in detail in Chapter 10, was introduced shortly after the passage of the Family Law Act 1996. It provides remedies which overlap with those provided by Part IV of the 1996 Act, and it is unclear why Parliament did not attempt to distinguish between the two statutes.

# CHAPTER TWO

# Who May Apply for Orders?

## Introduction

**2.1** One of the difficulties in framing legislation on a subject such as domestic violence is deciding who is entitled to take proceedings against whom. Clearly, there has to be some nexus, or connection between a potential applicant and respondent. What may have been regarded as a 'deserted wife's equity' some years ago has been expanded to cover changing social conditions, and to take account of the practical problems encountered in the operation of the previous law.

The nature of the orders for which applicants may apply are considered in greater detail in Chapters 3 and 4. Here, it will suffice to say that the two principal classes of orders contained in Part IV of the Act are 'occupation orders' and 'non-molestation orders'; the meaning of such orders in general terms is obvious from these descriptions. Non-molestation orders, in terms of eligibility of applicants, are relatively uncomplicated, and are dealt with at para **2.21**. The bulk of this chapter will be taken up with consideration of eligibility to apply for occupation orders.

This chapter will set out in detail who may apply for which classes of orders. The chapter is divided into five parts, as follows:

Part A – Applications for occupation orders
Part B – Non-molestation orders
Part C – Applications by children
Part D – Separate representation of children
Part E – Application made by third parties on behalf of victims of domestic violence.

## Part A – Applications for occupation orders

### Preliminary

**2.2** As will be seen, whether or not an applicant is eligible to apply for certain classes of order will depend on whether she comes within a certain category; however, that category itself will partly be governed by the type of property in question. This will be considered in more detail at para **2.8**, but for the present, it will suffice to bear in mind that an occupation order cannot be made in respect of a property which never has been, nor was ever intended to be, the home of the parties involved. Therefore, a property which was for example always an investment property, and was never intended to be the residence of either party, could not be the subject of an occupation order.

**2.3**    Potential applicants for occupation orders fall into three categories, as follows:

(a)    entitled persons;
(b)    persons with matrimonial home rights;
(c)    non-entitled persons (subdivided into former spouses and cohabitants).

As will be seen below, the basic concept of matrimonial home rights is what used to be called 'right of occupation', and is imported, more or less unchanged, from the earlier legislation. The concept of entitled and non-entitled must be considered briefly at the outset.

### Entitled or non-entitled?

**2.4**    As will be seen in the next chapter, and as was mentioned at para **2.3** above, a potential applicant is either entitled or non-entitled; (a spouse who is non-entitled where her spouse is entitled may have in fact the same rights of application to the court as her entitled spouse, by virtue of matrimonial home rights, but a cohabitant or former spouse does not).

The simple distinction between entitled and non-entitled is that an entitled person is someone who has some legal right to occupy property, because of being the freehold owner, tenant or contractual licensee. A non-entitled person has no such entitlement.

The Law Commission justified the distinction between the two classes of applicants for two reasons. First, the grant of an occupation order can severely restrict the enjoyment of property rights, and its potential consequences to a respondent are therefore more serious than those of a non-molestation order. Such consequences may be acceptable when both parties are entitled to occupy, but are more difficult to justify when the applicant has no such right. Secondly, the purpose of an occupation order is usually different in the two classes of case; in the case of entitled applicants, the occupation order has a purpose beyond short-term protection, namely to regulate the occupation of the home until its medium or long-term destiny has been decided (Law Com para 4.7). When the 1995 Bill was introduced, it followed the division of applicants into entitled and non-entitled, as recommended by the Law Commission, and this remained the position throughout its Parliamentary history. However, in order to meet some of the objections which had been raised, and which had caused the downfall of the Bill, the Government introduced a further distinction when the provisions re-emerged in the Family Law Bill. The position of entitled applicants remains the same, but non-entitled applicants are now divided into those who are former spouses and those who are cohabitants or former cohabitants. As will be seen when these provisions are considered in detail, the difference in fact is not very great; the matter was well put by the Parliamentary Secretary to the Lord

Chancellor's Department during the final debate on the Family Law Bill in the House of Commons:

> '... the government believe that there is a difference between cohabitation and marriage, and we believe that it is proper that the difference is reflected in the considerations of the court. We believe that that is the overwhelming view of the House. However, that does not mean that the court will necessarily come to different conclusions in the two cases, given the concern of the court in these matters to afford effective protection from domestic violence.' (Official Report (HC) 17 June 1996 col 641)

Accordingly, the type of order for which the applicant may apply will depend on her status as either entitled or non-entitled and, in the latter case, on whether she was married to the respondent. The former will apply for an order under s 33, the latter under ss 35, 36, 37 or 38. The respective positions of entitled and non-entitled applicants will be considered in detail below, but first it may be convenient to consider the meaning of matrimonial home rights.

**Matrimonial home rights**

**2.5** The term 'matrimonial home rights' replaces the term 'rights of occupation' contained in the MHA. It will be remembered that the main purpose of the MHA 1967 was to protect the right of occupation of the deserted spouse. Section 30 of the Act therefore re-enacts, with minor amendments, the corresponding provisions in the Acts of 1967 and 1983. The added significance of matrimonial home rights in the context of the new Act should become clear when the concepts of 'entitled' and 'non-entitled' persons are considered.

Since matrimonial home rights can determine whether or not a person is in the same position as one who is 'entitled', they are a vital part of the structure of the Act. It will be noted that they are limited to spouses; they cannot survive decree absolute unless an order to that effect is made before decree absolute – see ss 31(8) and 33(5). They arise by virtue of the marriage.

**2.6** By s 30(1), matrimonial home rights are conferred where:

> '(a) one spouse is entitled to occupy a dwelling-house by virtue of—
>
>    (i) a beneficial estate or interest or contract; or
>
>    (ii) any enactment giving that spouse the right to remain in occupation; and
>
> (b) the other spouse is not so entitled.'

These rights are conferred on the spouse 'not so entitled', and consist of the following:

> '(a) if in occupation, a right not to be evicted or excluded from the dwelling-house or any part of it by the other spouse except with the leave of the court given by an order under section 33;

(b)   if not in occupation, a right with the leave of the court so given to enter into and occupy the dwelling-house.'

Certain other consequential provisions are contained in the section, and these will be considered at more appropriate places in this book. For the moment, it is necessary only to mention s 30(7), which provides that the section does not apply to:

'a dwelling-house which has at no time been, and which was at no time intended by the spouses to be, a matrimonial home of the spouses in question.'

The words 'and which was at no time intended by the spouses to be' represent a change in the law effected by the Act. Under the MHA, there was no power to regulate the occupation of a property which the parties intended to be their home, but in which they had never actually lived together. The Law Commission gave the example of a couple who had sold their existing house and were living in temporary rented accommodation while renovating a new house bought in the sole name of the husband. In such a case, the wife would have had no occupation rights over the new property if the relationship broke down in the meantime, since they had never lived in it together (Law Com para 4.4). Section 30(7) corrects this gap in the law, so that matrimonial home rights may be acquired in respect of such a property.

**2.7**   The effect of matrimonial home rights is, therefore, that a spouse who occupies a dwelling-house which is, has been, or was intended to be the matrimonial home, and which is vested in the sole name of the other spouse, whether as beneficial owner or tenant, has a right of occupation and a right not to be evicted by the other spouse; where she is not in occupation, for example if the other spouse had evicted her, she is entitled to apply to the court for an order under s 33 of the Act.

In summary, therefore, a spouse always has matrimonial home rights provided her spouse is entitled and the dwelling-house in question is not excluded by virtue of s 30(7).

**Entitled applicants**

**2.8**   Section 33(1)(a) defines a 'person entitled' as one who:

'(i)   is entitled to occupy a dwelling-house by virtue of a beneficial estate or interest or contract or by virtue of any enactment giving him the right to remain in occupation, or

(ii)   has matrimonial home rights in relation to a dwelling-house . . . '

The meaning of (i) is clear; it refers to a person who is a freehold or beneficial owner of a dwelling-house, or is a tenant or contractual licensee. The meaning of 'matrimonial home rights' has already been discussed at para **2.5** et seq above.

Section 33(1)(b) then makes the important qualification about the type of dwelling-house in respect of which a s 33 application may be made, the significance of which has already been discussed at para **2.6** above. The section applies (only) where the dwelling-house:

> '(i) is or at any time has been the home of the person entitled and of another person with whom he is associated, or
>
> (ii) was at any time intended by the person entitled and any such other person to be their home, . . . '

## Associated persons

**2.9** A new concept is introduced here, namely that of 'associated person'. This is one of the key concepts of the legislation. When non-molestation orders are considered later in this chapter, it will be seen that eligibility to apply is based on the two parties being associated. Since the principle is the same in both classes of application, what is to be said here will apply equally to occupation orders and non-molestation orders.

In the context of applications for occupation orders made by an entitled person, the applicant has to show that she and the other party were associated. This term is defined by s 62(3) of the Act, which provides that a person is associated with another person if:

(a) they are or have been married to each other;

(b) they are cohabitants or former cohabitants;

(c) they live or have lived in the same household, otherwise than merely by reason of one of them being the other's employee, tenant, lodger or boarder;

(d) they are relatives;

(e) they have agreed to marry each other (whether or not that agreement has been terminated);

(f) in relation to any child, they are both persons falling within sub-s (4). Subsection (4) provides that a person falls within its scope if:

> '(a) he is a parent of the child; or
>
> (b) he has or has had parental responsibility for the child.';

(g) they are parties to the same family proceedings (other than proceedings under this Part of the Act).

This definition introduces further terms, some of which must themselves be defined.

**2.10** Sub-paragraph (a) presents no problems. The first term requiring definition is 'cohabitant'. Section 62(1) defines 'cohabitants' thus:

> '(a) "cohabitants" are a man and a woman who, although not married to each other, are living together as husband and wife; and
>
> (b) "former cohabitants" is to be read accordingly, but does not include cohabitants who have subsequently married each other.'

This, too, is clear; the parties must be of the opposite sex and have lived together as if husband and wife. This would involve a shared life and living arrangements and, normally, a sexual element in the relationship. In most cases, the meaning of cohabitant will be clear enough, although it has to be said that, given the almost infinite variety of conditions of married life, there may be room for interesting arguments about what does and does not come within 'living together as husband and wife'.

The question of what constitutes cohabitation is not only relevant in the field of family law; there is a body of jurisprudence on the subject in social security law, which is frequently overlooked by family practitioners. The issue to be determined is normally whether an applicant for income support is disqualified because of cohabitation.

In *Crake v Supplementary Benefits Commission* [1982] 1 All ER 498, Woolf J approved six factors as 'admirable signposts' for the existence of cohabitation. These are membership of the same household, stability, financial support, sexual relationship, children and public acknowledgment. However, in *Re J (Income Support: Cohabitation)* [1995] 1 FLR 660, a Social Security Commissioner held that to consider only these factors placed a wholly inadequate emphasis on the parties' 'general relationship'. The parties' sexual and financial relationship was relevant only for the light it cast on this general relationship. Where there had never been a sexual relationship there must be strong alternative grounds for holding that there existed a relationship akin to that of husband and wife.

**2.11**  Sub-paragraph (c) introduces a new class of applicants into the law. The previous law, taken as a whole, recognised present or former spouses and cohabitants as potential applicants; this provision broadens the range of applicants. A brief consideration of the background may assist.

The Law Commission saw its task as being to widen the range of applicants to include anyone who was associated with the respondent by virtue of a family relationship or something closely akin to such a relationship. Other solutions might exclude, for example, people who had a genuine need for protection in circumstances which most people would regard as family relationships in the broadest sense, such as two people who had lived together on a long-term basis, whether as close friends or in a homosexual relationship. In practice, many of the same considerations applied to persons in 'family relationships' as to married or cohabiting couples; the proximity of the parties gave unique opportunities for molestation and abuse; the heightened emotions of all concerned gave rise to a particular need for sensitivity and flexibility in the law; there was frequently a possibility that the relationship would continue; and there was, in most cases, the likelihood that they would share a common budget, making financial remedies inappropriate (Law Com para 3.19).

As will be seen, the 1995 Bill introduced by the Government did not accept the totality of The Law Commission recommendations. On the second reading, the Lord Chancellor explained:

'The other significant policy departure from the recommendations of the Law Commission concerns the categories of people entitled to apply for orders. The categories proposed by the Law Commission of – persons who had at any time agreed to marry each other; and persons who have or have had a sexual relationship with each other were rejected, because the persons within them may not have the same domestic link as those in the other categories. In some cases, the relationship might have been brief and the parties would never have lived together. There might also be problems for the courts of definition and proof, which would not apply to the other categories. If that happened, it would undermine the principle that domestic violence remedies should be able to be obtained swiftly in emergencies. Of course, that does not mean that there would not be other remedies available to such people; but it means that the simplified form of procedure available under the Bill would not be available to them for the reasons that I have given.' (Official Report (HL), 23 February 1995)

The essential characteristic of this class of person is, therefore, that they have lived in the same household as the other person.

**2.12** 'Household' was considered by The Law Commission, which, when defining the relationships to be protected in addition to spouses and cohabitants, began with:

'anyone who lives or has lived in the same household as the respondent, otherwise than merely by reason of one of them being the other's employee, tenant, lodger or boarder. This is intended to include people who live in the same household, other than on a purely commercial basis. It would, for example, exclude a student renting the spare bedroom or a live-in nanny employed to care for children. The phrase "living in the same household" may be expected to retain the usual meaning which it has acquired in matrimonial proceedings. Thus, it is possible for people to live in different households, although they are actually living in the same house. The crucial test is the degree of community life which goes on. If the parties shut themselves up in separate rooms and cease to have anything to do with each other, they live in separate households. But if they share domestic chores and shopping, eat meals together or share the same living room, they are living in the same household, however strained their relations may be.' (Law Com para 3.21)

The term implies some shared living arrangements; people living under the same roof, for example by occupying flats or bedsits in the same building, would not be living in the same household. The class clearly could overlap with cohabitants, in the sense that someone could qualify under this classification and as a cohabitant; however, one could not qualify as a cohabitant without being of the opposite sex to the other party, and without the relationship being similar to that of husband and wife.

In the same way, the class would overlap with that of relatives, so it must be taken that, in attempting to define those intended to qualify here, relatives should be excluded. Section 62(3)(c) specifically excludes people who live in the same household 'merely by reason' of their being employer and employee, landlord and tenant (although it is difficult to see how a landlord and tenant, properly so called, could live in the same household), and 'landlord' and lodger or boarder. It would be possible for someone to argue that, although he or she was an employee or boarder, that was not the only reason for living in the same household as someone else; for example, it might be argued that there was some sexual relationship which made it convenient for them to be close at hand.

It seems, therefore, that people who might be associated with each other would include homosexual couples, and people who share a home for reasons of friendship, convenience or some other reason. To qualify as an applicant for an occupation order, such a person would have to be 'entitled'; for the purpose of this subsection, spouses and cohabitants, past or present, are to be ignored, so the applicant would have to establish a right to live in the property by virtue of some freehold, leasehold or contractual interest.

**2.13**   'Relative' is defined in s 63(1). In relation to a person, 'relative' means:

'(a)   the father, mother, stepfather, stepmother, son, daughter, stepson, stepdaughter, grandmother, grandfather, grandson or granddaughter of that person or of that person's spouse or former spouse, or

(b)   the brother, sister, uncle, aunt, niece or nephew (whether of the full blood or of the half blood or by affinity) of that person or of that person's spouse or former spouse,

and includes, in relation to a person who is living or has lived with another person as husband and wife, any person who would fall within paragraph (a) or (b) above if the parties were married to each other;'

The significance of this last provision is, therefore, that the word 'cohabitant' or 'former cohabitant' can be substituted for 'spouse' in the definition. Apart from this, the definition needs little further elaboration, save for a consideration of the effect of s 62(4) and (5).

Section 62(4) begins 'A person falls within this subsection in relation to a child. . .'. Pausing there, it will be remembered that the purpose of the section is to define 'associated persons', relatives are associated persons, and, of course, parents are relatives of their children. It is unsurprising, therefore, to find that sub-s (4) continues:

'if—

(a)   he is a parent of the child; or

(b)   he has or has had parental responsibility for the child.'

By s 63(1), 'parental responsibility' has the same meaning as in the Children Act 1989.

Section 62(5) deals with the position where a child has been adopted or freed for adoption by virtue of any of the enactments mentioned in s 16(1) of the Adoption Act 1976. In such circumstances, two persons may be associated for the purposes of this Act if:

> '(a) one is a natural parent of the child or a parent of such a natural parent; and
>
> (b) the other is the child or any person—
>
>> (i) who has become a parent of the child by virtue of an adoption order or has applied for an adoption order, or
>>
>> (ii) with whom the child has at any time been placed for adoption.'

**2.14** Section 62(3)(e) introduces another class of associated persons, namely the former engaged couple. This was an area of some controversy during the legislative passage of the 1995 Bill. The Law Commission recommended the inclusion of a further group, described as 'difficult to define in legislative terms' including:

> 'people who have been boyfriend and girlfriend in a romantic relationship which might have varying degrees of sexual involvement. Such relationships are possibly easier to recognise than to describe, but we envisage that there would have been a degree of mutuality and some participation in consensual sexual activity, although not necessarily amounting to sexual intercourse.' (Law Com para 3.24)

The recommendations of The Law Commission were resisted by the Government. Repeated attempts were made to amend the 1995 Bill to restore what had originally been proposed, by limiting the category to those who had been engaged to be married. This too met initial resistance. One noble Lord, agreeing that it was very important that these proceedings should be despatched expeditiously, continued:

> 'There is no difficulty about the courts deciding whether two people have agreed to marry. They have been doing that at least since *Bardell v Pickwick* and, indeed, earlier than that. However, *Bardell v Pickwick*, if I remember, was a case which took rather a long time. It is not the kind of time schedule that we have in mind for these proceedings.' (Lord Archer – Public Bill Committee, 24 April 1995)

Eventually, the Government had a partial change of view. At Report stage in the House of Lords, the Lord Chancellor referred to his initial doubts, and to his fears that problems of definition might lead to long preliminary enquiries, which would defeat the objective of quick and simple justice. He continued:

> 'As the evidence before the Committee developed, it seemed plain that there might be cases where it would be easy to prove that entitlement. It may have been a bit harsh, unnecessary and unwise to exclude those. If we could find some way of satisfactorily differentiating between the cases

in which the entitlement could be proved readily and those in which it would take a great deal of time, that would be the best answer to the problem.' (Official Report (HL) vol 564 no 95, col 1061)

So it was that what is now s 62(3)(e) of the 1996 Act was introduced. However, that was not an end of the matter, because of the difficulty of proving an agreement to marry; this had been one of the stumbling blocks all along. There was further debate about this, which ended in a form of wording which met with universal approval on Third Reading of the 1995 Bill, being described by the Lord Chancellor as 'a neat way to accommodate an enlargement of the circumstances which might be covered', and, by Lord Archer, as 'hardly short of genius' (Official Report (HL) vol 565 no 106, cols 219 and 220).

Section 44, the marginal note of which is 'Evidence of agreement to marry', provides, in sub-s (1), that the court shall not make an order under s 33 (an occupation order in favour of an entitled person) or s 42 (a non-molestation order) by virtue of s 62(3)(e) unless there is produced to it evidence in writing of the existence of an agreement to marry. However, this is subject to sub-s(2), which provides as follows:

'Subsection (1) above does not apply where the court is satisfied that the agreement to marry was evidenced by—

(a)   the gift of an engagement ring by one party to the agreement to the other in contemplation of their marriage, or

(b)   a ceremony entered into by the parties in the presence of one or more other persons assembled for the purpose of witnessing the ceremony.'

**2.15**   The practical circumstances under which these provisions are likely to have to be considered are, therefore, either where an applicant entitled by some freehold, leasehold or contractual interest in a property is seeking an occupation order against a person to whom he was engaged, or where someone seeks a non-molestation order against someone to whom he was engaged; the latter is likely to be the more common. In either case, the court will have to be satisfied of the agreement to marry, and s 44 establishes that there are only three ways to do this.

First, the applicant may produce written evidence of the agreement; this does not mean a written agreement as such, but some written evidence of the fact that there was an agreement to marry. This could take the form of letters passing between the parties referring to their engagement, press announcements, wedding invitations or such other evidence as might satisfy the court; it would be for the court in each case to find as a fact that the written evidence put before it tended to prove the existence of the agreement, and this would have to be considered together with the oral evidence of the parties. The written evidence would be necessary but not, of itself, sufficient.

Secondly, where no such written evidence existed, the applicant could seek to prove that an engagement ring had changed hands, by way of gift. This would be a matter of evidence, no doubt oral in most cases. It would be helpful if the ring still existed. There might be room for argument as to whether a ring was an engagement ring, a mere gift, or a demonstration of affection and intent falling short of a commitment to marry.

Thirdly, the applicant could seek to prove that there had been a ceremony in the presence of others at which the agreement to marry had been made. This would be most likely to have happened where the parties belonged to one of the minority ethnic communities. The important element is that the agreement to marry itself is made at a formal ceremony; this would distinguish it from, say, an engagement party.

Where none of these three possibilities exists, the court may not entertain an application under ss 33 or 42. There could be an army of witnesses to prove an agreement to marry, but without proof in one of the three specified ways the court would be precluded from acting. What would happen if there was no such evidence but the respondent appeared before the court and admitted the engagement is unclear. At the very least, his verbal admission would be of no effect if he did not commit it to writing. If he did so, could it be argued that the court should not have allowed the matter to proceed so far in the absence of the pleading of one of the three specified grounds, and that the application should have been refused ad limine? This may be a matter for future debate.

**2.16** With these definitions in mind, it will be seen that an entitled person can apply for a s 33 order against a larger class of persons than merely spouses, former spouses, cohabitants and former cohabitants. Most members of a potential applicant's family would qualify as potential respondents, provided, of course, the two parties had shared, or intended to share, a home together, and the various other classes of persons set out in ss 62 and 63 would also be eligible.

A checklist or flowchart for cases involving both entitled and non-entitled applicants is set out at para **2.22** below.

**Non-entitled persons**
**2.17** The next class of potential applicants to be considered is those who have no existing right to occupy a particular dwelling-house. These people can apply for an occupation order under one of three sections, depending on their status and on whether the respondent is entitled or non-entitled. The importance of whether or not the non-entitled applicant is a former spouse, and the reasons for this distinction, where discussed at para **2.4** above. The non-entitled applicant will therefore fall into one of four categories, namely:

(a) former spouse-respondent entitled (s 35);
(b) cohabitant, or former cohabitant-respondent entitled (s 36);
(c) former spouse-respondent not entitled (s 37);
(d) cohabitant or former cohabitant-respondent not entitled (s 38).

The Law Commission had not anticipated the division of applicants into former spouses and others, and addressed only the distinction between the two types of respondent. It recommended that non-entitled applicants should only be able to apply for occupation orders against former spouses, cohabitants or former cohabitants (it will be remembered that a spouse is always, by definition, an entitled applicant). The report stated (Law Com para 4.10):

> 'It should, however, be borne in mind that there are two different sorts of non-entitled applicants, those who are seeking an order against an entitled respondent and those who are seeking an order against a respondent who is also non-entitled. In the latter case, the court is only adjusting occupation rights as between the parties themselves, both of whom may well be subject to almost immediate ejection at the behest of a third party.'

The different characteristics of the various kinds of orders will be examined in the next chapter; here, it is only necessary to define the different classes of applicant.

**2.18**    The first class of applicant to be considered is the former spouse where the respondent is entitled. Section 35(1) applies if:

> '(a)   one former spouse is entitled to occupy a dwelling-house by virtue of a beneficial estate or interest or contract, or by virtue of any enactment giving him the right to remain in occupation;
> (b)   the other former spouse is not so entitled; and
> (c)   the dwelling-house was at any time their matrimonial home or was at any time intended by them to be their matrimonial home.'

By sub-s (2), in such circumstances the former spouse who is not entitled may apply for an order under s 35 against the other former spouse. The four essential elements are, first, that the applicant is a former spouse, secondly, that she is not entitled, thirdly, that the respondent is entitled and, fourthly, that the dwelling-house in question is, or was intended by them to be, their matrimonial home.

**2.19**    If the conditions set out above are not met, the next stage would be to see whether ss 36, 37 or 38 applied. Where the applicant was not a former spouse, it would be to s 36 or s 38 that she would turn. Where the applicant was a former spouse, and the issue was the respondent's entitlement, the only remedy would lie in s 37. Where the third requirement set out above was not fulfilled, ie the dwelling-house had never been nor was intended to be the joint home, there would be no right to apply in any event.

Section 36 provides that it applies if:

> '(a)   one cohabitant or former cohabitant is entitled to occupy a dwelling-house by virtue of a beneficial estate or interest or contract or by virtue of any enactment giving him the right to remain in occupation;

(b)  the other cohabitant or former cohabitant is not so entitled; and
(c)  that dwelling-house is the home in which they live together as husband and wife or a home in which they at any time so lived together or intended to live together.'

If these conditions are fulfilled, the non-entitled party may apply for an order under s 36.

**2.20**  If the applicant cannot fulfil any of these requirements, it must be the case that the respondent is non-entitled also. The next stage is therefore to go to s 37 (in the case of a former spouse), or s 38 (in the case of a cohabitant or former cohabitant).

Section 37(1) applies if:

'(a)  one spouse or former spouse and the other spouse or former spouse occupy a dwelling-house which is or was the matrimonial home; but
(b)  neither of them is entitled to remain in occupation—
  (i)   by virtue of a beneficial estate or interest or contract; or
  (ii)  by virtue of any enactment giving him the right to remain in occupation.'

In such a case, either may apply to the court for an order under this section.

The essence of this class of parties is, therefore, that they are or have been married to each other, and neither of them is entitled, whether as freeholder, tenant or contractual licensee to occupy the dwelling-house. It is also a condition of s 37 that both parties are residing in the dwelling-house. No relief can be granted if one of them is out of occupation. When the powers of the court are considered in the next chapter, it will be seen that they are considerably less extensive than those available under the provisions already examined.

**2.21**  If the parties have never been married to each other, the only remedy available would be under s 38. This applies where:

'(a)  one cohabitant or former cohabitant and the other cohabitant or former cohabitant occupy a dwelling-house which is the home in which they live or lived together as husband and wife; but . . .'

Subsection (b) is identical to that set out in s 37 above. The requirements are, therefore, identical with those in s 37 save that the parties have never been married.

**Checklist for occupation orders**
**2.22**  The various criteria considered so far are interlinked, quite complicated and potentially confusing. It may be helpful, therefore, if at this stage a form of checklist is suggested, so that the busy practitioner may see quickly into which class of applicant a client may fall.

**Checklist**

| Question | Answer |
|---|---|

**1. Preliminaries**

| Is the property a dwelling-house? | Must answer YES to all three questions. If NO to any, no eligibility |
|---|---|

Did the parties occupy it, or intend to occupy it as their home?

Are the parties associated? (see para **2.25**)

**2. Section 33 orders**

Is applicant either:

| (i) entitled, or | If YES to any, apply under s 33. |
|---|---|
| (ii) married to respondent, or | If NO to all, proceed to 3. |

(iii) divorced but retaining matrimonial home rights by virtue of court order?

**3. Sections 35 and 36 orders**

| Is respondent entitled? | If NO, proceed to 4. If YES: |
|---|---|

| Are the parties former spouses? | If YES, apply under s 35. If NO, apply under s 36. |
|---|---|

**4. Sections 37 and 38 orders**

| Is the property the present or former matrimonial home (of spouses for former spouses) or the home where parties last lived together (where cohabitants)? | If NO – no entitlement. If YES: |
|---|---|

| Are the parties former spouses? | If YES, apply under s 37 If NO: |
|---|---|

| Are they cohabitants or former cohabitants? | If NO – no entitlement. If YES, apply under s 38. |
|---|---|

# Part B – Applications for non-molestation orders

**2.23** As has been seen, the qualifications for the various classes of occupation orders are quite involved. Entitlement to apply for a non-molestation order is much less complicated.

The Law Commission had to decide which classes of persons it should recommend as being entitled to the protection of the law under the proposed statute. Its original inclination was to limit this to spouses, former spouses, cohabitants, former cohabitants, parents and some children. However, it went on to conclude that a wider range of people should be eligible:

'there is no doubt that harassment and violence can occur in many types of relationship. For example, abuse of the elderly by members of the family with whom they are living is coming increasingly to be recognised as a social problem and significant numbers of women find it difficult or impossible to obtain protection from their violent teenage or adult sons.' (Law Com para 3.8)

It was therefore decided to base eligibility on association through family relationships; some of the reasons for this have already been discussed, in the context of occupation orders, in Part A above, to which reference should be made for a full discussion of the meaning of 'associated persons'; the matter is also set out, in summary form, at para **2.25** below.

**2.24**  All these factors resulted in s 42(2) of the Act, which provides that the court may make a non-molestation order:

> '(a)  if an application for the order has been made (whether in other family proceedings or without any other family proceedings being instituted) by a person who is associated with the respondent; or
>  (b)  if in any family proceedings to which the respondent is a party the court considers that the order should be made for the benefit of any other party to the proceedings or any relevant child even though no such application has been made.'

'Associated person' is defined by s 62(3), which has already been considered at some length in Part A, and a summary or checklist appears at para **2.25** below.

'Family proceedings' are defined by s 62(3) as any proceedings under the inherent jurisdiction of the High Court in relation to children, and any under the following enactments:

(a)  Part II of the 1996 Act
(b)  Part IV of the 1996 Act
(c)  the Matrimonial Causes Act 1973
(d)  the Adoption Act 1976
(e)  the Domestic Proceedings and Magistrates' Courts Act 1978
(f)  Part III of the Matrimonial and Family Proceedings Act 1984
(g)  Parts I, II, and IV of the Children Act 1989
(h)  s 30 of the Human Fertilisation and Embryology Act 1990.

'Family proceedings' also includes proceedings in which the court has made an emergency protection order under s 44 of the Children Act 1989 which includes an exclusion requirement as defined in s 44A(3) of that Act (see Chapter 6).

By s 62(2), 'relevant child' means:

> '(a)  any child who is living with or might reasonably be expected to live with either party to the proceedings;

(b) any child in relation to whom an order under the Adoption Act 1976 or the Children Act 1989 is in question in the proceedings; and

(c) any other child whose interests the court considers relevant.'

The Law Commission had concluded that it was unnecessary for the court to have to have regard to the interests of every child of every party; it was clearly desirable for the court to have a discretion to make orders on relation as wide a range of children as possible, without necessarily being required to consider the position of children whose interests might be completely unaffected by the matters before the court; hence the somewhat broad definition (Law Com para 3.27).

**Checklist**

**2.25** It may be helpful to set out in summary form the classes of persons against whom an applicant may apply for a non-molestation order under this legislation. Such application may be made if the respondent is:

(a) In relation to the applicant, in one of the following categories:
Spouse
Former spouse
Cohabitant
Former cohabitant

(b) In relation to the applicant or to any class of person in (a):
Father
Mother
Stepfather
Stepmother
Son
Daughter
Stepson
Stepdaughter
Grandmother
Grandfather
Grandson
Granddaughter
Brother
Sister
Half or stepbrother or sister
Uncle
Aunt
Niece
Nephew

(c) In relation to any of the persons in (b):
Spouse
Former spouse
Cohabitant

Former cohabitant

(d)  Someone who lives, or has lived, in the same household (for detail see para **2.12**).

(e)  Someone whom the applicant has agreed to marry (for detail see para **2.14**); where agreement terminated, only within 3 years of termination.

(f)  Where the applicant is the parent of a child or has parental responsibility for a child, any other parent or person having parental responsibility.

(g)  Where a child has been adopted or freed for adoption,

    (i)  a natural parent, or the parent of such a natural parent,
      is associated with

    (ii)  the child, or
      a parent of the child by virtue of an adoption order, or
      a person who has applied for an adoption order, or
      any person with whom the child has at any time been placed for adoption.

    Anyone in class (i) may apply for an order against anyone in class (ii).

(h)  The other party to any family proceedings (see para **2.22** for definition).

**2.26**  Procedure will be considered more fully in Chapter 9. It should merely be noted here that there are three possible sets of circumstances in which a non-molestation order may be made under Part IV. The first is where there are no existing family proceedings, and the applicant makes a 'free-standing' application.

The second is where there are existing family proceedings, and the applicant applies within those proceedings.

The third is where there are existing family proceedings, neither party applies for a non-molestation order, but the court sees fit to make such an order of its own motion. The court may only do so if it considers that the order should be made for the benefit of any other party to the proceedings or of any relevant child.

## Part C – Applications by children

**2.27**  In principle, a child is eligible to apply for an occupation order or a non-molestation order. A mere glance at the checklist set out at para **2.25** above reveals a long list of persons with whom a child may be associated. It is unlikely that a person under 16 will be entitled, and thus able to apply under s 33, but the remainder of the list of possible applications is open.

Applications by a child are governed by s 42(1) which provides that a child under the age of 16 may not apply for an occupation order or a non-molestation order except with the leave of the court. Section 42(2) provides that such leave may only be granted if the court is satisfied that the child has sufficient understanding to make the proposed application.

This requirement for leave is similar to that which exists in relation to applications under the Children Act 1989, and will be exercised in the same way. Rule 3.8(2) provides that an application for an occupation order or a non-molestation order made by a child under the age of 16 shall be made in Form FL401 (the standard application form) but shall be treated in the first instance as an application to the High Court for leave.

## Part D – Separate representation of children

**2.28**   A subject which overlaps with, but is in reality separate from, the last topic is the separate representation of children. This was achieved by an Opposition amendment, accepted by the Government, during the final stages of the Family Law Bill debates. Section 64 now provides as follows:

> '(1)   The Lord Chancellor may by regulations provide for the separate representation of children in proceedings in England and Wales which relate to any matter in respect of which a question has arisen, or may arise, under—
>
> . . .
>
> (b)  Part IV;
>
> . . .
>
> (2)   The regulations may provide for such representation only in specified circumstances.'

It remains to be seen what regulations are introduced to implement this provision. As yet, none have been introduced. The intention is, clearly, that the voice of the child should be heard and that, in some cases, it may be necessary for that voice to be heard independently of that of its parents.

## Part E – Provision for third parties to act

**2.29**   One of the recommendations in the Law Commission report was that in some cases a third party, such as a police service, should be able to bring proceedings on behalf of a victim of domestic violence who was, for some reason, unable to bring the proceedings herself. This was resisted by the Government during the debates on the 1995 Bill and, initially, during the progress of the Family Law Bill. However, during the final stages of debate on the Family Law Bill, when the Opposition proposed an amendment to implement the Law Commission recommendation, the Parliamentary Secretary to the Lord Chancellor's Department found that he was 'delighted to support the amendment enthusiastically' (Official Report (HC) 17 June 1996 col 598) and, what is now s 60, was accepted.

**2.30**   Section 60 provides as follows:

> '(1)   Rules of court may provide for a prescribed person, or any person in a prescribed category, ("a representative") to act on behalf of another in relation to proceedings to which this Part applies.

(2) Rules made under this section may, in particular, authorise a representative to apply for an occupation order or for a non-molestation order for which the person on whose behalf the representative is acting could have applied.

(3) Rules made under this section may prescribe—

    (a) conditions to be satisfied before a representative may make an application to the court on behalf of another; and

    (b) considerations to be taken into account by the court in determining whether, and if so how, to exercise any of its powers under this Part when a representative is acting on behalf of another.'

Moving the amendment, Mr Paul Boateng MP, observed that the new clause:

'... will enable a third party – usually, but not necessarily, a police service – to take legal action on the part of the victim of domestic violence. The need is obvious, because all too often the victim of domestic violence feels peculiarly vulnerable and therefore unable, because of the oppression she faces daily, to take action herself.' (Official Report (HC) 17 June 1996 col 596)

It was proposed that several pilot schemes should be conducted by the Lord Chancellor to investigate the resources implications; such schemes would be conducted in areas where there was already good practice, including a multi-agency approach.

As yet, no rules have been introduced pursuant to s 60.

# CHAPTER THREE

# Occupation Orders

## Introduction

**3.1**   In the previous chapter, the question of the different classes of persons entitled to apply for various orders was considered. It was seen that there are five types of occupation orders, namely those available under ss 33, 35, 36, 37 and 38.

In this chapter, the nature of these different classes of order will be considered, as will the matters to which the court is directed to have regard when exercising its discretion in deciding which, if any, orders it should make. At the outset, it may be helpful to recall the classification of orders which was recommended by The Law Commission, and which therefore governed the drafting of Part IV of the Act.

The Law Commission distinguished between declaratory orders and regulatory orders. Declaratory orders were those:

> '(i)   declaring pre-existing occupation rights in the home;
> (ii)   extending statutory occupation rights beyond the termination of the marriage on divorce or death;
> (iii)   granting occupation rights in the home to non-entitled applicants ("an occupation rights order").' (Law Com para 4.2)

Regulatory orders were those:

> '(iv)   requiring one party to leave the home;
> (v)   suspending occupation rights and/or prohibiting one party from entering or re-entering the home, or part of the home;
> (vi)   requiring one party to allow the other to enter and/or remain in the home;
> (vii)   regulating the occupation of the home by either or both of the parties;
> (viii)   terminating occupation rights; and
> (ix)   excluding one party from a defined area in the vicinity of the home.' (Law Com para 4.2)

These were the classes of orders which the legislation was intended to implement. With this in mind, the various classes of orders can now be considered.

# The nature of section 33 orders

**3.2** It will be remembered that the only persons who may apply for s 33 orders are those who are entitled to occupy the dwelling-house either by virtue of the general law (normally because they are a freehold or beneficial owner or tenant), or because they have matrimonial home rights under s 30. In effect, therefore, a s 33 applicant has to be either a person with a legal right to occupy the house, a spouse of such a person, or a former spouse whose matrimonial home rights have been extended by order of the court. Where the applicant has a legal right to occupy, the other party need not be a spouse or even a cohabitant; the only qualification is that they should be associated and have shared, or intended to share the house in question as their home.

By s 33(1), the order may contain any of the provisions specified in sub-ss (3), (4) or (5). It may be helpful to consider sub-s (4) first; this provides that:

> 'An order under this section may declare that the applicant is entitled as mentioned in subsection (1)(a)(i) above or has matrimonial home rights.'

This merely provides, therefore, that the exact nature of the applicant's entitlement to a s 33 order may be specified in the order; this might perhaps be useful where there had been some issue as to entitlement to apply. (In such a case, a magistrates' court would not, normally, have jurisdiction – see s 59(1) and Chapter 9.)

**3.3** Subsection (3) sets out what the order may do, as follows:

> '(a)  enforce the applicant's entitlement to remain in occupation as against the other person ("the respondent");
>
> (b)  require the respondent to permit the applicant to enter and remain in the dwelling-house or part of the dwelling-house;
>
> (c)  regulate the occupation of the dwelling-house by either or both parties;
>
> (d)  if the respondent is entitled as mentioned in subsection (1)(a)(i) above, prohibit, suspend, or restrict the exercise by him of his right to occupy the dwelling-house;
>
> (e)  if the respondent has matrimonial home rights in relation to the dwelling-house and the applicant is the other spouse, restrict or terminate those rights;
>
> (f)  require the respondent to leave the dwelling-house or part of the dwelling-house; or
>
> (g)  exclude the respondent from a defined area in which the dwelling-house is included.'

The effect of these provisions will be considered in turn.

It should be noted that whatever order is made must conform to one of the precedents set out in Form FL404. This Form is set out in full in Appendix III.

*(a) Enforce the applicant's entitlement to remain in occupation*
An order in these terms would be required where the respondent had interfered, or threatened to interfere with the applicant's right to occupy the dwelling-house. The order would, where necessary, declare the applicant's right of occupation, and take the form of an injunction restraining the respondent from interfering with that right. It would be for the court to decide whether any of the other classes of order contained in sub-s (3) should also be made.

*(b) Require respondent to permit application to enter and remain in dwelling-house or part*
This would apply where the applicant had been excluded from the home, or where the respondent threatened to exclude her. It would take the form of a mandatory order requiring the respondent to allow the applicant back into possession, and/or a restraining order requiring him not to exclude her.

Such an order could direct that the applicant be permitted to occupy part only of the house; this might be appropriate where, for example, the house was large enough for the respective quarters of the parties to be defined, and it was in their best interests to be kept apart.

*(c) Regulate the occupation of dwelling-house by either party*
This overlaps, to some extent, with the final comments in para (b) above. In theory, to 'regulate' the occupation of a house could involve excluding one party from it. However, the fact that there is specific provision in this section for exclusion suggests that this provision is designed to enable the court to dictate which parts of a house may be used by one or other party, and to prescribe areas which one party may not enter.

*(d) If respondent entitled, prohibit, suspend or restrict the exercise of his right to occupy*
This applies where the respondent is 'entitled' under s 33(1)(a)(i); that is to say, he is entitled to occupy because he is a freehold or beneficial owner, or tenant, or contractual licensee. He does not need the protection of the Act in order to occupy; he occupies as of right.

This provision, therefore, enables the court to override his legal property rights, and to deny him the right to occupy the house. This can be a complete denial ('prohibit'), a temporary denial ('suspend'), or a partial denial ('restrict').

*(e) If respondent has matrimonial home rights, restrict or terminate those rights*
To some extent, this is a mirror image of the previous provision. Whether or not a person has matrimonial home rights is a matter of law, not discretion. Where the parties are spouses, and one of them is 'entitled' because of general legal rights, the other automatically acquires matrimonial home rights by virtue of s 30(2). If these rights could not be interfered with, there would be

the absurd position that such a person would be in a stronger position than the spouse who was 'entitled'.

Accordingly, this provision permits the court to order that a person with matrimonial home rights may be excluded from the home either partially, temporarily or permanently.

*(f) Require respondent to leave the dwelling-house or part thereof*
This is self-explanatory, and clearly fits in with the general array of powers conferred on the court. This provision would be the specific authority for making an ouster order.

*(g) Exclude respondent from a defined area in which the dwelling-house is included*
This is a power which derives from the DVMPA, there being no corresponding provision in the MHA; it is clearly sensible that it is to be included in the unified powers of the court. The tendency has been for courts to approach such orders with caution. On the one hand, it may obviously be wise to prevent a potential molester from lurking in the vicinity of the home and intimidating by his very presence. However, it is necessary to have regard to and protect the liberty of the subject, and also to avoid the possibility of unintentional breaches of orders. Accordingly, it is submitted, any order of this kind should only be made where a clear need for it, in order to protect the applicant and family, had been demonstrated, and then only in the most limited terms consistent with the safety of the applicant. Having said that, it must also be said that the specimen orders attached to Form FL404 (see Appendix III at p 211) include, at nos 12, 19 and 23, an appropriate order for use in such cases.

**3.4** It has been noted already, on several occasions, that only a spouse is entitled to matrimonial home rights. Her rights end on decree absolute, when she becomes a former spouse. If she is not entitled by virtue of s 33(1)(a)(i) she becomes a non-entitled person, whose only remedy is to apply under s 35, where the powers of the court are significantly less than under s 33.

For this reason, s 33(5) permits the court to order that matrimonial home rights shall not be terminated by the termination of the marriage.

Subsection (5) provides that:

> 'If the applicant has matrimonial home rights and the respondent is the other spouse, an order under this section made during the marriage may provide that those rights are not brought to an end by—
>
> (a)   the death of the other spouse; or
> (b)   the termination (otherwise than by death) of the marriage.'

Two points for applicants' advisers to note, therefore, are first that the court should be invited to make such an order, and, secondly, that the application must be made before the grant of decree absolute. It must, of course, be borne in mind that where the parties are married and are contemplating, or in the throes of, divorce, and one of them has freehold or leasehold property, it is more likely than not that their long-term positions will be determined by a property adjustment application rather than an application under this Act. As to whether the court should accede to a request for an order under sub-s (5), the court must look to sub-s (8) which provides that:

'The court may exercise its powers under subsection (5) in any case where it considers that in all the circumstances it is just and reasonable to do so.'

The court therefore has the widest discretion. This follows a recommendation of The Law Commission, which thought that the previous law could be expressed with greater clarity.

'Giving the court express jurisdiction to make an order extending matrimonial home rights beyond divorce or death would resolve these uncertainties, although if the court were to make an order extending rights of occupation beyond death, it would generally be appropriate for some time limit or condition to be imposed on it.' (Law Com para 4.3)

In a footnote to this passage, The Law Commission adds:

'For instance, the spouse might be permitted to occupy the dwelling house for a certain length of time, or until a certain event occurred, such as the conclusion of a claim under the Inheritance (Provision for Family and Dependants) Act 1975.'

## How should the court exercise its discretion under section 33?

**3.5** As was seen when discussing the pre-1996 law, (see Chapter 1), the MHA gave limited guidance as to how the courts should exercise their discretion and the DVMPA gave none. The Law Commission thought it right that fairly detailed criteria should be established, and this approach has been followed in the Act. (At least one distinguished commentator has questioned the wisdom of this,[1] but that issue has been resolved by Parliament.)

The Law Commission recognised that a wide variety of cases had to be dealt with, and, accordingly, that the system had to be flexible:

'Hence the remedy itself may be of extreme seriousness, for example where the application is for the immediate exclusion of a person who has no alternative accommodation available from a home in which he is firmly established. The courts have frequently emphasised that such a grave step is not to be taken lightly or without proper regard for the due processes of the law. Of course, however serious the remedy, it may nevertheless be proper to grant it in the particular circumstances of the

---

[1] Dr SM Cretney, in his evidence to the House of Lords Select Committee.

case. In other cases, the remedy sought, or the circumstances in which it is sought, may not be of the same degree of gravity. The criteria to be applied by the courts have to be sufficiently flexible to cater appropriately for the very broad range of cases which may arise.' (Law Com para 4.21)

Originally, The Law Commission had suggested a 'balance of hardship' test. After consultation, this was changed to a 'balance of harm' test, and it is that approach which is adopted by the Act.

What has been said so far indicates the general approach in the Act. However, there are several different kinds of occupation orders, and the approach will vary in detail in each class. Since s 33 orders are currently being examined, it is s 33(6) which must now be considered.

**3.6**   Section 33(6) provides as follows:

'In deciding whether to exercise its powers under subsection (3) and (if so) in what manner, the court shall have regard to all the circumstances including—

(a)   the housing needs and housing resources of each of the parties and of any relevant child;

(b)   the financial resources of each of the parties;

(c)   the likely effect of any order, or of any decision by the court not to exercise its powers under subsection (3), on the health, safety or well-being of the parties and of any relevant child;

(d)   the conduct of the parties in relation to each other and otherwise.'

Pausing there, and before turning to sub-s (7), it will be seen that sub-s (6) concentrates on three broad areas; first, the housing needs and financial and other resources (including access to housing) of the parties. If the matter ended there, the competing claims of the parties would be resolved in favour of the more financially disadvantaged of them.

Secondly, however, the court must have regard to the health, safety and well-being of the parties and of any relevant child. 'Health' is defined by s 63(1) as including mental and physical health. 'Safety' may be clear enough; one of the purposes of the Act is to protect from molestation and violence, and the court would be concerned to ensure that a victim of violence was not compelled to reside with the perpetrator, nor to have to flee the home because of it.

'Well-being' may be more debatable. Both parties could argue that their well-being required that they continue to occupy their home; the well-being of both would suffer if they were to be ejected.

The final matter to which the court is directed to have regard is the conduct of the parties in relation to each other and otherwise. This is a new provision which was not in the 1995 Bill, and which appeared for the first time in the Family Law Bill. It was clearly designed to meet the objection that the 1995 Bill had been concerned with social engineering on a valueless basis. The court is now entitled to base its decision, in part, on a value judgement as to how the parties have behaved. Conduct is only one of the considerations, and should not be given undue weight in comparison with the others, but, in appropriate cases, it may well play an important part.

In passing, it should be noted that conduct reappears below in the context of the 'greater harm' test. Significant harm is only a relevant factor if it is attributable to the conduct of one of the parties; this, too, was an innovation in the Family Law Bill, and was not contained in the 1995 Bill.

**3.7**    It is, no doubt, in an effort to guide the court through these competing considerations that sub-s (7) provides as follows:

'If it appears to the court that the applicant or any relevant child is likely to suffer significant harm attributable to conduct of the respondent if an order under this section containing one or more of the provisions mentioned in subsection (3) is not made, the court shall make the order unless it appears to it that—

(a)    the respondent or any relevant child is likely to suffer significant harm if the order is made; and

(b)    the harm likely to be suffered by the respondent or child in that event is as great as, or greater than, the harm attributable to conduct of the respondent which is likely to be suffered by the applicant or child if the order is not made.'

A number of matters arise out of this. First, the subsection imposes on the court a positive duty to make one of the seven classes of order contained in sub-s (3) in certain circumstances. Secondly, those circumstances establish, in effect, a balance of harm test, provided the court is satisfied that the harm is significant.

In its report, The Law Commission explained the reasoning behind its recommendation, and how this would work in practice:

'In cases where the question of significant harm does not arise, the court would have power to make an order taking into account the three factors set out above; but, in cases where there is a likelihood of significant harm, this power becomes a duty and the court must make an order after balancing the degree of harm likely to be suffered by both parties and any children concerned. This approach would still work in the case of cross applications, where the court would firstly consider who would suffer the greatest risk of harm if the order were not made. In the event of the balance of harm being equal, the court would retain power to make an order, but would have no duty to do so, and so would still be able to reach the right result. Harm has a narrower meaning than hardship. It is defined as "ill-treatment or impairment of physical or mental health". In relation to children, the term will attract the definition used in section 31 of the Children Act 1989. It is likely that a respondent threatened with ouster on account of his violence would be able to establish a degree of hardship (perhaps in terms of difficulty in finding or unsuitability of alternative accommodation or problems in getting to work). But he is unlikely to suffer significant harm, whereas his wife and children who are being subjected to his violence or abuse may very easily suffer harm if he remains in the house. In this way the court will be treating violence or other forms of abuse as deserving immediate relief, and will be directed to make an order where a risk of significant harm exists. However, by placing an emphasis on the need for a remedy rather than on the conduct which gave rise to that need, the criteria will not actually put a premium on allegations of violence and thus may avoid the problems which would be generated by a scheme which focuses upon it. The proposed test also has the advantage that it will avoid giving rise to a situation in which the court is put in the undesirable position of having to choose between the interests of a child and those of an adult, as, in cases where there is a risk of significant harm to a child, the duty to make an order will come into operation and the child's welfare will effectively become the paramount consideration.' (Law Com para 4.34)

**3.8** It will be seen, therefore, that the first decision which the court has to make is whether or not to make any order at all; having decided to make an order, it must then decide which of the menu of orders contained in sub-s (3) it should make. If the decision-making process anticipated by The Law Commission is adopted, the chain of reasoning would be as follows:

(1)   The first consideration will be the direction contained in sub-s (7), namely to decide whether the applicant has established that she, or a relevant child, is likely to suffer significant harm attributable to conduct of the respondent if an order is not made; (the meaning of 'significant harm' is considered below). The harm which may be taken into account is limited to harm which is attributable to the conduct of the respondent; other harm is not to be taken into consideration.

(2)   Next, the court would have to consider whether the respondent had established that he or any relevant child would suffer significant harm if the order were made. Here, there is no requirement that the harm to be considered be attributable to the conduct of the applicant; the court may consider harm in the widest sense, for example, the harm which might be suffered as a result of being evicted.

(3)   Finally, the court would have to decide which party would suffer the greater harm; the applicant or a child if the order were not made, or the respondent or child if the order were made.

The process therefore has a cumulative effect; if the applicant fails to clear the first hurdle, sub-s (7) does not apply at all, and sub-s (6) alone would govern the decision. If the applicant passed that stage, but the respondent failed to satisfy the court as to the second test, the court would have to find in favour of the applicant. It would only be if both hurdles were crossed that the court would be faced with the balance of harm test.

**3.9**  As the extract from The Law Commission report envisaged, 'harm' is defined by s 63(1), which provides that 'harm':

'(a)  in relation to a person who has reached the age of eighteen years, means ill-treatment or the impairment of health; and

(b)  in relation to a child, means ill-treatment or the impairment of health or development;'

It was originally intended to define harm by reference to the Children Act 1989. In fact, an identical definition is now given, in the case of a child, in this Act.

'Development' is defined as 'physical, intellectual, emotional, social or behavioural development'. 'Health' means 'physical or mental health', and 'ill-treatment' includes 'sexual abuse and forms of ill-treatment which are not physical'.

Section 63(3) provides that where the question of whether harm suffered by a child is significant turns on the child's health or development, his heath or development shall be compared with that which could reasonably be expected of a similar child. As to the general question of when harm should be regarded as significant, some further guidance may be derived from Hershman and McFarlane's *Children Law and Practice* (Family Law), which, of course, has had to consider the meaning of 'significant harm' in the context of the Children Act 1989. There, at para **C[126]**, the matter is dealt with as follows:

'It will be a matter for the court to determine, on the balance of probabilities, whether the harm in a particular case is significant. . . . It is the harm which must be significant, rather than any act or omission which leads to the harm occurring or being likely to occur. . . . It is difficult for a qualitative term such as "significant" to be accurately defined. The guidance relies upon a dictionary definition of "significant", meaning "considerable, noteworthy or important"[2]; this definition has received judicial endorsement.[3] "Significant harm" is harm which the court should take into account when considering a child's future.[4] The assessment of whether harm in a particular case is significant may involve the court considering whether, on an objective general view, the harm would be significant if it occurred to any child. Equally, it seems that the court must also consider the particular characteristics of the child concerned to determine whether harm, which may not be significant in the general context, is nevertheless significant in the case of the particular child. . . . Not all harm will be significant. Even if a court is satisfied, for example, that sexual abuse has occurred, it must consider whether the

---

[2] *The Children Act 1989 Guidance and Regulations Volume 1 Court Orders*, para 3.19.
[3] *Humberside County Council v B* [1993] 1 FLR 257.
[4] *Re B (A Minor) (Child Abuse: Custody)* [1990] 2 FLR 317.

harm occasioned by the ill-treatment is significant. . . . The court may also consider the significance of the harm from a cultural, racial or social perspective. Harm which may be significant in some circumstances may not be significant in others.'

It is submitted that this may be additional guidance to the manner in which, *mutatis mutandis*, the court should approach the question of 'significant harm' in cases of occupation orders.

**3.10**    The court therefore has clear guidelines to follow where it is satisfied that significant harm has been established. The approach where this has not been established, and the process is governed by s 33(6) only, is less clear. What was said at the conclusion of para **3.6** is repeated; one wonders whether the reference to 'the health, safety or well-being of the parties' contained in s 33(6)(c) would be particularly important in the absence of a positive finding under s 33(7).

When a relationship, such as a marriage, breaks down, it is normally very uncomfortable for the parties to go on residing under the same roof. However, the predecessors to this Act were not intended for mere social engineering, and orders were never made on the basis of convenience; one presumes that, notwithstanding the fact that the guidelines are now wider, this will continue to be the case. In the case of spouses, presumably the long-term question of which party, if either, continues to occupy the matrimonial home will be dealt with by the vehicle of a property adjustment order and not by this Act.

## Duration of orders

**3.11**    The final matter in relation to s 33 which must be mentioned, and which may also be relevant in relation to para **3.8**, above, is sub-s (10), which deals with the duration of orders. It is provided that an order under s 33:

'may, in so far as it has continuing effect, be made for a specified period, until the occurrence of a specified event, or until further order.'

Subsection (10) therefore does not contemplate the possibility of an order which would last for an indeterminate period. There must either be some date or event which will terminate the rights given by the order, or those rights must be stated to subsist 'until further order'.

No s 33 order can, therefore, be said to be a final order, in the same way that, for example, a property adjustment order is final.

## Orders which can be made under section 35

**3.12**    The orders which have so far been considered have been those which may be granted to an applicant who is either 'entitled' or has matrimonial home rights. Non-entitled applicants are dealt with under ss 35, 36, 37 or 38, depending on whether the respondent is or is not entitled and on whether or not the applicant is a former spouse.

Section 35 deals with cases where the applicant is non-entitled, the respondent is entitled and the applicant is a former spouse. Subsection (1) applies where:

'(a) one former spouse is entitled to occupy a dwelling-house by virtue of a beneficial estate or interest or contract or by virtue of any enactment giving him the right to remain in occupation; and

(b) the other former spouse is not so entitled; and

(c) the dwelling-house was at any time their matrimonial home or was at any time intended by them to be their matrimonial home.'

Subsection (2) then provides that, in such cases, the former spouse, not so entitled, may apply for an order under this section against the entitled former spouse.

Entitlement to apply under s 35 was considered in more detail at para **2.18** above. Here, it is merely necessary to comment that the section will never apply to spouses, since they have matrimonial home rights. Applicants under this section will therefore always be former spouses; the respondent will always be 'entitled'.

**3.13** Subsections (3) to (5) prescribe what a s 35 order must, and may contain. By sub-s (3) every order under s 35 must contain the following provision if the applicant is in occupation:

'(a) giving the applicant the right not to be evicted or excluded from the dwelling-house or any part of it by the respondent for the period specified in the order; and

(b) prohibiting the respondent from evicting or excluding the applicant during that period.'

By subsection (4), if the applicant is not in occupation, the order must contain provision:

'(a) giving the applicant the right to enter into and occupy the dwelling-house for the period specified in the order; and

(b) requiring the respondent to permit the exercise of that right.'

These requirements are mandatory; if the court decides to make any order at all, these provisions must be included. It will be seen that the provisions of sub-ss (3) and (4) are similar to, but not identical with, matrimonial home rights. The similarities are obvious, and may be demonstrated by comparing this subsection with s 30(2), (see para **3.2** above).

The differences are as follows. First, there is no mention of 'leave of the court'. The reason for this is that matrimonial home rights are an entitlement conferred by statute, whereas the protection under a s 35 order is always contained in an order of the court.

Secondly, whereas matrimonial home rights are a general protection, with no time-limit (save that they disappear on decree absolute), the rights under a s 35 order will subsist only for 'the period specified in the order'. Courts will,therefore, have to ensure that every order under s 35 specifies a period for the duration of the rights conferred.

**3.14**  Subsection (5) prescribes the provisions which a s 35 order may contain, in addition to the mandatory matters set out above. An order under s 35 may:

> '(a) regulate the occupation of the dwelling-house by either or both parties;
> (b) prohibit, suspend or restrict the exercise by the respondent of his right to occupy the dwelling-house;
> (c) require the respondent to leave the dwelling-house or part of the dwelling-house;
> (d) exclude the respondent from a defined area in which the dwelling-house is included.'

These provisions are identical to those found in s 33(3)(c), (d), (f) and (g). Comment on all these provisions will be found at para **3.3** above.

## Guidelines for court's discretion under section 35

**3.15**  As is the pattern in this Act, clear guidelines are laid down to guide the court in the exercise of its discretion. However, this is complicated by the fact that different guidelines are prescribed depending on what type of order the court has it in mind to make.

First, sub-s (6) provides that when deciding whether to exercise its powers under sub-ss (3) or (4), (that is to say, the mandatory contents of a s 35 order which are roughly equivalent in effect to matrimonial home rights), the court shall have regard to:

> '... all the circumstances including—
>
> (a) the housing needs and housing resources of each of the parties and of any relevant child;
> (b) the financial resources of each of the parties;
> (c) the likely effect of any order, or of any decision by the court not to exercise its powers under subsection (3) or (4), on the health, safety or well-being of the parties and of any relevant child;
> (d) the conduct of the parties in relation to each other and otherwise;
> (e) the length of time that has elapsed since the parties ceased to live together;
> (f) the length of time that has elapsed since the marriage was dissolved or annulled; and
> (g) the the existence of any pending proceedings between the parties—

(i)   for an order under section 23A or 24 of the Matrimonial Causes Act 1973 (property adjustment orders in connection with divorce proceedings etc);

(ii)  for an order under paragraph 1(2)(d) or (e) of Schedule 1 to the Children Act 1989 (orders for financial relief against parents); or

(iii) relating to the legal or beneficial ownership of the dwelling-house.'

The matters set out above are, therefore, those which the court must consider when deciding whether or not to make an order under sub-s (3) or (4) (that is, in effect, whether to make any s 35 order at all).

**3.16** Subsection (7) then deals with the matters to which the court must have regard when considering orders under sub-s (5), referred to as 'a subsection (5) provision'. However, it may be helpful at this stage to pause to consider the matters which must be considered by the court when deciding whether or not and, if so, in what terms, to make an order under sub-ss (3) or (4); this is the first step for the court. The meaning of sub-ss (6)(a), (b) and (c) have already been considered at para **3.6** above in the context of s 33, and need not be examined further here. However, sub-s (6) raises a number of new issues which are worthy of comment. First, however, it is worth remembering that what the court would be considering at this stage would be whether or not to make a s 35 order at all. Although sub-s (6) applies when the court is:

' . . . deciding whether to make an order under this section containing provision of the kind mentioned in subsection (3) or (4) and (if so) in what manner,'

there is in fact no power in the court to decide 'in what manner' such an order should be made because the provisions of sub-ss (3) and (4) are mandatory once the decision has been taken to make a s 35 order. Therefore, the only way in which the court could exercise its discretion is in deciding whether or not to make any order at all.

The Law Commission favoured a discretionary approach:

' . . . which would permit the court to make orders which reflect what might be the parties' legitimate expectations according to the circumstances of each particular case.' (Law Com para 4.12)

In deciding such a matter, the court is therefore directed to have regard to four areas; (a), (b) and (c) are similar to those in s 33, which have already been discussed (see para **3.6** above). It is then necessary to go on to consider the conduct of the parties; again, this has been discussed already.

The second is the lapse of time since the separation and the third is the lapsed time since the dissolution of the marriage. The court is being directed to have regard to the reality of the case, and, by implication, not to make an order where the nexus between the parties is a thing of the past.

Finally, the court must take account of any other pending proceedings between the parties. There is no guidance as to how the court should regard these proceedings; this would depend entirely on the circumstances of the case. It is suggested that the significance of this provision is that the court should consider whether the issues between the parties could be more conveniently dealt with in other proceedings.

These may all be regarded as matters additional to the factors set out in sub-ss (a), (b) and (c), and as such have no greater weight than those matters, but they clearly temper them to some extent.

**3.17**  Having made its decision to make a s 35 order, the court must then decide which, if any, of the menu of orders available by virtue of sub-s (5) it should make. Its decision in this respect is governed by sub-s (7), which provides that the court must have regard to 'all the circumstances including the matters mentioned in subsection (6)(a) to (e)'. Those matters have already been discussed above.

Subsection (8) then goes on to provide that if the court decides to make an order under this section, and it appears to it that if the order does not contain a subsection (5) provision the applicant or any relevant child is likely to suffer significant harm attributable to the conduct of the respondent:

'the court shall include the subsection (5) provision in the order unless it appears to the court that—

(a)    the respondent or any relevant child is likely to suffer significant harm if the provision is included in the order; and'

Subsection (7)(b) of s 33 is repeated.

The effect of this is that the greater harm test, the full significance of which was discussed at para **3.7** above, is repeated here and is again an overriding requirement in deciding whether or not any of the menu of orders in s 35(5) is to be included.

## Duration of section 35 orders

**3.18**  Sub-sections (9) and (10) deal with the duration of s 35 orders. By sub-s (9), such an order may not be made after the death of either party, and ceases to have effect on the death of either party.

Subsection (10) limits the duration of the order, providing that any order must be limited 'so as to have effect for a specified period not exceeding six months'. The parties, and the court, must therefore ensure that this period is not exceeded. However, it is also provided that a s 35 order:

' . . . may be extended (on one or more occasions) for a further specified period not exceeding six months.'

No s 35 order can be for longer than six months; any number can be made; none may be regarded as a final order.

# Occupation orders involving cohabitants

**3.19**  Having dealt with cases where the applicant is either entitled, a spouse or a former spouse (leaving on one side the position where no-one is entitled – as to which see para **3.27** below), we must pass on to cohabitants. It should be mentioned here that the 1995 Bill made no distinction between former spouses and cohabitants which, no doubt, was one of the reasons for its downfall. Part IV of the Act is careful to make a clear distinction between the parts of the Act which apply to former spouses and those applicable to cohabitants (although whether the end result is much different is another matter).

This, therefore, may be a convenient moment to set out s 41 which has to be considered whenever the parties are cohabitants or former cohabitants, and which therefore has an overriding effect.

Section 41(1) states that it applies if the parties are cohabitants or former cohabitants. Subsection (2) then provides that:

> 'Where the court is required to consider the nature of the parties' relationship, it is to have regard to the fact that they have not given each other the commitment involved in marriage.'

**3.20**  It has to be said that it is not immediately clear what subsection (2) means, nor how it is likely to be interpreted by the courts. Each section, affecting each class of applicant, has its own set of guidelines to which the court is directed to have regard, and, as has been seen, the significant harm test is an overriding factor which runs through all of them. Quite what sub-s (2) adds to this is somewhat of a mystery; why it came into being is clear enough, but, for the moment, one can only await further interpretation.

# Occupation orders under section 36

**3.21**  It is now appropriate to pass on to consider the first class of case involving cohabitants or former cohabitants, namely, that where the applicant is non-entitled and the respondent is entitled. Section 36(1) provides that s 36 applies if:

> '(a)  one cohabitant or former cohabitant is entitled to occupy a dwelling-house by virtue of a beneficial estate or interest or contract or by virtue of any enactment giving him the right to remain in occupation;
>
> (b)  the other cohabitant or former cohabitant is not so entitled; and
>
> (c)  that dwelling-house is the home in which they live together as husband and wife or a home in which they at any time so lived together or intended so to live together.'

These provisions need no comment; the general thrust has already been discussed.

Subsection (2) then provides that the cohabitant or former cohabitant not so entitled may apply for an order under s 36 against the other party.

**3.22**   Subsections (3) and (4) then set out what an order under s 36 *must* contain. These are identical with sub-ss (3) and (4) of s 35, which is set out at para **3.13** above.

Subsection (5) contains the matters which an order under s 36 *may* contain; once again, these are identical to sub-s (5) of s 35, discussed at para **3.14** above.

The reader may, therefore, wonder why it has been necessary to create the subdivision of what was, in the 1995 Bill, one section, and to draw a distinction between a former spouse and a cohabitant. The answer lies in the guidelines which are laid down for the exercise of the court's discretion.

**3.23**   Subsection (6) governs the exercise of the court's discretion in deciding whether to make an order of the kind mentioned in sub-ss (3) and (4) ie, in effect, whether to make an order at all. Many of the matters set out in the guidelines in s 36(6) are identical with those contained in s 35(6) (see para **3.15** above). Paragraphs (a) to (d) are exactly the same in both subsections. Section 36(6)(i) is identical to s 35(6)(g), save that it omits reference to orders under the MCA 1973, for obvious reasons.

The differences are in s 36(6)(e) to (h), which are as follows:

'(e)   the nature of the parties' relationship;
(f)   the length of time during which they have lived together as husband and wife;
(g)   whether there are or have been any children who are children of both parties or for whom both parties have or have had parental responsibility;
(h)   the length of time that has elapsed since the parties ceased to live together.'

Comparison with s 35(6) shows that (h) has its counterpart in sub-s (6)(f) of that section. The real differences are therefore contained in (e), (f) and (g). Given that the parties have never married, the court has, in effect, to make a value judgement on the nature of the relationship; cohabitants may vary from those who have entered into a fleeting relationship to those who have lived together in a stable relationship for many years and have brought up children together. In deciding who is to occupy the home, and for how long, the court will have to take these matters into account.

**3.24**   A potentially more significant difference from the s 35 provisions is contained in s 36(7), which deals with whether or not to include any of the sub-s (5) provisions in an order which the court has decided to make which contains the matters mentioned in sub-s (3) or (4); this is, essentially, the significant harm test. By sub-s (7), the court is directed to have regard to:

'. . . all the circumstances including—

(a) the matters mentioned in subsection (6)(a) to (d); and

(b) the questions mentioned in subsection (8).'

By sub-s (8), the questions are:

'(a) whether the applicant or any relevant child is likely to suffer significant harm attributable to conduct of the respondent if the subsection (5) provision is not included in the order; and

(b) whether the harm likely to be suffered by the respondent or child if the provision is included is as great as or greater than the harm attributable to conduct of the respondent which is likely to be suffered by the applicant or child if the provision is not included.'

This is similar in some respects to the greater harm test contained in s 35, discussed at para **3.17** above. However, there is one obvious difference. Under s 35(8), which applies the greater harm test to former spouses, the court must include a sub-s (5) provision where the first limb of the greater harm test is satisfied, unless satisfied as to the second limb; once significant harm is established, the onus passes to the respondent to show why a sub-s (5) provision should not be included.

Under s 36(8), applicable to cohabitants or former cohabitants, there is no such requirement on the court. The issue of the balance of significant harm is a 'question' for the consideration of the court; the court must consider it, but there is no obligation on the court to exercise its discretion in any particular direction once it has made a finding.

It might be argued that the court would be acting unreasonably, or unjudicially, if it did not include a sub-s (5) provision after making a finding in favour of one party as to one of the sub-s (8) questions. However, the difference in wording between the two provisions is deliberate and it might be thought, therefore, that the intention of Parliament was that the protection to be afforded to a cohabitant is less than that which the court is obliged to afford to a former spouse.

**3.25** Subsection (9) contains provisions identical to those in s 35(9). Subsection (1) provides that an order under s 36 must be limited so as to have effect for a specified period not exceeding six months, but may be extended on one further occasion for a further specified period not exceeding six months. This is the second principal difference between these provisions and the s 35 provisions. A cohabitant or former cohabitant is limited to an occupation order for one year; then she must leave.

The intention is clearly that, if the applicant is unable to justify occupation on other grounds in other proceedings (eg under the Children Act, or by proving a beneficial or equitable interest), an occupation order should not in the long term displace the interest in the property of the entitled party.

**3.26** Finally, sub-s (13) provides that, so long as the order remains in force, sub-ss (3) to (6) of s 30 apply in relation to the applicant as if he were a spouse entitled to occupy the dwelling-house by virtue of that section and the respondent were the other spouse. These provisions relate to payment of rent, mortgage etc.

## Occupation orders where neither party entitled

**3.27**    The final class, or classes, of occupation orders is applicable where neither party is entitled. The categories were set out in Chapter 2 at para **2.20**; the requirements are that the parties must still occupy the dwelling-house (there is no entitlement to apply if one is not in occupation) and the dwelling-house must be the matrimonial home in the case of spouses or former spouses, or the home in which they live or lived together as husband and wife in the case of cohabitants or former cohabitants. These provisions would apply where, for example, the parties were squatters, or where their right of occupation had been terminated. It is intended that any order should be of a short-term nature.

**3.28**    Spouses and former spouses are covered by s 37 and cohabitants and former cohabitants by s 38. Subsection (3) of both sections sets out in identical terms what orders the court may make. These are to:

'(a)   require the respondent to permit the applicant to enter and remain in the dwelling-house or part of the dwelling-house;
 (b)   regulate the occupation of the dwelling-house by either or both of the parties;
 (c)   require the respondent to leave the dwelling-house or part of the dwelling-house; or
 (d)   exclude the respondent from a defined area in which the dwelling-house is included.'

The differences are to be found in the guidelines for the exercise of the court's discretion.

**3.29**    Section 37(4), which applies to spouses and former spouses provides that sub-ss (6) and (7) of s 33 apply to the exercise by the court of its powers under this section as they apply to the exercise by the court of its powers under sub-s (3) of that section. These provisions are set out at para **3.6** above, and contain the obligation to include one or more of the orders set out therein on the greater harm test, unless the respondent succeeds on that test.

   Section 38(4), which applies to cohabitants and former cohabitants, provides that in the exercise of its discretion the court must have regard to all the circumstances including the matters which it goes on to set out. These are, in fact, identical to those contained in s 36(7) and (8) (see para **3.24** above), with five exceptions.

   There is no reference to:

(i)    children;

| (ii) | the nature of the relationship; |
|---|---|
| (iii) | the length of the relationship; |
| (iv) | the length of time since they ceased to live together; |
| (v) | other proceedings. |

This, in effect, leaves needs, resources, effect of order and conduct as the relevant factors. Significant harm is dealt with as a 'question' the court must consider but, as in s 36, there is no requirement on the court to make any particular order as a result of that inquiry.

**3.30** By s 37(5), an order in respect of spouses or former spouses must be limited to six months, with the possibility of one extension of a further six months. Section 38(6) makes identical provision for cohabitants or former cohabitants.

## Supplementary and additional provisions

**3.31** Section 39 contains certain supplementary provisions relating to any occupation order.

First, by sub-s (2), an application for an occupation order may be made in any other family proceedings, or without any other family proceedings being instituted. In other words, if proceedings, for example for divorce, already exist the application may be made in those proceedings; if not, they may be 'free-standing' proceedings in their own right. This is merely to repeat the pre-1996 Act position.

Subsection (3) provides that if:

'(a) an application for an occupation order is made under section 33, 35, 36, 37 or 38, and

(b) the court considers that it has no power to make the order under the section concerned, but that it has power to make an order under one of the other sections,

the court may make an order under that other section.'

The effect of this is that an application will not be defeated by having been brought under the wrong section.

Finally, sub-s (4) provides that the fact that someone has applied for or been granted an occupation order shall not affect his right to claim a legal or equitable interest in the property in any subsequent proceedings.

**3.32** Section 40 deals with the important question of additional provisions which may be included in occupation orders made under ss 33, 35 or 36. Before the 1996 Act, the court had power to make such orders in MHA proceedings, but not otherwise. The Law Commission recommended that the court should have power to make ancillary orders as to the discharge of rent, mortgage instalments and other outgoings in all cases. This should not be the principal relief in emergency cases, but might be particularly useful when an occupation order continued for some time, perhaps awaiting the outcome of proceedings under the MCA 1973 or under the ordinary law of property. The court should also have power to make orders about the use of furniture; it was not expected that these would be frequently used, but they did occasionally arise in matrimonial cases at present (Law Com paras 4.38 and 4.40).

Section 40 therefore provides that on making an order under ss 33, 35 or 36, or at any time thereafter, the court may:

'(a)   impose on either party obligations as to
>    (i)     the repair and maintenance of the dwelling-house; or
>    (ii)    the discharge of rent, mortgage payments or other outgoings affecting the dwelling-house;
(b)   order a party occupying the dwelling-house or any part of it (including a party who is entitled to do so by virtue of a beneficial estate or interest or contract or by virtue of any enactment giving him the right to remain in occupation) to make periodical payments to the other party in respect of the accommodation, if the other party would (but for the order) be entitled to occupy the dwelling-house by virtue of a beneficial estate or interest or contract or by virtue of any such enactment;
(c)   grant either party possession or use of furniture or other contents of the dwelling-house;
(d)   order either party to take reasonable care of any furniture or other contents of the dwelling-house;
(e)   order either party to take reasonable steps to keep the dwelling-house and any furniture or other contents secure.'

Either party, whether the one in occupation or the one denied occupation, may therefore be ordered to pay outgoings on the property. In addition, or alternatively, a party in occupation may be ordered to pay an occupation charge to the party not in occupation, provided the party not in occupation is 'entitled'. Finally, the court may decide which party is entitled to use the furniture or other effects. This need not be the party in occupation; a situation can be foreseen in which a party ordered to leave the home would be in need of certain basic effects to take with him.

It will be noted that these provisions do not apply to ss 37 or 38 orders; the reason is that in those cases neither party has any legal right of occupation, and therefore the question of liability for outgoings does not arise.

**3.33**   Section 40(2) contains guidelines to govern the exercise of the court's discretion. It is provided that in deciding whether and, if so, how to exercise its powers, the court shall have regard to all the circumstances of the case, including:

'(a)   the financial needs and financial resources of the parties; and

(b) the financial obligations which they have, or are likely to have in the foreseeable future, including financial obligations to each other and to any relevant child.'

No particular comment is needed on these provisions.

By sub-s (3), any order under this section ceases to have effect when the occupation order to which it relates ceases to have effect.

## Ex parte orders, powers of arrest and undertakings

**3.34**  Occupation orders may, in exceptional circumstances, be made on an ex parte basis. Further discussion of this will be found at Chapter 4.

A power of arrest may be attached to an occupation order. This is dealt with in Chapter 5.

**3.35**  In any case where the court has power to make an occupation order, it may accept an undertaking (s 46(1)). Undertakings are considered in detail in Chapter 4.

# CHAPTER FOUR

# Non-molestation Orders

## Introduction

**4.1** As was seen in Chapter 1, the power of the court to protect against molestation originally derived from the inherent jurisdiction of the court to protect the subject, in particular, children, from wrongdoing at the hands of others. This assumed statutory form in the DVMPA and DPMCA. One of the purposes of the new legislation is to unify this jurisdiction with that relating to occupation orders.

In its report, The Law Commission said that molestation was an umbrella term which covered a wide range of behaviour.

> 'Although there is no statutory definition of molestation, the concept is well established and recognised by the courts. Molestation includes, but is wider than violence. It encompasses any form of serious pestering or harassment and applies to any conduct which could properly be regarded as such a degree of harassment as to call for the intervention of the court.' (Law Com para 3.1)

Examples given by The Law Commission were *Horner v Horner* [1982] Fam 90, in which it was held that handing the plaintiff menacing letters and intercepting her on her way to work amounted to molestation, and *Johnson v Walton* [1990] 1 FLR 350, where sending partially nude photographs of the plaintiff to a national newspaper for publication with the intent of causing her distress was held to come within a prohibition against molestation.

One question which The Law Commission had canvassed was whether there should be some statutory definition of molestation. Their conclusion was that there was no evidence of problems having been caused in practice by the lack of such definition, and, indeed, concern was expressed that a definition might become over restrictive or lead to borderline disputes. Accordingly, they recommended that there should be no statutory definition of molestation. The court should have power to grant a non-molestation order where this was just and reasonable having regard to all the circumstances including the need to secure the health, safety or well-being of the applicant or a relevant child (Law Com para 3.6).

It will be observed that the Protection from Harassment Act 1997, considered in detail in Chapter 10, likewise contains no definition of harassment.

# What is a non-molestation order?

**4.2**   A 'non-molestation order' is defined by s 42(1) as:

'... an order containing either or both of the following provisions—

    (a)   provision prohibiting a person ("the respondent") from molesting another person who is associated with the respondent;

    (b)   provision prohibiting the respondent from molesting a relevant child.'

As was seen in para **4.1** above, it was thought that 'molesting' needed no further definition. The next question, therefore, is that of who may apply for a non-molestation order. This question has been considered at some length in Chapter 2, but it may be helpful to summarise the position briefly here.

There has to be a definable nexus between the applicant and the respondent; for example, if one were trying to think of classes of persons who might need to come before the court for protection from intimidation, neighbours might be an obvious category. The draftsman of Part IV of the Act, which itself is in narrower terms than those recommended by The Law Commission, was concerned to avoid ambiguities and not to provide blanket relief to a very wide category of potential applicants. Accordingly, neighbours are certainly not within the definition and neither is one of the somewhat broad categories favoured by The Law Commission (see Chapter 2 for further discussion of the point). For protection, such people would have to invoke the Protection from Harassment Act 1997 (see Chapter 10).

The test which has been adopted is twofold; either the applicant must be 'associated' with the respondent, or the applicant and respondent must be parties to the same family proceedings. The meaning of 'associated' is defined by s 62(3) and has already been considered at length in Chapter 2, as were 'relevant child' and 'family proceedings'; a checklist for deciding who are associated persons will be found at para **2.20**.

Broadly speaking, therefore, there has to be, or have been, some link such as marriage, cohabitation, family tie, or a decision to share a home. This is still a considerable extension of the range of possible applicants, compared with what went before, and may produce some quite surprising results, as may be seen from the discussion at para **2.17** et seq above.

**4.3**   By sub-s (2), the court may make a non-molestation order:

    '(a)   if an application for the order has been made (whether in other family proceedings or without any other family proceedings being instituted) by a person who is associated with the respondent; or

    (b)   if in any family proceedings to which the respondent is a party the court considers that the order should be made for the benefit of any other party to the proceedings or any relevant child even though no such application has been made.'

Much of this follows from what has already been said. Sub-paragraph (a) establishes that the application may be made in the course of other family proceedings or as a 'free-standing' application.

Sub-paragraph (b) might mean that the court could make a non-molestation order of its own motion, even where no one had applied for it. This was considered by The Law Commission, whose view was that it would be less appropriate for orders regulating the lives of adults, where it might reasonably be expected that they could decide for themselves when an application was necessary. In relation to children, it might be desirable in the interests of those children for the court to react immediately to a situation which had arisen and make an appropriate order. A non-molestation order was different from an occupation order in that it was often truly ancillary to some other remedy, and the need for it might only become apparent during the proceedings. Further, such an order would not prejudice the respondent's interests to any significant extent. Also, an own motion power could be useful on occasions where the victim was intimidated or for some other reason reluctant to apply for a non-molestation order herself. Accordingly, it was recommended that the court should have power to make non-molestation orders of its own motion, and this is what appears in the Act (Law Com para 5.2).

Sub-paragraph (b) also means that the court may make such an order in the course of other family proceedings at the request of one of the parties, even though no formal application had been made. The court will therefore not be constrained by the lack of an application on paper, although, where the respondent was not present, it would need to be convinced that an ex parte order was appropriate.

**4.4** Subsection (3) provides that 'family proceedings' includes proceedings in which the court has made an emergency protection order under s 44 of the Children Act 1989 which includes an exclusion requirement. This topic is considered in more detail in Chapter 6, but it may be noted here that the effect of this provision is that, where the court excludes a suspected abuser from a dwelling-house as part of an emergency protection order, it may also make a non-molestation order.

**4.5** There are no time-limits on the making of a non-molestation order except that where an applicant claims to be entitled because of an agreement to marry, in which case no application may be brought after the end of the period of 3 years beginning with the day on which the agreement to marry was terminated (s 42(4)).

**4.6** By subsection (6), a non-molestation order may be expressed so as to refer to molestation in general, to particular acts of molestation, or to both. In other words, the order may forbid the respondent from 'molesting the applicant', or, for example, from 'assaulting the applicant' or 'harassing or threatening or pestering the applicant', or whatever is appropriate in the particular case.

By subsection (7), a non-molestation order may be made for a specified period or until further order. This follows the recommendation of The Law Commission, which stated that:

> 'No distinction should be drawn on the basis of the class of applicant as protection should be available when and for as long as it is needed. Fixed time limits are inevitably arbitrary and can restrict the court's ability to react flexibly to problems arising within the family. In particular, it is important that non-molestation orders should continue to be capable of enduring beyond the end of a relationship, although in some cases, short-term relief will be all that is necessary or desirable.' (Law Com para 3.28)

Under the pre-1996 law, it was unusual to make an 'open ended' domestic violence injunction which might run indefinitely, and the forms prescribed by the County Court Rules contained provision for the insertion of the date until which the order was to remain in force (see Form N16, CCR). The practice has been for such an order to remain in force for not more than 6 months in the first instance, and although there is no reason to think that this will change, the specimen non-molestation orders attached to Form FL404 (see Appendix III at p 211) contain no provision for the insertion of a date on which the order will cease to have effect. It may be that when the printed forms of order appear they will contain such provision; in any event, there seems to be no reason why the court should not amend Form FL404 to that extent.

## How will the court exercise its discretion?

**4.7**   Section 42(5) sets out the matters to which the court must have regard. It is provided that:

> 'In deciding whether to exercise its powers under this section and, if so, in what manner, the court shall have regard to all the circumstances including the need to secure the health, safety and well-being—
>
> (a)   of the applicant or, in a case falling within subsection (2)(b) above, the person for whose benefit the order would be made, and
> (b)   of any relevant child.'

As has been seen, sub-s (2)(b) referred to cases where an order is made without a formal application having been made.

Section 42(5) is in broad terms, and appears to give the court wide discretion. It would appear that 'health, safety and well-being' is to be regarded as a term which is to be read together, rather than broken up into its constituent parts (it does not say 'health *or* safety *or* well-being'). By s 63, 'health' is defined as including physical or mental health. Otherwise, these terms are not defined by the Act, and so must be taken to have their normal dictionary meaning.

However, it will be seen that when the court is deciding whether or not to make an ex parte order, or to attach a power of arrest, somewhat more positive guidelines are given.

# Ex parte orders

**4.8** As was seen in Chapter 1, under the pre-1996 law, case-law had developed to govern the making of ex parte orders, that is to say, orders of which the respondent had been given no notice. Such orders should only be made in 'cases of real urgency, where there has been a true impossibility of giving notice'; see Chapter 1 for a fuller discussion.

This case-law has now been superseded by the statutory provisions contained in s 45. It should be noted that these provisions apply to both non-molestation orders and to occupation orders.

This question had been considered at some length by The Law Commission. It was decided that the power to make ex parte orders should extend to occupation orders, while accepting that ex parte occupation orders, particularly ouster orders, were extremely rare. It appears therefore that no change in the existing approach to occupation orders is envisaged (Law Com para 5.5).

The Law Commission quoted approvingly from, and, implicitly, adopted the judgment of Ormrod LJ in *Ansah v Ansah* [1977] Fam 138, in the following terms:

> 'the power of the court to intervene immediately and without notice in proper cases is essential to the administration of justice. But this power must be used with great caution and only in circumstances in which it is really necessary to act immediately. Such circumstances do undoubtedly tend to occur more frequently in family disputes than in other types of litigation because the parties are often still in close contact with one another and particularly when a marriage is breaking up, in a state of high emotional tension; but even in such cases the court should only act ex parte in an emergency when the interests of justice or the protection of the applicant or a child clearly demands immediate intervention by the court. Such cases should be extremely rare.'

**4.9** The Law Commission pointed out that while general rules of court existed in the High Court and in county courts to deal with ex parte orders, no such rules existed in magistrates' courts.

> 'One of our principal aims in undertaking this project has been to remove unnecessary distinctions between different courts and where possible, to give them uniform powers within a unified jurisdiction. We think this can be best achieved by providing an overall statutory framework which

contains common principles and procedures with a standard test and have therefore made express provision for this. ... The standard test would be that applied at present in the higher courts, that the court should have a general discretion to grant orders where in all the circumstances it would be just and convenient to do so.[1] Including this in the legislation has the further advantage of permitting some indication to be given of the special features which should be taken into account when the courts are dealing with ex parte applications in these cases, thus providing a degree of consistency between courts and also some guidance for the lay magistrates who will be called upon to exercise these powers. These factors will not be exclusive: the court should in each case take into account any other relevant circumstances. They are, however, cumulative, and any one of them might be decisive in a particular case.' (Law Com para 5.7)

**4.10**   Thus it is that s 45(1) provides that:

'The court may, in any case where it considers that it is just and convenient to do so, make an occupation order or a non-molestation order even though the respondent has not been given such notice of the proceedings as would otherwise be required by rules of court.'

This is, therefore, the statutory power to make an ex parte order.
  Section 45(2) sets out the guidelines, as follows:

'In determining whether to exercise its powers under subsection (1) above the court shall have regard to all the circumstances including—

(a)   any risk of significant harm to the applicant or a relevant child, attributable to conduct of the respondent if the order is not made immediately;

(b)   whether it is likely that the applicant will be deterred or prevented from pursuing the application if an order is not made immediately; and

(c)   whether there is reason to believe that the respondent is aware of the proceedings but is deliberately evading service and that the applicant or a relevant child will be seriously prejudiced by the delay involved—

  (i)    where the court is a magistrates' court, in effecting service of the proceedings; or

  (ii)   in any other case, in effecting substituted service.'

  The final point in sub-s (2), relating to substituted service, reflects the fact that substituted service is not available in magistrates' courts. Summonses under the DPMCA had to be served personally unless the court was satisfied

---

[1] Supreme Court Act 1981, s 37(1) and (2).

by evidence that prompt personal service of the summons was impracticable (Magistrates' Courts Rules 1981, r 99(7)).

Little further comment on these provisions is required. It will be seen that the court 'may' make an ex parte order; the power is discretionary and, although guidelines are given for the exercise of this discretion, there is no mandatory element. (Contrast the position as to powers of arrest, set out in Chapter 5.)

Rule 3.8(5) requires an applicant for an ex parte order to state the reasons for no notice having been given in the sworn statement which must accompany the application.

As will be seen in Chapter 5, a power of arrest may be attached to an ex parte order, but the discretion of the court as to whether to do so is not fettered, as it is when considering an application on notice.

Section 45(3) provides that when the court exercises its power to make an ex parte order:

> '... it must afford the respondent an opportunity to make representations relating to the order as soon as just and convenient at a full hearing.'

It is therefore mandatory to give what is known as a 'return day' so that the matter may be reconsidered in the presence of both parties.

**4.11**   Subsection (4) contains provisions to govern the manner in which any time provided for in an ex parte order (described in this context as an 'initial order') is to be taken into account when a 'full order' is made at a 'full hearing'. The various sections under which occupation orders are made stipulate maximum times for the subsistence of such orders. The effect of sub-s (4) is that, for this purpose, any full order is deemed to have commenced when the initial order commenced, so that time begins to run from the date of the initial order.

## Undertakings

**4.12**   An undertaking is a promise which a party makes to the court to do, or, more commonly, not to do certain things. Examples of undertakings which are frequently given are:

- not to molest, assault or harass the other party;
- not to enter or attempt to enter a certain property;
- [sometimes] not to come within a certain distance of a property;
- to vacate a certain property by a certain date and time and not thereafter to return.

The advantage of accepting an undertaking from the point of view of the court is that this represents a method of allowing the parties to 'settle' their dispute. From the point of view of the parties, the complainant is not required to give evidence and the person giving the undertaking may do so on the basis that no admissions are made regarding the allegations made against him.

In county courts, the disposal of domestic violence cases by means of undertakings has become very common; in fact, it is the norm. There is no reason to think that this will change under the new Act. Moreover, the practice is now extended to magistrates' courts.

**4.13**   Section 46(1) provides that in any case where the court has power to make an occupation order or a non-molestation order, the court may accept an undertaking from any party to the proceedings. This is the statutory power to accept an undertaking; it replaces what was previously based on practice and rule.

The amended forms prescribed for use under Part IV contain a new Form FL422 which is the general form of undertaking; it is identical to CCR Form N117 which has been in use in county courts for some years. From the wording of Form FL422, it might seem that it is designed for use in magistrates' courts only, but this is of no significance.

**4.14**   By s 46(2), a power of arrest may not be attached to an undertaking; moreover, the court may not accept an undertaking where, apart from this section, a power of arrest would be attached to the order.

The court must, therefore, consider in every case in which it is proposed that undertakings be offered, whether it is a case in which a power of arrest should have been attached to certain provisions of the order. If it appears to the court that, if an order had been made, a power of arrest would have been attached, it should not accept the undertaking.

The court must, therefore, make a finding as to whether violence had been used or threatened. If it finds that this is the case, the court has to attach a power of arrest unless satisfied 'in all the circumstances of the case' that the applicant will be adequately protected without it; this means that the court should not accept an undertaking unless so satisfied.

In coming to this decision, the court must consider all the circumstances. It is arguable that the circumstances must include the wishes of the applicant who, if properly advised, may be the best person to know whether the respondent can be trusted to honour his undertaking. If, therefore, the applicant is prepared to accept an undertaking, it might be argued that it would be unreasonable for the court to refuse to accept it unless there was clear evidence that the applicant was being hopelessly optimistic, and that the court would be entitled to form the view that the applicant would not be adequately protected by the undertaking.

Where the respondent offered an undertaking which the applicant was not willing to accept, the position would be different, and the court would be bound to hear all the evidence on the issue before making a decision.

A respondent who was unwilling to submit to a power of arrest would have, of course, to accept the fact that even where no such power is attached, the standard method of enforcement of any undertaking is now going to be arrest in one form or another.

**4.15** Section 46(4) provides that an undertaking is enforceable as if it were an order of the court. This means, of course, an order of the court to which a power of arrest has not been attached. The method of enforcement would, therefore, be to apply for a warrant for arrest under s 47(8). The procedure for this is set out in more detail in Chapter 5.

# CHAPTER FIVE

# Arrest and Enforcement

## Introduction

**5.1**  Before 1976, the only effective way of enforcing an injunction order which had been broken was by way of applying on notice to commit the wrongdoer to prison for contempt of court. This was a somewhat blunt instrument and could lead to delay, and so the DVMPA introduced the remedy of the power of arrest. Where an injunction restrained a person from using violence or contained an exclusion order, then, provided certain criteria were met, a power of arrest could be attached to those parts of the order and a constable could arrest without warrant anyone whom he had reasonable grounds for suspecting of being in breach of the order. This has been a much used and effective provision, but has only been available under the DVMPA and not the MHA. Certain discrepancies also existed between the powers of magistrates and those of other courts. A further problem was that the circumstances under which a power of arrest might be attached were quite strictly defined, and if a court declined to attach a power of arrest, the only remedy for breach remained an application to commit.

**5.2**  The Law Commission therefore examined how powers of arrest could be incorporated in and improved in the new system. A number of options were proposed, but the preferred solution was that powers of arrest should generally be attached in cases where there had been violence or threatened violence. The Law Commission favoured this alternative which:

> '... proposed a presumption in favour of powers of arrest in cases where there has been violence and threatened violence. There are a number of advantages in this. A power of arrest is seen as a simple, immediate and inexpensive means of enforcement which underlines the seriousness of the breach to the offending party. It was felt that threatened violence should be included because it is wrong in principle that women and children should have to wait to be injured before the law can offer effective protection. However it could be wrong to provide for an absolutely automatic power of arrest as there may well be some cases in which it is inappropriate. We therefore *recommend* that where there has been violence or threatened violence the court should be required to attach a power of arrest to any specified provisions of an order in favour of any eligible applicant unless in all the circumstances the applicant or

child will be adequately protected without such a power.' (Law Com para 5.13)

## Attaching a power of arrest

**5.3**   Section 47(1) begins by defining a 'relevant order' as 'an occupation order or a non-molestation order'. Subsection (2) then provides that where:

'(a)   the court makes a relevant order; and

(b)   it appears to the court that the respondent has used or threatened violence against the applicant or a relevant child,

it shall attach a power of arrest to one or more provisions of the order unless the court is satisfied that in all the circumstances of the case the applicant or child will be adequately protected without such a power of arrest.'

The term 'one or more provisions' is not defined by the Act, so it may be taken that this means no more than that the order must make it clear to what parts of the order the power of arrest applies. However, in view of the fact that the Act imposes a positive obligation on the court, it may seem unfortunate that no guidance is given on this issue. Will the court have fulfilled its obligations if it attaches the power to selected parts of the order only?

The pre-1996 practice was to attach the power only to those parts relating to ouster and to violence, and not, for example, to 'mere' harassment. One presumes that this will continue to be the case, but the Act does not help (The Law Commission had in fact mentioned this – see the final sentence of the extract at para **5.6** below, but there is nothing specific in the Act).

It will be seen that the court must now approach powers of arrest in a different manner from that which was the case under the pre-1996 law. Previously, this was entirely discretionary, and the normal judicial approach was not to attach such a power unless it appeared absolutely necessary. By s 47(2), the imposition of a power of arrest becomes mandatory in certain circumstances.

Clearly, the question of power of arrest does not arise if the court does not make a relevant order. Having made that decision, the court must make a finding of fact on the issue of whether the respondent has 'used or threatened violence'. The Act does not say when this violence or threat thereof must have occurred, but it would be reasonable to take the view that it must have been within the timescale of the events which have led the court to make the relevant order. The Act does not give guidance as to the amount of violence which must have been used or threatened; if the words in s 47(2)(b) are followed, therefore, it must be the case that any violence or threat of violence will be sufficient to satisfy sub-s (2)(b). A raised fist on one occasion would be sufficient. This must be contrasted with the previous law, under which it was necessary to prove that actual bodily harm had been caused. On any reading, therefore, the standard required has been relaxed by the new Act.

Once the court has found as a fact that violence has been used or threatened, the burden of proof changes. The court must attach a power of arrest unless satisfied that the applicant or child will be adequately protected without this. How can the court be satisfied as to this? The answer, presumably, is in the same way that the court satisfies itself of anything, namely by evidence. The court would also be entitled to use its commonsense which would, perhaps, dispose of the 'raised fist' point made above. If the court cannot be satisfied that the evidence shows that the applicant or child would be adequately protected, it must attach the power of arrest. It seems likely, therefore, that powers of arrest will be attached in many more cases than has happened in the past.

**5.4** It should be noted that a power of arrest can, indeed in certain circumstances, must, be attached to any relevant order, no matter what the standing of the applicant. This is a radical departure from the pre-1996 law, where it was necessary to show that the applicant and respondent had been married or had cohabited. Now, to take an extreme example, the applicant could be the respondent's stepson's former cohabitant;[1] if the court were satisfied that some violence had been threatened, the presumption would be in favour of a power of arrest.

**5.5** The question of the period during which the power of arrest should subsist is dealt with in s 47(4) and (5). The pre-1996 practice has been that the power of arrest should normally last for a shorter period than the injunction or order itself.

Subsection (4) provides that the court may provide that the power of arrest is to have effect for a shorter period than the other provisions of the order. It is therefore clearly contemplated that the previous practice may continue.

Subsection (5) provides that any such period may be extended on one or more occasions on an application to vary or discharge the relevant order.

Form FL406, which is the prescribed form for a power of arrest, clearly indicates that the date on which the power expires must be stated.

# Ex parte orders

**5.6** What has been said so far applies to applications of which notice has been given to the respondent. As was seen in Chapter 4, both non-molestation orders and, less commonly, occupation orders, may be made on an ex parte basis, and the matters to which the court must have regard are set out in Chapter 4. A 'relevant order', as defined by s 47(1) can include an ex parte order. It was always accepted under the pre-1996 law that the consequences of a power of arrest could be so drastic that one should be attached to an ex parte order only in the most unusual circumstances, if at all.

---

[1] I am indebted to Dr SM Cretney for this example.

The Law Commission argued that different standards had to apply:

'We do however see a case for differentiating between powers of arrest granted after an inter partes hearing and those granted ex parte. It must be appropriate to take a more stringent approach to the latter, as the court is being asked to grant a power of arrest against someone who has not yet had an opportunity of stating his case. We therefore *recommend* that in the case of ex parte orders, the court should not be under any obligation to attach a power of arrest but should be able to do so in cases where there has been actual or threatened violence, provided that it is also satisfied that there is a risk of significant harm to the applicant or child if the power is not attached immediately. In all cases, the particular breach which will give rise to the operation of the power of arrest should be clearly specified.' (Law Com para 5.14)

**5.7**   This approach is reflected in s 47(3), which first provides that sub-s (2) does not apply where the order is made ex parte, and goes on to provide that in such a case the court may attach a power of arrest to specified provisions of the order if it appears to the court:

'(a)   that the respondent has used or threatened violence against the applicant or a relevant child; and

(b)   that there is a risk of significant harm to the applicant or child, attributable to conduct of respondent, if the power of arrest is not attached to those provisions immediately.'

It will be seen, therefore, that this power is always discretionary; the court may only attach a power of arrest if the conditions of both (a) and (b) are satisfied, and even then has a discretion as to whether or not to do so.

## Undertakings

**5.8**   The question of undertakings generally is dealt with in Chapter 4.

By s 46(2), a power of arrest may not be attached to an undertaking; indeed, an undertaking may not be accepted by the court in any case where 'apart from this section a power of arrest would be attached to the order'. The court must, therefore, always consider whether a power of arrest is appropriate, and, if so, should not accept an undertaking. This is discussed at para **4.15** above.

Section 46(4) provides that an undertaking shall be enforceable as if it were an order of the court. This point will arise when warrants for arrest are considered at para **5.9** et seq below.

## Warrant for arrest

**5.9**   One of the helpful innovations of the 1996 Act is that if the court decides not to attach a power of arrest at the time of making the order, that is not necessarily the end of the matter; under certain circumstances a warrant for arrest may be issued which will have the same effect.

The Law Commission thought that:

> 'The use of powers of arrest should be confined to serious cases where it is necessary to give extra weight to an order to drive home to the respondent the need to keep within its terms. Powers of arrest can be counter-productive and may exacerbate tensions unless they are reserved for cases in which they are shown to be necessary to prevent future injury. But applicants should have open to them methods of enforcement which are as effective as possible when breaches of non-molestation or occupation orders occur. Short of attaching a power of arrest, the High Court and county courts have at present no power to involve the police in the enforcement of orders made under the domestic violence legislation. Yet the police will already have been involved in incidents between the parties in many cases. They are the obvious agency to use and will generally be more effective at and experienced in handling domestic violence issues than either the High Court tipstaff or the county court bailiffs who are the only present resources of the higher courts in the event of committal proceedings. The magistrates' courts, however, have a useful power to involve the police, as they may issue a warrant on application where there are reasonable grounds for believing that the respondent has disobeyed an order. We *recommend* that this power to issue warrants should be extended to the High Court and county courts.' (Law Com para 5.15)

Accordingly, s 47(8) provides as follows:

> 'If the court has made a relevant order but—
>
> (a)  has not attached a power of arrest under subsection (2) or (3) to any provisions of the order, or
> (b)  has attached that power only to certain provisions of the order,
>
> then, if at any time the applicant considers that the respondent has failed to comply with the order, he may apply to the relevant judicial authority for the issue of a warrant for the arrest of the respondent.'

**5.10**  By s 46(4), considered at para **5.8** above, an undertaking is enforceable in the same way as an order. It might seem to follow, therefore, that breach of an undertaking is enforceable by the issue of a warrant of arrest in the same way as an order. This certainly seems to have been the intention of the legislature. When the 1995 Bill was under consideration by the House of Lords Special Public Committee, the Lord Chancellor was asked about the enforcement of undertakings (the wording of the corresponding sections in the 1995 Bill being identical with ss 46 and 47 of the 1997 Act). His reply was as follows:

'My intention would be that the undertaking would not have a power of arrest attached to it; but, on the other hand, the powers of the court to deal with the matter as if it were a contempt would arise on the breach of the undertaking ... The ordinary way in which that would be developed, if it was wanted to go down that road, would be, of course, to apply for a warrant of arrest. That is my intention and I believe it is what was wanted. (HL Paper 55 col 20)

It is also relevant that the Forms annexed to the FPR (Amendment No 3) Rules 1997 clearly contemplate that breach of an undertaking will be enforceable by a warrant for arrest (see Form FL407, the application for a warrant for arrest, which refers to the order or undertaking which has been broken).

Conversely, it may be argued that s 47 refers to a 'relevant order' which it then defines as an occupation order or a non-molestation order. This appears to be a mere defining provision for the purpose of that section, and, it may be asked, if an undertaking is not enforceable as if it were an occupation order or non-molestation order, what type of order could the draftsman have had in mind? However, it may also be argued that, if the draftsman had intended to say occupation order or non-molestation order in s 46, he would have done so.

The position is, therefore, not entirely free from doubt. If an undertaking is not enforceable by warrant for arrest, it will be necessary to do so by means of notice to show cause (Form N78 in the county court).

**5.11** By s 63(1), 'the relevant judicial authority' is defined as:

'(a) where the order was made by the High Court, a judge of that court,
(b) where the order was made by a county court, a judge or district judge of that or any other county court, or
(c) where the order was made by a magistrates' court, any magistrates' court.'

**5.12** The procedure to be followed on the issue of a warrant is set out in s 47(9). The judge, district judge or magistrates' court may not issue a warrant unless:

'(a) the application is substantiated on oath; and
(b) the relevant judicial authority has reasonable grounds for believing that the respondent has failed to comply with the order.'

The question therefore arises of whether a warrant should be issued after breach of any order, or whether the breach would have to be sufficiently serious to justify the drastic remedy of the issue of a warrant for arrest. It might be argued that it would only be appropriate to issue a warrant where a power of arrest might have been attached to the original order, but, for some reason, was not. On the other hand, this is not what the Act says; the only requirement is that the court must be satisfied that the respondent is in breach of 'the order'.

In the very nature of things, the case would not have been sufficiently grave for the attaching of a power of arrest in the first instance.

The reference in the extract from The Law Commission report set out above to bring the higher courts into line with the powers exercised by magistrates is not, of itself, helpful, because a footnote to the report indicates that this power was introduced when:

> 'Some reinforcement of magistrates' powers was therefore considered necessary in cases where the applicant or a child may have suffered physical injury and be at risk of a further attack.' (Law Com fn 26 at p 45)

The position, therefore, remains potentially ambiguous. A possible approach might be that courts should not issue a warrant for arrest except in cases where, under the pre-1996 law, committal proceedings would on the face of it have been justified, even if they might not have led to immediate committal; this would be in keeping with the spirit of the Act and The Law Commission report, which appear to contemplate the disappearance of committal applications in respect of breaches of injunction and their replacement by the procedures contained in the Act.

**5.13** A person who alleges breach of an undertaking or of an order to which a power of arrest was not attached must, therefore, apply to a court at the same level (but not necessarily the same court) as the court which made the order. This application is made ex parte. Application is made on Form FL407, which requires the applicant to set out in what way it is alleged that the respondent has breached the order or undertaking. The application must be supported by sworn evidence (r 3.9A(3) and Forms FL407 and FL408).

This sworn evidence may be given by means of a sworn statement, which may well become the most common method, or by the sworn evidence of the complainant.

If the court is satisfied that there is evidence of breach, a warrant for arrest in Form FL408 is issued.

# Arrest

**5.14** The effect of a power of arrest is set out in s 47(6):

> 'If, by virtue of subsection (2) or (3) above, a power of arrest is attached to certain provisions of an order, a constable may arrest without warrant a person whom he has reasonable cause for suspecting to be in breach of any such provision.'

By r 3.9A(1)(a), where a power of arrest is attached to one or more provisions (called 'the relevant provisions') of an order, the relevant provisions must be set out in Form FL406; this form does not include any provisions of the order to which the power of arrest was not attached. A copy of Form FL406 must then be delivered to the officer for the time being in charge of any police station for the applicant's address or such other police station as the court may direct, accompanied by a statement (normally from the applicant's solicitor) showing that the respondent has been served with the order or informed of its terms (whether by being present when the order was made or by telephone or otherwise).

When an order is made varying or discharging any of the relevant provisions, the court (in the person of the proper officer or justices' Clerk) must immediately inform the police station and deliver a copy of the new order (r 3.9A(2)).

Where a power of arrest is attached, a constable may arrest without warrant any person whom he has reasonable cause for suspecting of being in breach of any of the relevant provisions (s 47(6)).

If a respondent is arrested pursuant to s 47(6), sub-s (7) provides that:

> '(a)  he shall be brought before the relevant judicial authority within the period of 24 hours beginning at the time of his arrest, and
> (b)  if the matter is not then disposed of forthwith, the relevant judicial authority before whom he is brought may remand him.'

The meaning of 'relevant judicial authority' has already been discussed. In reckoning the period of 24 hours, no account is to be taken of Christmas Day, Good Friday or any Sunday.

The Act does not specify a time within which a person arrested under a warrant issued under sub-s (8) must be brought before the court, but this is a matter of general law and in fact the period in such a case would also be 24 hours. Form FL408 directs the constable or other person arresting the respondent to bring him before the court immediately. Subsection (10) provides that where a person is brought before the court by virtue of a warrant under sub-s (8), the court may remand him.

# Remand

**5.15**  When a respondent is arrested, whether under a power of arrest or warrant of arrest, he must be brought before the relevant judicial authority, ie judge, district judge or magistrates' court, as may be appropriate. This court will then have to deal with him.

Rule 3.9A(4) provides that the court before which a person is brought following his arrest may:

(a)  determine whether the facts, and the circumstances which led to the arrest, amounted to disobedience of the order, or

(b)  adjourn the proceedings and, where such an order is made, the arrested person may be released and –

   (i)   be dealt with within 14 days of the day on which he was arrested; and

(ii)  be given not less than 2 days' notice of the adjourned hearing.

By sub-s (10) the court 'may remand him'. In the High Court and county courts, the power to remand is governed by Sch 5 to the Act, which is introduced by sub-s (11); this confers on those courts the same powers as those already exercised by magistrates' courts under ss 128 and 129 of the Magistrates' Courts Act 1980.

Schedule 5 is set out in full in Appendix I at p 150, and it is not proposed to repeat it in full here. However, it may be useful to summarise the various options open to the court, pursuant to Sch 5 and r 3.9A(4) and (5), which are as follows.

## Remand in custody

The court may commit the respondent to custody to be brought before the court at the end of the period of remand or at such earlier time as the court may require (para 2(1)(a)). Such remand in custody may not be for a longer period than 8 clear days (para 2(5)), except by way of further remand (as to which, see below). Where the remand in custody is for a period not exceeding 3 clear days, the respondent may be committed into the custody of a constable (para 2(6)).

## Remand on bail

The court may remand the respondent on bail on his own recognisance, with or without sureties (para 2(1)(b)). Where both parties consent, the remand may be for a longer period than 8 days; otherwise, it cannot exceed 8 clear days. In any event, when a person is released on bail, the adjourned hearing cannot be more than 14 days (as opposed to clear days) after his arrest.

Where an arrested person is not dealt with within the required period, an application to show cause may still be issued under CCR Ord 29, r 1(4) (r 3.9A(4)). (For magistrates' courts, see r 20(8)–(10).)

By s 47(12), where a person is remanded on bail, he may be required by the relevant judicial authority to comply, before release on bail or later, with such requirements as appear to that authority to be necessary to secure that he does not interfere with witnesses or otherwise obstruct the course of justice.

Rule 3.10 contains detailed provisions as to the procedure for dealing with bail applications. These provisions are set out in Appendix II, and, apart from noting that the application may be made orally or in writing, it is unnecessary to set out the detail here.

## Further remand

Paragraph 2(2) provides that where a person is brought before the court after remand, the court may further remand him.

Where a person has been remanded on bail, and cannot appear on the return day because of illness or accident, the remand may be extended. Further, anyone remanded on bail may be remanded for a further period by the court enlarging his recognisances to a later time (para 3).

**Remand for medical report**

In addition to these powers, s 48 confers a further power. By s 48(1), the power to remand may be exercised for the purpose of enabling a medical examination and report to be made. Where this is done, the remand may not be for longer than 3 weeks if the respondent is committed to custody, or 4 weeks where he is on bail.

Section 48 enables the court to make an order under s 35 of the Mental Health Act 1983 remanding the respondent for report on his mental condition, where there is reason to suspect that he is suffering from mental illness or severe mental impairment.

The motive behind this part of the legislation is presumably a recognition of the fact that some, if not many, contemnors in domestic violence cases appear to act out of some irrational compulsion or obsession and would benefit from medical help. When the Special Public Committee took evidence on this part of the 1995 Bill, there was an interesting debate as to the persons to whom any medical report should be disclosed. The opinion of one distinguished authority was that it was necessary to draw a distinction between the position before a finding of contempt and that after such a finding:

> 'I think before a finding of contempt the report should only be available to legal advisors. A report commissioned after a finding of contempt should be commissioned by the court so that the court can take it into account when deciding the disposal. In that case, I think that the contemnor, who has now been found guilty of contempt, would probably need to consent.' (evidence of His Honour Judge Fricker – *HL Paper 55*, para 383)

This view was accepted by the Committee, and it was decided to deal with the problem in the rules. However, it seems that the rules contain no specific reference to this issue.

# Hospital orders and guardianship orders

**5.16** Pursuant to what was said in the last section, the relevant judicial authority may deal with an arrested person by making a hospital order or a guardianship order. The forms of order are Form FL413 and Form FL414 respectively.

# Committal

**5.17** Whether or not an arrested person is dealt with at the first hearing or is remanded on bail or in custody, the court at some time has to perform two functions. The first is to make a determination as to whether or not he has broken the terms of the order or undertaking; this is a matter of evidence. The second is to decide how, if at all, to punish any breach; this is a matter of discretion.

The relevant judicial authority has the jurisdiction, and the duty, to deal with both functions; previous restrictions on the jurisdiction of a district judge have been removed by s 58 and by the Allocation to Judiciary Directions 1997.

By r 3.9A(6), the court may adjourn consideration of the penalty to be imposed for contempts found proved, and such consideration may be restored if the respondent does not comply with any conditions imposed by the court. This enables the court, in effect, to impose a suspended sentence.

Committal is ordered in Form FL419.

## Special provisions for magistrates' courts

**5.18** Section 50 was introduced to ensure that the powers of magistrates' courts were the same as those of the High Court and county courts. By s 50(1), if a magistrates' court has power to commit to custody for breach of 'a relevant requirement' (ie occupation orders, non-molestation orders or exclusion requirements), it may direct that the execution of the order be suspended for such period or on such terms and conditions as it may specify.

By s 51(1), it is provided that a magistrates' court shall have the like power to make a hospital order or guardianship order under s 37 of the Mental Health Act 1983, or an interim hospital order under s 38 in the case of a person suffering from mental illness or severe mental impairment who could otherwise be committed to custody for breach of a relevant requirement as a magistrates' court has under those sections in the case of a person convicted of an offence punishable on summary conviction with imprisonment.

**5.19** One of the important results of these provisions is that, for the first time, a magistrates' court has the power to commit for breach of an undertaking. Undertakings generally are dealt with in Chapter 4, where it was noted that an undertaking is enforceable as if it were an order of the court. The effect of s 50 is that occupation orders and non-molestation orders are now included in the category of orders in respect of which magistrates may commit, and an undertaking therefore has the same effect.

## Conclusion

**5.20** It seems likely that the enforcement of occupation orders and non-molestation orders will be improved by the 1996 Act. The court now has much more positive encouragement to attach a power of arrest, which will be an obligation in some cases, and, at the very least, will be much more frequent than has been the case in the past. It also seems likely that the issue of a warrant for arrest will come to be regarded as the routine way to deal with breaches of non-molestation orders and occupation orders.

The provision for arrest and remand is intended to replace the previous procedure of applications to commit for breach of injunction, although the Act does not specifically say this. However, if a person is arrested and brought before the court, this in itself is frequently sufficient to defuse the situation and, in many cases, no more need be done; this is even more the case when the court remands the person concerned in custody for one week. The great majority of committals for contempt do not exceed that period, so it would probably be the case that no more would need to be done at the end of that period. The court would, arguably, be entirely justified in committing a person to custody for 7 days, using the remand provisions, to enable him to 'cool off' and reflect on the error of his ways.

Having said that, it will, of course, always be necessary to dispose of a contemnor by making a final order of some sort. The definition of 'relevant judicial authority' gives the courts the flexibility to do this in the most efficient way.

If the Act is operated in this way, it should provide a valuable and imaginative way to deal with these problems.

# CHAPTER SIX

# Amendments to the Children Act

## Introduction

**6.1**   Section 52 of, and Sch 6 to, the 1996 Act effect changes to the Children Act 1989 which are appropriate to be considered here since they introduce a new set of circumstances in which an ouster, or exclusion requirement may be made. It has been recognised since the introduction of the 1989 Act that one of its defects was that it provided no machinery for ousting a suspected child abuser from the family home; the only remedy in such circumstances was to remove the child by way of an interim care order, which might seem to be punishing the child for the misdeeds of others.

This issue was raised by The Law Commission in its consultations, and formed part of the recommendations in the report (Law Com paras 6.15 to 6.22). These recommendations may be summarised as follows:

(1)   A court dealing with a child protection case should have power to make an ouster order for the protection of children.
(2)   This should be a short-term remedy only; in the short term the needs of the child should take precedence over those of the adults but, in the longer term, considerations of property and the competing claims of adults must play a part.
(3)   The power to oust should be ancillary to an interim care order or emergency protection order, and not an alternative to it.
(4)   The purpose of the order was the protection of the child, and nothing else. Accordingly, if the applicant or local authority placed the child outside the home, the order should lapse.
(5)   Criteria for making such orders should be set out in the Act; these are dealt with below. The time for the duration of the orders should be limited.

These recommendations are incorporated in Sch 6 to the Act as a result of s 52, and will now be considered in detail.

An important factor to bear in mind when considering this part of the Act is that the court may make the exclusion order against anyone (that is to say, in reality, any suspected abuser). It is not necessary to prove the 'nexus' of, for example, associated persons.

# Interim care orders

**6.2**   The essential first step when considering the power to make an exclusion requirement ancillary to an interim care order is that the court must be satisfied that it is appropriate to make an interim care order; this may seem obvious, but it is important to make the point that this procedure is not some 'half-way house'. The threshold criteria must be satisfied.

Accordingly, the new s 38A(1) of the Children Act 1989 (introduced by para 1 of Sch 6) provides that where:

'(a)   on being satisfied that there are reasonable grounds for believing that the circumstances with respect to a child are as mentioned in section 31(2)(a) and (b)(i), the court makes an interim care order with respect to a child, and

(b)   the conditions mentioned in subsection (2) are satisfied,

the court may include an exclusion requirement in the interim care order.'

Section 31(2)(a) and (b)(i) of the Children Act 1989 are the threshold criteria which must be satisfied before a care order or supervision order may be met; s 31(2)(b)(ii), which enables the court to make a care or supervision order where a child is beyond parental control is not mentioned, so it would not be possible to make an exclusion requirement where that was the basis of the application.

Therefore, the court must have decided to make an interim care order before it turns its mind to the question of an exclusion requirement.

**6.3**   The next matter on which the court must make a decision is whether the conditions mentioned in s 38A(2) are satisfied. These conditions are:

'(a)   that there is reasonable cause to believe that, if a person ("the relevant person") is excluded from a dwelling-house in which the child lives, the child will cease to suffer, or cease to be likely to suffer, significant harm, and

(b)   that another person living in the dwelling-house (whether a parent of the child or some other person)—

(i)    is able and willing to give to the child the care which it would be reasonable to expect a parent to give him, and

(ii)   consents to the inclusion of the exclusion requirement.'

The meaning of sub-s (2)(a) is as clear as it can be; the person to be removed must be the cause, or one of the causes, of the significant harm which the child is suffering or is likely to suffer, and his removal would make it likely that the child would cease to suffer such harm.

To satisfy sub-s (2)(b), it is necessary that there should be in the house a person who is able and willing to care for the child; clearly, there would be no point in leaving the child alone and uncared for. It is implicit in all this that the applicant, and the court, consider it appropriate for the child to remain in its home if at all possible, rather than being removed into care.

It is important to note that the proposed carer must not merely consent to care for the child, but must also consent to the exclusion requirement against the 'relevant person'. Where there was doubt about this, the court would not be able to include an exclusion requirement, and would have to decide whether the child should be removed (see para **6.13** below on procedure).

Jurisdiction to make such an order would be vested in a person who was capable of making the interim care order; this would be a judge, a family proceedings court and, subject to limitations on jurisdiction, a district judge when giving directions.

## Exclusion requirements

**6.4** Section 38A(3) of the Children Act 1989 defines an exclusion requirement as any one or more of the following:

'(a) a provision requiring the relevant person to leave a dwelling-house in which he is living with the child,

(b) a provision prohibiting the relevant person from entering a dwelling-house in which the child lives, and

(c) a provision excluding the relevant person from a defined area in which a dwelling-house in which the child lives is situated.'

In short, if the relevant person lives in the home, he may be ousted and, if he is a visitor, he may be required to keep away.

By sub-s (4), the court may provide for the exclusion requirement to have effect for a shorter period than the other provisions of the interim care order. This enables the court to approach the matter with the maximum flexibility.

**6.5** The Act makes no distinctions based on the status of the person to be excluded; he could be a lodger, tenant, or joint or sole owner of the property or an occasional visitor.

Section 38A(10) provides, in effect, that if the local authority removes the child from the house from which the relevant person is excluded for a continuous period of more than 24 hours, the exclusion requirement shall cease to have effect. The effect of the provision for 24 hours is that the order would not cease to have effect if, for example, the child were removed for a medical examination.

A person against whom an exclusion requirement has been made may well not be a person eligible to apply for the discharge or variation of the care order in which the exclusion requirement is contained; accordingly, a new s 39(3A) of the Children Act 1989 provides that a person to whom an exclusion requirement applies may apply to vary or discharge the care or supervision order insofar as it imposes the exclusion requirement. Such application would be made to the court which had made the order containing the exclusion requirement, or, where the case had been transferred, to the court in which the case was proceeding.

## Emergency protection orders

**6.6**   The circumstances in which the court may make an emergency protection order are set out in s 44(1)(a), (b) and (c) of the Children Act 1989. Briefly, the court must be satisfied that:

(a)   there is reasonable cause to believe that the child is likely to suffer significant harm if he is not removed to accommodation provided by the applicant, or he does not remain in the place where he is being accommodated (s 44(1)(a)); or

(b)   enquiries are being made by a local authority under s 47(1)(b) (cause to suspect child suffering or likely to suffer significant harm) which are being frustrated and there are reasonable grounds to think that access to the child is required as a matter of urgency (s 44(1)(b)); or

(c)   facts similar to (b) where enquiries are being made by an authorised person (s 44(1)(c)).

Paragraph 3 of Sch 6 inserts a new s 44A into the Children Act 1989. Once again, the court must first determine that the statutory grounds for making, this time, an emergency protection order exist. Having done so, it may then consider whether an exclusion requirement should be inserted in the order; exclusion requirement is defined by s 44A(3) in exactly the same terms as in s 38A(3), set out at para **6.4** above, and the same provisions as to the timing of such an order apply. Exactly the same provisions for the termination of the exclusion requirement in the event of the removal of the child for longer than 24 hours, and the right of the relevant person to apply to vary or discharge are made in relation to emergency protection orders.

**6.7**   By s 44A(2), the court may include an exclusion requirement where:

'(a)   . . . there is reasonable cause to believe that if a person ("the relevant person") is excluded from a dwelling-house in which the child lives, then—

   (i)   in the case of an order made on the ground mentioned in section 44(1)(a), the child will not be likely to suffer significant harm, even though the child is not removed as mentioned in section 44(1)(a)(i) or does not remain as mentioned in section 44(1)(a)(ii), or

   (ii)   in the case of an order made on the ground mentioned in paragraph (b) or (c) of section 44(1), the enquiries referred to in that paragraph will cease to be frustrated, and

(b)   [Section 44A(2)(b) need not be repeated, since it is in precisely the same terms as s 38A(2)(b), set out above.]'

**6.8**   In the very nature of things, emergency protection orders are frequently made by magistrates on an ex parte basis. A decision will therefore often have to be made as to whether the drastic step of including an exclusion requirement, or even a power of arrest (see below) should be taken without hearing the person to be excluded. The Act gives no guidance on this, but the rules of procedure clearly contemplate the probability of orders being made in the absence of the person to be excluded (see para **6.13** et seq below on procedure). No doubt the reasoning behind this is that an emergency protection order would only be granted in exceptional circumstances. Perhaps the principles contained in s 45(2) governing the making of ex parte occupation orders should be applied by way of analogy (see Chapter 3).

## Powers of arrest

**6.9**   The new ss 38A and 44A of the Children Act 1989 each contain sub-ss (5) to (9) which contain identical provisions, *mutatis mutandis*, as to powers of arrest in respect of exclusion requirements contained in interim care orders and emergency protection orders respectively.

Subsection (5) provides that where an exclusion requirement is ordered, the court may attach a power of arrest to the exclusion requirement. By sub-s (6), such a power of arrest may have effect for a shorter period than the interim care order or emergency protection order; however, any such period may be extended on one or more occasions on an application to vary or discharge the interim care order or emergency protection order (sub-s (7)).

By sub-s (8), where a power of arrest is attached to an exclusion requirement, a constable may arrest without warrant anyone whom he has reasonable cause to believe to be in breach of the requirement. It is then provided that the provisions applying to a person arrested under sub-s (8) are those which apply when a person is arrested pursuant to a power of arrest under s 47(6) of the 1996 Act. This is set out in detail in Chapter 5.

## Undertakings

**6.10**   The general effect of undertakings was considered in Chapter 4.

The new s 38B(1) of the Children Act 1989, introduced by Sch 6 to the 1996 Act, provides that in any case where the court has power to include an exclusion requirement in an interim care order, the court may accept an undertaking from the relevant person. Such an undertaking would, presumably, normally be to vacate the property, but there is no limitation in the Act as to the terms of any undertaking which the court might accept.

By sub-s (2), a power of arrest may not be attached to an undertaking; if, therefore, the court thought it appropriate that there be a power of arrest, it should not accept an undertaking.

By sub-s (3), an undertaking is enforceable as if it were an order of the court. Enforcement of undertakings is dealt with in Chapter 5, para **5.8**. An undertaking ceases to have effect if the child in question is removed from the home by the local authority for a continuous period of more than 24 hours.

**6.11**    Section 44B makes exactly the same provisions in respect of undertakings relating to emergency protection orders as those applicable to interim care orders.

# Final orders

**6.12**    It will have been noted that the power to include exclusion requirements in public law Children Act cases extends only to interim orders. There is no power to include such a requirement in a final order.

This was a point which was discussed when the Special Public Committee took evidence in respect of the 1995 Bill. One distinguished author had described the omission as 'loopy'. Addressing the point, the Lord Chancellor said that the omission of the exclusion requirement at the final order stage was:

> '. . . because it would not make much sense to do it at the care order stage. That is more a final situation. This is the interim care order or the examination order; the one which is required for examination. These are interim solutions . . . ' (*HL Paper 55*, col 408)

Later, the Lord Chancellor added:

> 'Underlying all this is the question of the extent to which a local authority should have rights to take action of this kind in particular situations, and I wondered whether at the final stage it is not appropriate for the local authority, who would have the right one assumes to go for an exclusion order in all the circumstances to leave the choice to the carer.' (ibid, col 414)

What might seem to emerge from this is that whereas the court may impose emergency requirements at an interim stage, by the time the court comes to consider making a final care order, a proposed carer who had not been able to secure the exclusion of an abuser by the use of her own remedies should not look to the court or the applicant local authority to do it for her.

# Procedure

**6.13**    Procedure for applications for exclusion requirements in interim care orders or emergency protection orders is governed by r 4.24(1) and (2) and r 4.24A. It may be summarised as follows.

### (a)   The application
The applicant (normally a local authority) must prepare a separate statement of the evidence in support of the application for the exclusion requirement (r 4.24A(2)). It appears (see (e) below) that this statement is principally required for service on the person to be excluded (referred to as 'the relevant person' pursuant to s 44A and s 44B of the Children Act 1989); the relevant person is not, therefore, served with all the evidence before the court in respect of the full application.

It seems likely that the full application before the court would contain sufficient evidence to support the application for the exclusion requirement and it might not be necessary to have completed the summary for service at that stage; nevertheless, it might be regarded as good practice to have the statement of evidence ready for the court.

### (b)   The hearing
It is clearly envisaged from what follows that the application for an exclusion requirement is made without notice to the relevant person.

### (c)   Consents
An order will not be made unless the proposed carer consents to the exclusion requirement. Rule 4.24(1) provides that such consent may be given either orally in court (ie before the judge, district judge or magistrates) or in writing. If it is in writing, no form is prescribed but whether in writing or oral it must include a statement that the person giving consent:

(1)   is able and willing to give to the child the care which it would be reasonable to expect a parent to give him; and

(2)   understands that the giving of consent could lead to the exclusion of the relevant person from the dwellinghouse in which the child lives (r 4.24(2)).

### (d)   The order
The emergency protection order or interim care order will be in the usual form (Form C23 or Form C33). These will have an additional clause to the effect that the court directs that [the relevant person] be excluded from [the property] so that the child may continue to live there, consent to the exclusion requirement having been given by [a named person]. A power of arrest may be attached to the exclusion requirement.

### (e)   Service on the relevant person
Once the order containing the exclusion requirement has been made, the applicant must serve it on the relevant person. At the same time, the applicant must prepare and serve a separate statement of the evidence in support of the application for an exclusion requirement; no separate form is prescribed for this. The position is slightly different where the court has made the exclusion requirement of its own motion; here, it is not necessary to serve a statement of evidence in support.

The applicant must also inform the relevant person of his right to apply to vary or discharge the exclusion requirement (r 4.24A(2)).

The usual rules as to delivery to the local police station of an order bearing a power of arrest apply to these orders (r 4.24A(3) and see para **5.14**).

### (f) Application to vary or discharge

When a relevant person applies to vary or discharge an exclusion requirement, he must serve all parties to the proceedings with the application (r 4.24A(5)).

# CHAPTER SEVEN

# The Effect on Third Parties

## Introduction

**7.1**   This chapter is concerned almost entirely with the effect of occupation orders on persons other than the parties to the proceedings, in particular, persons who may have, or wish to acquire, a legitimate interest in a dwelling-house in respect of which an occupation order has been made. The fact that someone may have the right to occupy a house may have an important effect on a person such as an intending purchaser, a landlord or mortgagee who may be unaware of the existence of the person in whose favour the occupation order has been made.

In Chapter 1, it was shown that Part IV of the Act is the successor of the MHA 1983, which was itself the successor of the MHA 1967. The 1967 Act was brought about to reverse the effect of the decision of the House of Lords in *National Provincial Bank Ltd v Ainsworth* [1965] AC 1175, in which it had been held that a married woman's common law right to be provided with a home by her husband was no more than a personal right incapable of binding a third party. One of the intentions of the 1967 Act was to give a wife a right of occupation in the former matrimonial home; this came to be known as the 'deserted wife's equity'.

Both the 1967 Act and the 1983 Act contained complex provisions designed to ensure a just balance between the various competing interests. Most of these provisions are repeated, and, if anything, made even more complex by the 1995 Act.

**7.2**   The structure of those parts of the Act which relate to this aspect can be summarised as follows:

Section 30 generally deals with matrimonial home rights, and, generally, repeats s 1 of the MHA 1983.

Section 30(3) to (5) deals with payment of rent etc by a spouse with matrimonial home rights.

Section 31 deals with the effect of matrimonial home rights as a charge on the dwelling-house.

Section 32 gives effect to Sch 4, which deals with the conveyancing aspects of a spouse's rights of occupation of a former matrimonial home.

Section 34 deals with the effect of a s 33 occupation order, where rights of occupation are a charge on the dwelling-house.

Section 35(11) deals with the position where a person with an equitable interest applies for a s 35 order.

Section 54 deals with the position of mortgagees of properties which are the subject of occupation orders.

These will all be considered, although not necessarily in turn.

**7.3**   An important preliminary point to bear in mind is that the Act draws a clear distinction between the rights of a spouse and the rights of cohabitants. Spouses have rights which can be registered and which may bind third parties. Cohabitants, and former cohabitants have personal rights which are not capable of binding third parties. This distinction flows from the classification of applicants into 'entitled' and 'non-entitled', and the different classes of orders which may be granted under ss 33, 35, 36, 37 and 38. As was seen in Chapter 3, occupation orders are not generally intended to govern the occupation of a house on a long-term basis; where the parties are or have been spouses the longer term would be governed by a property adjustment application, and where they have not been married the orders made by the court would not be expected to be permanent.

# Matrimonial home rights

**7.4**   The nature of matrimonial home rights was considered in detail in Chapter 3, and need not be set out here. This section will be concerned only with matrimonial home rights as a charge or incumbrance on the dwelling-house.

Section 31(1) applies where one spouse is entitled to occupy a dwelling-house by virtue of a beneficial estate or interest, and the other spouse has matrimonial home rights. It will be remembered that matrimonial home rights only apply to a dwelling-house which is, was, or was intended to be, the matrimonial home of the spouses in question (see s 30(7)).

In such a case, the matrimonial home rights of the non-entitled spouse are a charge on the estate or interest of the entitled spouse, having priority as if it were an equitable interest created at whatever is the latest of the following dates:

'(a)   the date on which the spouse so entitled acquires the estate or interest;

(b)   the date of the marriage; and

(c)   1st January 1968 (which is the date of commencement of the Matrimonial Homes Act 1967).' (s 31(3))

It follows from this that no matrimonial home rights can have any effect before 1 January 1968, which was when the MHA 1967 came into force (this whole section, in fact, repeats with some minor changes s 2 of the 1983 Act, which in turn repeated the 1967 Act). If H and W live together in H's house, and then marry, W's matrimonial home rights become a charge on H's estate or interest at the date of marriage; if H then buys another house, which is intended to be the parties' home, W's matrimonial home rights become a charge on H's estate or interest from the date of acquisition.

**7.5**  In general, an equitable interest is not binding on a third party unless registered. Hence, there are certain provisions in the Act concerning this. By s 31(10), where the entitled spouse's interest is registered land under the Land Registration Act 1925,

> '(a)  registration of a land charge affecting the dwelling-house by virtue of [Part IV of the 1996 Act] is to be effected by registering a notice under that Act, and
>
> (b)  a spouse's matrimonial home rights are not an overriding interest within the meaning of [the 1925] Act affecting the dwelling-house even though the spouse is in actual occupation of the dwelling-house.'

Subsection (10) deals with registered land; applications to register are made pursuant to the Land Registration (Matrimonial Homes) Rules 1990, r 3, Schedule, Form 99.

Where the title is not registered, the charge may be registered as a Class F land charge under the Land Charges Act 1972, s 2(1) and (7).

In *Barnett v Hassett* [1982] 1 All ER 80, [1981] 1 WLR 385, it was held that a spouse who had no intention of occupying the house in question, and wished only to freeze the other spouse's assets was not entitled to register a charge. The spirit of this decision is now reflected in s 30(7); the only properties which can be affected are those which are, were, or were intended to be the home of the parties.

By sub-s (11), a spouse's matrimonial home rights do not entitle that spouse to register a caution under s 54 of the 1925 Act.

**7.6**  Subsection (12) deals with the position where a spouse has matrimonial home rights over an estate or interest which is subject to mortgage. If the spouse's charge is registered under s 2 of the 1925 Act after the date of the mortgage, it will, for the purposes of s 94 of the Law of Property Act 1925 (which regulates the rights of mortgagees to make further advances ranking in priority to subsequent mortgages), be deemed to be a mortgage subsequent in date to the mortgage of the other spouse's interest.

Finally, there are subsections in s 31 which deal with matters of (potentially important) detail. Where the entitled spouse has an interest under a trust, and there are no other persons, living or unborn, who are or could be beneficiaries under the trust, the matrimonial home rights of the non-entitled spouse are a charge on the estate or interest of the trustees for the entitled spouse (sub-s (4)); any potential exercise of a general power of appointment shall be disregarded (sub-s (7)).

Subsection (9) deals with the position where the entitled spouse's estate or interest is surrendered to merge in some other estate or interest; such surrender will be subject to the charge.

**7.7**   The provisions of Sch 4 deal in detail with some of the conveyancing aspects of matrimonial home rights and the registration thereof, and are therefore beyond the scope of this book, and its author. A practical point which may be noted, however, is para 4 which deals with cancellation of registration after termination of marriage. In principle, a charge will be cancelled by production to the Chief Land Registrar of a death certificate of the spouse with matrimonial home rights, a decree absolute, or an order of the court that the matrimonial home rights have been terminated (para 4(1)). However, this is subject to the rights being extended under s 33(5), and para 4(2) deals with this.

The procedure for release of matrimonial home rights is contained in Sch 4, para 5.

# Payment of outgoings

**7.8**   Section 30 contains provisions to deal with the position where a spouse with matrimonial home rights is in possession of a property and wishes to pay outgoings in order to maintain security of occupation. Were it not for these, a landlord or mortgagee would be entitled to refuse payment on the ground that his contractual relationship was with the other party, which might threaten the spouse's occupation.

Subsection (3) applies where a spouse is entitled under s 30, (ie by virtue of matrimonial home rights) to occupy a dwelling-house or part of a dwelling-house. In such a case,

> '. . . any payment or tender made or other thing done by that spouse in or towards satisfaction of any liability of the other spouse in respect of rent, mortgage payments or other outgoings affecting the dwelling-house is, whether or not it is made or done in pursuance of an order under section 40, be as good as if made or done by the other spouse.'

Section 40 will be found in Chapter 3. It deals with the power of the court to make orders for payment of outgoings when an occupation order is made.

Section 30(3) does not assist a wife once a husband's statutory tenancy has been ended by an order for possession being made (*Penn v Dunn* [1970] 2 QB 686).

By sub-s (4), a spouse's occupation by virtue of s 30:

> '(a)   is to be treated, for the purposes of the Rent (Agriculture) Act 1976 and the Rent Act 1977 (other than Part V and sections 103 to 106 of that Act), as occupation by the other spouse as the other spouse's residence, and

(b) if the spouse occupies the dwelling-house as that spouse's only or principal home, is to be treated, for the purposes of the Housing Act 1985 and Part I of the Housing Act 1988, as occupation by the other spouse as the other spouse's only or principal home.'

The significance of this is that the statutory entitlements of one party under landlord and tenant law will be kept alive by a spouse with matrimonial home rights who is in occupation.

## Effect of a section 33 order

**7.9** Section 34(1) of the Act repeats, in effect, s 2(5) of the MHA 1983. It provides that, where a spouse's matrimonial home rights are a charge on the estate or interest of the other spouse or of trustees for the other spouse—

'(a) an order under section 33 against the other spouse has, except so far as a contrary intention appears, the same effect against persons deriving title under the other spouse or under the trustees and affected by the charge, and

(b) sections 33(1), (3), (4) and (10) and 30(3) to (6) apply in relation to any person deriving title under the other spouse or under the trustees and affected by the charge as they apply in relation to the other spouse.'

This, therefore, sets out the general position. Where a spouse with matrimonial home rights obtains a s 33 order against the other spouse, that order binds anyone deriving title from the other spouse, for example a purchaser; it would, of course, be necessary that the rights or order should have been registered.

Section 34(2) provides that the court may make an order under s 33 'by virtue of subsection (1)(b)' (ie against a person deriving title under the other spouse) 'where it considers that in all the circumstances it is just and reasonable to do so'; in other words, it has the widest possible discretion.

## Rights of non-entitled parties

**7.10** So far, the position of those entitled to matrimonial home rights has been considered. Such people are always spouses, or former spouses whose rights have been extended by an order under s 33(5). However, what about the position of cohabitants or former cohabitants or former spouses whose rights have not been so extended?

The answer is that nothing has changed under this Act. A non-entitled person who has obtained an occupation order against her cohabitant, former cohabitant or former spouse cannot protect these rights against a third party.

The Law Commission addressed this issue as follows:

'The great majority of respondents tended to see occupation remedies for non-entitled applicants as a relatively short term measure of protection, just to give sufficient time to find alternative accommodation or to await the outcome of property proceedings. We did not suggest in the working paper that occupation rights granted to a non-entitled applicant should be capable of registration as a charge on the property itself as are spouses' rights by virtue of [MHA 1983]. Registration of rights which will have a time limit set by the court seems inappropriate. It has to be recognized that such a right would in consequence be merely personal and the owner could sell or mortgage over the head of the occupying applicant, unless the court were willing to grant an injunction to prevent this while the order was in force.' (Law Com para 4.19)

**7.11**    An anomalous situation might arise where a cohabitant was 'entitled' by virtue of a tenancy, perhaps of a short-term nature. Under s 33 the court could grant her an occupation order for the joint lives of the other party and herself. Nevertheless, this could not become binding on any third party.

An order made under ss 37 or 38 is not binding on any third party.

# Equitable owners

**7.12**    An equitable owner will, normally, be one who is able to show an intention on the part of the legal owner and herself to share the beneficial ownership or a record of contributions to the acquisition of the property; in such cases, the court might hold both parties to have beneficial interests in equity by way of implied, resulting or constructive trust. This might be the case in many longer-term cohabitation cases.

Section 35(11) provides that a spouse who has an equitable interest in a dwelling-house or its proceeds of sale, but it not entitled, is to be treated, only for the purpose of determining whether she has matrimonial home rights, as being not entitled.

Similar provisions, *mutatis mutandis*, are made in respect of applications for the various classes of occupation order; a former spouse, or cohabitant or former cohabitant, who has an equitable interest, is treated, for the purpose of the application, as not entitled.

The effect of this is that an equitable owner is, for the purposes of s 35(11), a non-entitled person and therefore able to apply under s 35. (The purpose of the section was originally, in the MHA 1983, to establish a wife's right to register her rights, but this significance has now been lost.) There is no doubt that the rights of an equitable owner who is not a spouse cannot be registered.

# Kaur v Gill

**7.13**   As has already been mentioned, the wording of ss 30, 31 and 34 of the Act closely follow ss 1 and 2 of the 1983 Act. However, they must be read with the rest of the Act. This may well produce results different from those which would have resulted from the earlier legislation. By way of example, if *Kaur v Gill* [1988] 2 All ER 288, CA was now before the court and governed by the 1996 Act, it would probably produce a different result.

The facts of *Kaur v Gill* were that the applicant wife left a matrimonial home which was vested in the sole name of her husband. He then agreed to sell the house to the respondent. A few days before completion, the applicant registered her right of occupation, of which, therefore, the respondent had constructive notice. Because the search was made by telephone, the respondent and his solicitors did not, in reality, know of the registration but they were bound by it. The applicant applied for orders declaring her right of occupation and prohibiting the respondent from occupying.

The judge held that he was entitled to take account of the interests of all parties, including the respondent. By s 2(5) of the 1983 Act, a person deriving title under the other spouse has all the rights of application to the court under s 1(2)-(8) as the spouse; he could therefore apply to the court to prohibit or restrict the wife's rights, and his interests had to be taken into account. This decision was upheld by the Court of Appeal. It appears to have been taken for granted in this case that, if the applicant could clear the hurdle of getting the court to consider his position with the position of the other parties, he was bound to succeed.

Under the 1996 Act, the applicant would have a similar right to be heard. The wife was married to the sole owner of the house and therefore had matrimonial home rights; the criteria to be considered by the court would be those contained in s 33(6). It would be necessary for the court to take account of the financial resources of the parties, and their housing needs. The wife and a young child were living in cramped accommodation, and certainly did not have the funds to buy a house. The court would have to apply the test as to greater significant harm. It would appear more likely than not that the court would have found in favour of the wife.

# Landlords

**7.14**   For the sake of completeness in considering the position of third parties, when transfers of tenancies are considered in Chapter 8, it will be seen that rules of court have been made to ensure that landlords are to be given notice of such applications and are entitled to be heard.

# CHAPTER EIGHT

# Transfer of Tenancies

## Introduction

**8.1**  The bulk of the provisions in Part IV of the 1996 Act are concerned with the regulation of the occupation of a dwelling-house which is, or has been a family home, and with the behaviour of the parties towards each other; longer-term issues, such as transfers of title to property are not dealt with, because they are normally the subject of proceedings under the MCA 1973.

The exception to this, namely the provisions dealing with transfer of tenancies, concerns the position of cohabitants or former cohabitants, and, in effect, adapts the existing law which had previously applied only to spouses. This reflects the fact that the previous law relating to the position of cohabitants was unsatisfactory and, in some cases, unfair.

As will be seen, the provisions as to transfer of tenancies repeat, and are designed to improve, the existing law relating to former spouses, and extend that law to cohabitants and former cohabitants. In each case, the rights previously enjoyed by spouses are extended to unmarried people. These will be considered in turn.

**8.2**  The power to transfer a tenancy from one party to another has existed for some time in the case of former spouses whose marriage has been dissolved or annulled, or spouses to whom a decree of judicial separation has been granted. It was arguable that this power existed by virtue of s 24(1) of the MCA 1973, although a potential difficulty was that the court could not compel an unwilling landlord to accept a transfer of tenant where there was a covenant against assignment. However, there was no doubt that by virtue of s 7 of and Sch 1 to the MHA 1983 the court did have the power to transfer tenancies between spouses or former spouses.

This power did not exist in the case of cohabitants, and The Law Commission considered that this anomaly should be rectified. Although the Family Law Reform Act 1987 gave the court jurisdiction to order the transfer or settlement of property between unmarried parents for the benefit of their children, this was thought to be unduly restrictive and unsatisfactory for a number of reasons (see Law Com para 6.5).

Such considerations led The Law Commission to:

'... the firm conclusion that the power to transfer tenancies at present contained in the Matrimonial Homes Act 1983 should be extended to cohabitants, whether they are joint tenants or whether one party is a sole tenant and the other is non-entitled. We therefore *recommend* accordingly. There would, of course, be no entitlement to such a transfer in any particular situation. The court would simply have power to make such an order if the merits of the case justified it. If they did not, it would not be done.' (Law Com para 6.6)

This change was, therefore, brought about by s 53 of the Act which provides that Sch 7 to the Act shall have effect.

It should be noted that, by virtue of para 15(1) of Sch 7, the court's powers under this Schedule are in addition to the court's powers to make occupation orders under whatever section is appropriate. These powers are therefore additional to those arising under the remainder of the Act. It is interesting to note that unmarried couples are, in this respect, placed in a more favourable position with respect to rented property than to property which one of them might have owned.

## Applicants for transfer of tenancy

**8.3**   The MHA 1983 is abolished in its entirety by the Act. As a result, the Act has to confer on spouses and former spouses the rights which they enjoyed under the earlier legislation, as well as extending those rights to others. This part of the legislation is, therefore, of considerable significance to divorced couples whose matrimonial home has been tenanted property, within the classes of tenancy covered by the Schedule.

Schedule 7 begins by defining some terms. 'Cohabitant', except in one limited case which will be considered later, includes a 'former cohabitant'. 'Landlord' includes any person deriving title under the original landlord. 'Relevant tenancy' means:

'(a)   a protected tenancy or statutory tenancy within the meaning of the Rent Act 1977;

(b)   a statutory tenancy within the meaning of the Rent (Agriculture) Act 1976;

(c)   a secure tenancy within the meaning of section 79 of the Housing Act 1985; or

(d)   an assured tenancy or assured agricultural occupancy within the meaning of Part I of the Housing Act 1988.'

'Tenancy' includes a sub-tenancy, and 'spouse', except in one case, includes a former spouse (Sch 7, Part I, para 1).

It will be noted that this list does not include assured shorthold tenancies, or long leases.

The orders for transfer which the court may make are collectively referred to as 'Part II orders'.

Paragraph 2 of Part I of Sch 7 goes on to define the cases in which the court may make an order. These are as follows.

## Spouses

Paragraph 2(1) applies if:

> '... one spouse is entitled, either in his own right or jointly with the other spouse, to occupy a dwelling-house by virtue of a relevant tenancy.'

Paragraph 2(2) goes on to provide that, at any time where it has power to make a property adjustment order under s 23A (divorce or separation) or s 24 (nullity) of the MCA 1973 with respect to the marriage, the court may make a Part II order.

It follows from this that a spouse may apply for a transfer of tenancy under Part II only when she is in a position to apply for a property adjustment order; when the whole of the Family Law Act 1996 comes into force, this will be, in the case of divorce or separation, at any time after the filing of a statement of marital breakdown. Until then, and in any event in the case of nullity, the appropriate time is on or after the grant of a decree. The applicant does not have to apply for a property adjustment order; the requirement is merely that she should be entitled to do so.

Paragraph 4 provides that the court shall not make such an order unless the dwelling-house is or was, in the case of spouses, a matrimonial home or, in the case of cohabitants, a home in which they lived together as husband and wife. A tenancy must therefore be contrasted with the much wider class of property which may be transferred under s 24 of the MCA 1973.

The 1995 Bill provided that only the court which granted the decree may make the order under Part II; that is no longer the case, so that the application may be brought in any county court.

Finally, it should be noted that para 13 of Sch 7 provides that a spouse who remarries cannot thereafter apply for an order under Part II. This has exactly the same effect as s 28(3) of the MCA 1973, which prevents a spouse who has remarried from applying for a capital order under s 24 of that Act; however, as will be seen, this restriction does not apply to cohabitants, who may marry with impunity and not lose the right to apply.

## Cohabitants

**8.4** Paragraph 3(1) of Part I of Sch 7 applies if:

> '... one cohabitant is entitled, either in his own right or jointly with the other cohabitant, to occupy a dwelling-house by virtue of a relevant tenancy.'

Paragraph 3(2) provides that:

> 'If the cohabitants cease to live together as husband and wife, the court may make a Part II order.'

As was seen above, by para 4, the court may not make an order unless the dwelling-house is or was a home in which the cohabitants lived together as husband and wife.

**8.5**   The meaning of 'cohabitant' has already been considered in Chapter 2 and need not be considered further here. There is, in the Act, no restriction on the time within which such an application may be made by a former cohabitant.

## Principles to be applied

**8.6**   The orders which the court may make are set out below at para **8.10**. Paragraph 5 of Part I of Sch 7 sets out the matters to which the court shall have regard; these are:

> '... all the circumstances of the case including—

>> (a)   the circumstances in which the tenancy was granted to either or both of the spouses or cohabitants or, as the case requires, the circumstances in which either or both of them became tenant under the tenancy;

>> (b)   the matters mentioned in section 33(6)(a), (b) and (c) and, where the parties are cohabitants and only one of them is entitled to occupy the dwelling-house by virtue of the relevant tenancy, the further matters mentioned in section 36(6)(e), (f), (g) and (h); and

>> (c)   the suitability of the parties as tenants.'

**8.7**   'All the circumstances of the case' gives the court a wide discretion to admit any evidence which may be relevant.

Sub-paragraph (a) directs the court to have regard to how the tenancy came into being, and to whom it was granted. It will, therefore, be relevant to consider which party is the tenant and how it was that he or she became the tenant.

Section 33(6)(a), (b) and (c) of the Act contains the matters to which the court is directed to have regard when deciding whether, and, if so, how, to exercise its powers to make an occupation order in favour of a person who is entitled or has matrimonial home rights; this is considered in more detail, in the context of occupation orders, in Chapter 3. It will be remembered that s 36 contains sub-s (7), which sets out the 'greater harm' test, but it might be thought that, if Parliament had intended sub-s (7) to apply, it would have said so, and the wording of para 5(b) of this Schedule seems to incorporate only s 33(6)(a), (b) and (c). It might seem, therefore, that the greater harm test is not applicable.

In all cases, therefore, the court will have to have regard to the respective housing needs of the parties and of any relevant child, and the respective financial resources of the parties. By s 33(6)(c) the court must also have regard to:

> '... the likely effect of any order, or of any decision by the court not to exercise its powers under subsection (3) above, on the health, safety or well-being of the parties and of any relevant child;'

Subsection (3) of s 33 sets out the different kinds of occupation orders which a court may make. If the wording is read literally, it would seem that the court is directed to have regard to the consequences of making, or not making, an occupation order, which might broaden the scope of the court's enquiry. It may be that this difficulty is more apparent than real, since the consequences of an order for transfer of tenancy would be that the 'unsuccessful' party would have to leave, which would have the same effect as an occupation order; this provision would then be interpreted as meaning that the court must consider the effect on both parties of an order that one of them leave.

It is worth noting that s 33(6)(d) which directs the court to have regard to the conduct of the parties, is not applicable to Sch 7. Conduct, therefore, is irrelevant.

**8.8** Paragraph 5(b) of Part I of Sch 7 then sets out further matters to which the court must have regard when the parties are cohabitants and only one of them is the tenant (it would not, therefore, apply when both were tenants); 'cohabitant' includes 'former cohabitant'.

These matters are those contained in s 36(6)(e), (f), (g) and (h), which are the factors to be considered by the court when deciding whether, and, if so, in what manner, to make an occupation order where the applicant was non-entitled; they are set out and considered in detail in Chapter 3. They are, where the parties are cohabitants or former cohabitants, the nature of their relationship, the duration of the cohabitation, whether there are children for whom they are responsible and the length of time since they ceased to live together. Once again, the conduct of the parties, which is relevant to an issue of an occupation order, is not included as a relevant factor here.

These provisions are clearly designed to give the court wide discretion to make orders in accordance with the justice of the case.

**8.9** The final matter to which the court must have regard is the suitability of the parties as tenants. It will be seen below that landlords will be entitled to be heard on applications for transfer of tenancies, and this provision enables the court to take account of the landlord's interests as well as those of the parties. It would also have some relevance as between the parties, since there would be little point, for example, in transferring a tenancy to someone who was incapable of paying the rent or who had proved to be a nuisance or annoyance to his neighbours.

## Orders which may be made

**8.10** By para 1 of Part I of Sch 7, 'the court' does not include a magistrates' court. Applications will therefore have to be brought in a county court.

The orders which the court may make will depend on the nature of the tenancy; these orders are, therefore, set out by reference to the type of tenancy which is involved. Part II of Sch 7 begins with one clarification of terms;

whenever this part of the Schedule refers to a cohabitant or spouse being entitled to occupy a dwelling-house by virtue of a relevant tenancy, this applies whether the tenancy is sole or joint (para 6).

It is, perhaps, also worth noting here the restrictions which apply in respect of some former spouses. As has already been noted above, a spouse who has remarried is not entitled to apply for an order under Sch 7 (para 13). If this is interpreted in the same way as other claims under the pre-1996 law for ancillary relief, it will mean that a petitioner who has applied for a transfer of a tenancy in the prayer to her petition will be taken to have applied, and her claim will not be defeated by her remarriage. However, a respondent who had not filed an answer claiming relief would be barred from applying after remarriage. It remains to be seen what rules of court will provide for the new divorce law.

By para 12 of Sch 7, it is provided that the date on which an order for transfer of tenancy is to take effect may not be earlier than decree absolute.

Neither of these restrictions applies, of course, to cohabitants. A spouse whose marriage has not been dissolved, or to whom a decree of judicial separation has not been granted, has no right to apply under Sch 7.

The orders which the court may make are classified by reference to the nature of the tenancy to be transferred. This is not a textbook on the law of landlord and tenant; accordingly, no explanation is provided of the meaning of the various terms used, for example 'assured agricultural occupancy'. The reader who requires further information as to the rights and obligations attaching to such terms should therefore consult a more specialised publication.

In all cases, the interest to be transferred is the tenancy to which the transferor is entitled. They are as follows.

### Protected tenancy, secure tenancy, assured tenancy, assured agricultural occupancy

**8.11**   These terms are defined by reference to their meaning in the Rent Act 1977, the Housing Act 1985, and Part I of the Housing Act 1988 respectively. It will be noted that an assured shorthold tenancy is not one which may be transferred, but a 'council tenancy' is. (The most common form of tenancy in the private sector is therefore excluded.) What is to be transferred is the estate or interest which the entitled spouse had in the dwelling-house immediately before the order for transfer:

> '... by virtue of the lease or agreement creating the tenancy and any assignment of that lease of agreement, with all rights, privileges and appurtenances attaching to that estate or interest but subject to all covenants, obligations, liabilities and incumbrances to which it is subject, ...' (para 7(1)(a))

The transfer is effected by the order, and no further assurance or document in writing is needed (para 7(1)).

Paragraph 7(1)(b) provides that where the entitled party is an assignee, his liability under any covenant of indemnity, whether express or implied, may also be transferred.

**8.12** Paragraph 7(2) provides, in effect, that when an order for transfer is made, any liability or obligation to which the party whose tenancy has been transferred was liable shall no longer be enforceable against that party; this is only in respect of liabilities or obligations falling due to be discharged after the date of the transfer.

By para 7(3) and (4), where the entitled party is a successor within the meaning of Part IV of the Housing Act 1985, or of s 17 of the Housing Act 1988, his former spouse or cohabitant is also deemed to be a successor.

Paragraph 7(5) deals with the position where the transfer is of an assured agricultural occupancy. For the purposes of Chapter III of Part I of the Housing Act 1988, the agricultural worker condition shall be fulfilled with respect to the dwelling-house while the spouse or cohabitant to whom the occupancy is transferred continues to be the occupier under that occupancy, and that condition shall be treated as so fulfilled by virtue of the same paragraph of Sch 3 to the Housing Act 1988 as was applicable before the transfer.

## Statutory tenancy within the meaning of the Rent Act 1977

**8.13** The court may order that as from the date specified in the order, the entitled party shall cease to be entitled to occupy the dwelling-house, and that the other party shall be deemed to be the tenant, or, as the case may be, the sole tenant, under the statutory tenancy (para 8(1)).

Paragraph 8(2) deals with the question of whether the provisions of paras 1 to 3, or, as the case may be, paras 5 to 7 of Sch 1 to the Rent Act 1977, as to the succession by the surviving spouse of a deceased tenant, or by a member of the deceased tenant's family, to the right to retain possession, are capable of having effect in the event of the death of a person deemed by an order under these provisions to be the tenant or sole tenant under the statutory tenancy. It is provided that this question shall be determined according as those provisions have or have not already had effect in relation to the statutory tenancy.

## Statutory tenancy within the meaning of the Rent (Agriculture) Act 1976

**8.14** The court may order that, as from such date as may be specified in the order, the entitled party shall cease to be entitled to occupy the dwelling-house and that the other party shall be deemed to be the tenant, or, as the case may be, the sole tenant under the statutory tenancy (para 9). A spouse or cohabitant who is deemed under this provision to be the tenant under a statutory tenancy shall be (within the meaning of the 1976 Act) a statutory tenant in his own right, or a statutory tenant by succession, according as the other spouse or cohabitant was a statutory tenant in his own right or a statutory tenant by succession.

## Supplementary provisions

**8.15**   Part III of Sch 7 contains what are described as 'supplementary provisions'. These are orders which may be made supplementary to the order for transfer of tenancy in any case. They are, in fact, potentially more important than their description might indicate.

The first of these relates to payment in return for transfer. By para 10(1), the court may order a party to whom a tenancy is transferred to make a payment to the other party. In deciding whether to exercise this power, and, if so, in what manner, the court is directed by para 10(4) to have regard to all the circumstances including:

'(a)   the financial loss that would otherwise be suffered by the transferor as a result of the order;

(b)   the financial needs and financial resources of the parties; and

(c)   the financial obligations which the parties have, or are likely to have in the foreseeable future, including financial obligations to each other and to any relevant child.'

A wide discretion is therefore conferred on the court.

**8.16**   By para 10(2), the court may, in effect, order that the payment need not be made immediately. Instead, it may direct that payment of the sum, or part thereof, be deferred, or be paid by instalments. Further, by para 10(3), the court may vary any order for payment, or exercise its powers under para 10(2) at any time before payment in full has been made.

In deciding how to exercise its powers as to the method of payment, the court must have regard to the factors set out in para 10(4) above. However, this is subject to the overriding provision, contained in para 10(5), that the court shall not give any direction under para 10(2) unless it appears to the court that immediate payment of the sum required by the order would cause the transferee financial hardship which is greater than any hardship that would be caused to the transferor if the direction were given.

**8.17**   The second type of supplementary order relates to liabilities and obligations in respect of the dwelling-house. By para 11, the court may direct that both parties shall be jointly and severally liable to discharge and perform any obligation or liability in respect of the dwelling-house (whether arising under the tenancy or otherwise) which, before the order for transfer, may have fallen to be discharged or performed by only one of them, and which were due as at the date of the transfer. Where such a direction is given, the court may also direct that either party shall be liable to indemnify the other in whole or in part against any payment made or expenses incurred by the other in discharging or performing any such liability or obligation.

## Rights of landlords

**8.18** Paragraph 14(1) provides that rules of court shall be made requiring the court to give the landlord of any dwelling-house, to which any order for transfer of tenancy will relate, an opportunity to be heard. The principal provision in the Schedule which protects a landlord is para 5(c), which directs the court to have regard to the suitability of the parties as tenants when deciding how to exercise its powers.

For procedure, see para **8.20** below.

## Date when order takes effect

**8.19** There is no special provision as to when an order between cohabitants or former cohabitants is to take effect. However, provision has had to be made for orders made between spouses because of the provisions of the MCA 1973 introduced by the Family Law Act 1996 as to the date on which a property adjustment order may take effect. Paragraph 12 of Sch 7 provides that, in the cause of nullity, the order may not take effect before decree absolute, and, in the case of divorce or separation, the date on which it may take effect is to be determined as if the court were making a property adjustment order under s 23A of the MCA 1973, regard being had to the restrictions imposed by s 23B of that Act.[1]

## Procedure

**8.20** The procedure for applications for transfer of tenancies is different from the other applications under Part IV. By FPR, r 3.8(14), r 3.6(7)–(9) (which governs applications under the Married Women's Property Act 1882) applies to applications for the transfer of tenancy. The effect of this is as follows:

**(a) Issue and Application**
Rule 3.6(7) does not deal with applications for MWPA orders as such; this is dealt with by r 3.6(1), which is not deemed to apply to applications for transfer of tenancy. However, there is nothing in r 3.8 to govern applications for transfer of tenancy, nor any prescribed forms; Form FL401 (see Appendix III at p 201) is limited to applications for occupation orders or non-molestation orders.

---

[1] See, generally, Cretney and Bird, *Divorce: The New Law* (Family Law, 1996).

It would seem, therefore, that application should be made by originating application supported by affidavit.

### (b)   Respondent contesting

A respondent who wishes to contest an application must, within the time limited for sending the acknowledgement of service, file and serve an affidavit in reply (r 3.6(7)).

### (c)   Interlocutory orders

If no affidavit in reply is served, the applicant may apply for directions (r 3.6(8)). A district judge may grant an injunction if it is incidental to the relief sought (r 3.6(9)).

The court has jurisdiction to order, for example discovery, further particulars etc as if the application were for ancillary relief (r 2.62(4) to (6) and 2.63, applied by r 3.8(13)).

### (d)   Service on landlords

Rule 3.8(12) provides that an application for transfer of tenancy must be served on the other cohabitant or spouse and on the landlord. Any person so served is entitled to be heard on the application. This is, therefore, a different requirement from that relating to third parties in applications for occupation orders where a landlord or mortgagee must be served with notice of an application rather than the application itself.

# CHAPTER NINE

# Procedure

## Introduction

**9.1**   There are various references to procedure in the Act. It is frequently provided that the Lord Chancellor may make rules to govern certain matters; in other words, these matters are to be the subject of delegated legislation, which has now been promulgated, principally in amendments to the FPR effected by the Family Proceedings (Amendment No 3) Rules 1997 and in the Family Proceedings Courts (Matrimonial Proceedings etc) (Amendment) Rules 1997. In this chapter, all procedural questions will be considered.

**9.2**   The broad areas to be covered are as follows:

(1)   Jurisdiction of courts;
(2)   Mode of application;
(3)   Practice on application;
(4)   Appeals.

These will now be considered in turn.

## Jurisdiction of courts

**9.3**   As has been mentioned in earlier chapters, one of the purposes of the Act is to provide a unified system of courts in place of the fragmented system which was in place previously. When he introduced the Bill on second reading, the Lord Chancellor made his intentions clear. At the outset, on this point, he remarked:

> 'Perhaps I may say a word about the family court. I believe we have one.' (Hansard, 23 February 1995, col 1269)

Later, he added:

> 'The Children Act – particularly with its jurisdictional provisions – in effect set up a family court, because it allowed these proceedings to be taken either in the family proceedings court at the magistrates level or in the county court presided over by judges who have made special studies, and, finally, the Family Division. The result is that at every level one gets the necessary family jurisdiction.' (ibid, col 1270)

Finally, on this topic, he said:

'I believe that the family proceedings court at the magistrates level is an extremely effective way of dealing with family matters. This was one of the issues that we discussed when the Children Bill was before this House. I knew that more than one of your Lordships believed that a family court had to be based at least at the county court level. I did not share that view. I believe that in many matters, particularly those concerned with children, the law books and technical knowledge of the law, although helpful, have only limited value. I believe that the practical decisions about where a child should live and so on are just as well taken by the magistrates.' (ibid)

**9.4**  Section 27(1) defines 'the court' as 'the High Court, a county court or a magistrates' court'. Subsections (3) to (7) confer on the Lord Chancellor the power by order to specify the level of court at which proceedings may or must be commenced, and the circumstances in which that shall occur, and the circumstances in which proceedings may be transferred from one level of court to another. The three levels are defined as the High Court, any county court and any magistrates' court.

**9.5**  The detailed rules as to jurisdiction of courts are to be found in the Family Law Act 1996 (Part IV) (Allocation of Proceedings) Order 1997, hereinafter referred to as 'the Allocation Order'. This Order is set out in full in Appendix II at p 187, but may be summarised as follows:

(a)   Proceedings under Part IV may be issued in a county court or a Family Proceedings Court.

(b)   However, not all county courts have jurisdiction. Jurisdiction is limited to divorce county courts, family hearing centres, or care centres. For this purpose, the Principal Registry of the Family Division (PRFD) is classified as a county court. Jurisdiction is specifically conferred on the Lambeth, Shoreditch and Woolwich County Courts.

(c)   Magistrates' courts which have jurisdiction are limited to Family Proceedings Courts.

(d)   An application brought by an applicant who is under the age of 18, and for the grant of leave under s 43, must be commenced in the High Court.

(e)   There is considerable freedom to transfer cases laterally at the same level of court, vertically or downwards. In particular, a Family Proceedings Court must transfer to the county court proceedings where a child under the age of 18 is the respondent or wishes to become a party, or where one party is incapable of managing his property and affairs by reason of mental disorder under the Mental Health Act 1983.

**9.6**  When a case is issued in a magistrates' court, magistrates may, in appropriate cases, transfer to the county court. Rule 3A(8) of the FPR provides that when an application for an occupation order or a non-molestation order is pending, the magistrates' court must consider (on the application of one party or on its own motion) whether to transfer the hearing to another court (ie another magistrates' court or to a county court) and the clerk of the court shall make an order for transfer if it seems necessary or expedient).

Section 29(1) provides that:

> 'A magistrates' court shall not be competent to entertain any application, or make any order, involving any disputed question as to a party's entitlement to occupy any property by virtue of a beneficial estate or interest or contract or by virtue of any enactment giving him the right to remain in occupation, unless it is unnecessary to determine the question in order to deal with the application or make the order.'

In other words, where there is a dispute as to whether one or other party is 'entitled', and that issue will have a significant effect on the outcome (which will not always be the case) the magistrates' court must transfer the case, presumably to the county court.

**9.7**   The Act specifically excludes the jurisdiction of magistrates in one more case. This is Sch 4, which deals with applications for transfer of tenancies, and which provides that 'the court' does not include a magistrates' court.

**9.8**   When a case is to be heard in a county court, the question will arise of whether it is to be heard by a judge or a district judge. For some years, district judges have had power to hear and determine injunction applications, and this will not change. Indeed, the Act confers new powers on district judges by including them in the category of 'relevant judicial authority', with power to commit to prison for breach of orders or undertakings.

Any previous practices or guidelines, for example that committal applications should be heard only by experienced circuit judges and not by assistant recorders, must now be regarded as being overridden, so far as district judges are concerned, by the statutory provisions. This is further confirmed by the Family Proceedings (Allocation to Judiciary) Directions 1997 which confirm at para (i)(c) that proceedings under any of the provisions in Part IV may be dealt with by a circuit judge, a district judge of the PRFD or a district judge in all circumstances. The jurisdiction of a deputy district judge is limited; he may deal with all matters except enforcement.

## Mode of application

**9.9**   The Act contains various specific provisions as to the way in which applications may be made.

By s 11(2) an application for an occupation order may be made in other family proceedings or without any family proceedings being instituted. In the latter case, the application would be known as a free-standing application.

By s 13(2), in effect, the position is the same. In addition, the court may make a non-molestation order of its own motion in family proceedings if it considers that such an order should be made for the benefit of any party or any relevant child. It is unlikely that this latter power would be very often exercised, but it does mean that the court should be more prepared to make a non-molestation order at short, or no notice, when the occasion demanded, for example if matters became very heated in the course of an application for ancillary relief.

## Practice on application

**9.10**    Procedure for applications is governed as to county courts by the new FPR, rr 3.8 et seq, which were introduced by the Family Proceedings (Amendment No 3) Rules 1997 and in magistrates' courts by the Family Proceedings Courts (Matrimonial Proceedings etc) (Amendment) Rules 1997. The two sets of rules are virtually identical and, unless otherwise stated, references in the text are to the FPR. These come into force on 1 October 1997, and govern all applications made under Part IV, at all levels of court. In a few instances, the RSC and CCR continue to apply, but these cases will be identified.

## Issue of proceedings

**9.11**    Jurisdiction was considered at para **9.3** above. Rule 3.8(1) provides that an application for an occupation order or a non-molestation order must be made in Form FL401, whether the application is free-standing or made in other proceedings which are pending (see r 3.8(3)).

The application form is similar to the form used in Children Act applications. The applicant must tick a box to show in what way she claims to be associated with the respondent, and the notes accompanying the form set out at some length the requirements of the Act. It then provides space for a brief indication of the remedy sought.

Procedure on issue and subsequently for applications for transfer of tenancy is considered in Chapter 8.

**9.12**    An applicant who wishes to omit her address from the application form must complete Form C8. This provides for the actual address to be inserted on that form. No leave of the court is required for this.

## Statement in support

**9.13**    An application in Form FL401 must be supported by a sworn statement by the applicant (r 3.8(4)). This should set out all the facts and matters on which the applicant relies, and will be regarded as her evidence in chief. The rules for magistrates' courts are slightly different. Rule 3A(3) of those rules provides that an application in Form FL401 must be supported either by a statement which is signed and is declared to be true or, with leave of the court, by oral evidence.

Although the requirement for the statement is mandatory, and the rules do not provide for emergencies, it is expected that the court may allow an application to be issued and heard on an ex parte basis without a statement in cases of exceptional urgency. In such cases, it would be necessary to give an undertaking to file a statement within a certain time.

Where an application is made without giving notice, on an ex parte basis, the statement must state why this is necessary (r 3.8(5)).

## Application to discharge or vary

**9.14**  An application to vary, extend or discharge an order in existing proceedings is made on Form FL403, and the rules applicable to applications apply also to such applications (r 3.9(8)). Form FL403 is less complicated than Form FL401 since it is unnecessary to establish association, an order having already been made. Application to vary etc must be made to the court which made the original order.

## Application by child

**9.15**  An application for an occupation order or a non-molestation order made by a child under the age of 16 is also made on Form FL401. However, it must be treated in the first instance as an application to the High Court for leave (r 3.8(2)). (See para **2.27** above.)

## Service

**9.16**  An application made on notice must be served personally on the respondent by the applicant (normally the applicant's agent) not less than two days before the date on which the application will be heard (r 3.8(6)). The documents to be served are the application form itself, a copy of the statement in support and notice to the respondent in Form FL402.

**9.17**  An applicant acting in person may request the court to effect service of the application (r 3.8(8)).

The court has power to order substituted service.

**9.18**  Time for service may be abridged under r 3.8(7). The court may, therefore, substitute any time less than two days for service, and would make its decision in the light of the urgency of the case. However, the abridgement of time for service is always to be preferred to dealing with an application in the absence of one party, and there is no reason why service of an urgent application should not be effected, in the first instance at least, informally, for example by telephone informing the respondent that an application was to be made (see *G v G (Ouster: Ex Parte Application)* [1990] 1 FLR 395 CA).

A justices' clerk may abridge time for service.

## Service on Third Parties

**9.19**   Service of applications for occupation orders on third parties such as landlords or mortgagees is effected by the applicant by first class post (r 3.8(11)). At the same time, it is necessary to serve notice in Form FL416. This informs him of his right to make representations in writing or to attend the hearing.

This should not be confused with the requirement to serve a landlord in an application for transfer of tenancy. This is considered in Chapter 8.

## Proof of service

**9.20**   After service has been effected, the applicant must file Form FL415, which is the statement of service.

## Minors

**9.21**   Rule 3.8(10) provides that r 9.2A shall not apply to an application for an occupation order or a non-molestation order. Rule 9.2A is concerned with minors, and provides, in effect, that a minor may bring or continue proceedings without a next friend in the circumstances set out in the rule, namely with leave of the court or where a solicitor considers that the minor is capable of instructing him.

The fact that r 9.2A is disapplied means that the usual rules as to minors apply, and that a next friend or guardian ad litem as the case may be is required.

## The hearing

**9.22**   Hearings of applications for occupation orders or non-molestation orders are in chambers in the county court unless the court otherwise directs (r 3.9(1)). In the magistrates' court, the public will be excluded. The court has the duty to keep a record of the hearing on Form FL405.

The rules prescribe a form of undertaking, Form FL422, for use in magistrates' courts. No such new form is necessary in county courts since it already exists in Form N117 CCR. Form FL405 and Form N117 are in substance identical. In particular, both provide for the person giving the undertaking to sign the form to acknowledge what he has done. The forms provide for an endorsement as to service on the person undertaking of a copy of the undertaking; it is clearly sensible, and good practice, for that service to take place before he leaves court.

## Orders

**9.23**  Any order made must be in Form FL404 (r 3.9(6)). This form, which is set out in full in Appendix III at p 211, falls into two parts. The first contains Notices A and B which are notices to the respondent of the meaning of the order. The court must choose which of these is to apply, but the only difference relates to the penal notice. Where the order contains a non-molestation order the penal notice is mandatory and Notice A must be used. Where the order does not contain a non-molestation order, Notice B is used. This Notice contains provision for a penal notice if the court so chooses, but this is discretionary.

**9.24**  There will follow in the order one or more of the numbered options set out. For example, there is a list of various kinds of occupation orders under the various sections of the Act and of the additional provisions which may be included. There follows a menu of non-molestation orders.

These specimen orders are comprehensive and should cover the great majority of cases, and will be of benefit to judges, magistrates and court staff. The only omission appears to be that the specimen non-molestation orders contain no provision for insertion of the period during which the order will remain in force. In principle, a non-molestation order may be for a lifetime, but the usual practice is to limit its duration, for example for six months. There seems to be no reason why the form should not be amended for such a purpose; clearly, it will also have to be amplified to provide for orders for costs.

## Enforcement

**9.25**  The procedure on enforcement is considered in Chapter 5 on arrest at para **5.12**.

## Appeals

**9.26**  The route for appeals from orders made under Part IV is as follows:

From magistrates
>    To the High Court (normally a single judge)

From district judge
>    To circuit judge

From circuit judge
>    To the Court of Appeal

**9.27**   Appeals under Part IV are governed by r 8.1A, subpara (1) of which may be summarised as follows:

(a) Paragraphs (2), (3), (4), (5), (7) and (8) of r 4.22 apply. These paragraphs govern the procedure for giving notice of appeal, obtaining notes of evidence and so on. The time for appeal is 14 days from the date of the order under appeal, or later with leave of the appellate tribunal.

(b) Rule 8.1(5) and (6) are applied. These relate to appeals from district judges and provide that appeals are heard in chambers unless the court otherwise directs and that an appeal does not in itself operate as a stay of the order under appeal.

(c) In relation to appeals from magistrates, r 8.2(4)(e) and (6) are applied. Paragraph (6) provides that the court is not bound to allow an appeal on the ground merely of misdirection or improper rejection or reception of evidence unless in the opinion of the court substantial wrong or miscarriage of justice has thereby been occasioned.

**9.28**   A district judge may dismiss any appeal for want of prosecution and may deal with any question of costs arising therefrom (r 8.1A(5)).

**9.29**   Rule 8.1A(6) relates to appeals from district judges. The effect of this is that an appeal from any order or decision granting or varying an order or refusing to do so in applications for an occupation order or a transfer of tenancy shall be treated as a final order for the purposes of CCR Ord 37, r 6, and the judge may exercise his own discretion in substitution for that of the district judge.

# CHAPTER TEN

# The Protection from Harassment Act 1997

## Introduction

**10.1**   The protection available under Part IV of the Family Law Act 1996 is not the only remedy for the victim of domestic violence. Since the passing into law of the 1996 Act, two further statutory provisions have been enacted which may have some relevance when protection is being sought. The first of these, contained in s 145 and s 149 of the Housing Act 1996 is clearly intended to be used in situations of domestic violence; this provision is considered in more detail in Chapter 11.

It is open to doubt whether the second statute, to which reference must now be made, namely the Protection from Harassment Act 1997, was drafted with domestic violence in mind, but this seems to be its result.

**10.2**   The Protection from Harassment Act 1997 was introduced after widespread public concern over the apparent inability of the law to control the practice known as 'stalking'. The essential characteristics of this phenomenon are the obsessive harassment of a victim, normally female, by someone who pursues her by following her movements, telephoning and so on. Any relationship between the parties has ended, if, indeed, it ever existed outside the imagination of the perpetrator. Several well-publicised cases led to a pledge by the government of the day to legislate to provide protection from this form of harassment. Unfortunately, whether or not the Act succeeds in achieving the aims of its proponents, it provides a system of law and procedure which is overlapping and parallel with Part IV of the Family Law Act 1996, which may result in some confusion. Whether Parliament ignored the scope for confusion, or was unaware of the fact that it had recently debated at some length a measure providing very similar remedies is a matter for speculation.

The operation of the 1997 Act is further complicated by the fact that it creates an offence of harassment which is the subject of the criminal law, and also provides civil remedies for the restraining of and damages for such offences, so that an unusual hybrid has come into being.

## The new offences

**10.3**   The foundation of the Act is laid in s 1, which provides that:

'A person must not pursue a course of conduct—

(a)   which amounts to harassment of another, and
(b)   which he knows or ought to know amounts to harassment of the other' (s 1(1))

Section 1(2) then provides that, for the purposes of the section:

'the person whose course of conduct is in question ought to know that it amounts to harassment of another if a reasonable person in possession of the same information would think the course of conduct amounted to harassment of the other.'

In other words, the test of the reasonable person applies and an offender would not be able to pray in aid of any particular obsession from which he suffered.

Section 2(1) then provides that a person who pursues a course of conduct in breach of s 1 commits an offence. 'A course of conduct' must involve conduct on at least two occasions (s 7(3)), and 'conduct' includes speech (s 7(4)).

Harassment is not defined by the Act, so that the general legal interpretation discussed at para **1.2** above applies.

**10.4**   Section 1(3) prescribes certain defences to prosecution under s 1.

'Subsection (1) does not apply to a course of conduct if the person who pursued it shows:

(a)   that it was pursued for the purpose of preventing or detecting crime,
(b)   that it was pursued under any enactment or rule of law or to comply with any condition or requirement imposed by any person under any enactment, or
(c)   that in the particular circumstances the pursuit of the course of conduct was reasonable.'

**10.5**   Section 4(1) creates a distinct, though clearly overlapping, offence. A person whose course of conduct causes another to fear, on at least two occasions, that violence will be used against him is guilty of an offence if he knows or ought to know that his course of conduct will cause the other to fear on each of those occasions. By s 7(2), the person whose course of conduct is in question ought to know that it will cause another to fear violence will be used against him on any occasion if a reasonable person in possession of the same information would think the course of conduct would cause the other so to fear on that occasion.

Section 7(3) then also provides certain statutory defences to prosecution under s 4, for example that the course of conduct was pursued for the prevention or detection of crime or for the protection of property. A person found not guilty of an offence under s 4 may nevertheless be convicted of an offence under s 2 (s 4(5)).

# Criminal penalties

**10.6**  A person guilty of an offence under s 12 is liable on summary conviction to imprisonment for not more than six months or to a fine not exceeding level 5 on the standard scale or to both (s 2(2)). An offence under s 2 is an arrestable offence (s 24(2)(n) of PACE 1984, as amended by s 2(3) of the 1997 Act).

A person guilty of an offence under s 4 is liable on conviction on indictment to imprisonment for up to five years or a fine or both, and on summary conviction to imprisonment for up to six months or a fine not exceeding the statutory maximum or both (s 4(4)).

# Civil remedies

**10.7**  The civil remedies available under the 1997 Act all relate to ss 1 and 2, and not to s 4. Accordingly, it is no longer necessary to consider s 4, save to note that a court dealing with a person convicted under s 2 or s 4 may make a restraining order against such a person; a restraining order will prohibit the convicted person from further conduct which causes harassment or will cause a fear of violence (s 5). Breach of such a restraining order is an offence under s 5(6).

An order under s 5 would be made at the request of the prosecution, no doubt with the encouragement or acquiescence of the victim.

**10.8**  Civil remedies properly so-called arise under s 3, which provides as follows:

(1)  An actual or apprehended breach of s 1 may be the subject of a claim in civil proceedings by the person who is or may be the victim of the course of conduct in question.

(2)  On such a claim, damages may be awarded for (among other things) any anxiety caused by the harassment and any financial loss resulting from the harassment.

The 1997 Act therefore provides a cause of action in damages. The right to apply for an injunction, which will probably be the most common civil remedy to be sought, is not specifically mentioned in the 1997 Act, but the general law as to interlocutory and final injunction orders applies.

## Procedure

**10.9**   There are no new rules relating to applications under s 3(1), and the general rules of procedure apply. Proceedings may be issued in the High Court, but this is likely to be unusual and the procedure to be considered here will be that of the county courts, to which the great majority of applications are likely to be made. It appears that the Principal Registry of the Family Division will not have jurisdiction since its jurisdiction is limited to family business.

Proceedings may be issued as follows.

(a)   Liquidated claim where no injunction sought.
      Default summons (Form N1).
(b)   Unliquidated claim, or liquidated claim with an injunction application.
      Fixed date summons (Form N2 or N3).
(c)   Free-standing injunction (not linked to damages claim).
      Form N16a (as amended).

The requirements for applications for injunctions will be the same as those for any other injunction.

**10.10**   Where the damages sought are limited to £3,000, and a defence is filed, the action will be dealt with as a small claim. Where damages are limited to £5,000 (or such sum as is the district judge's current trial jurisdiction), or no damages are sought, the district judge will have jurisdiction.

## Enforcement

**10.11**   Enforcement is dealt with in s 3(3)–(6). There is no provision for the attachment of a power of arrest to the order itself, and the procedure is very similar to that prescribed for the issue of a warrant of arrest under s 47 of the Family Law Act 1996 (see para **5.9** above).

Where the court grants an injunction for the purpose of restraining a defendant from pursuing any course of conduct which amounts to harassment, and the plaintiff considers that the defendant has done anything which he is prohibited from doing by the injunction, the plaintiff may apply for a warrant for the arrest of the defendant (s 3(3)). Where the injunction is granted by a county court, application may be made to a judge or district judge of that or any other county court (s 3(4)).

The judge or district judge may only issue a warrant if the application is substantiated on oath, and he has reasonable grounds for believing that the defendant has done anything which he is prohibited from doing by the injunction (s 3(5)).

**10.12**   The procedure set out above is of course in addition to what was the usual method of dealing with contempt, namely a notice to shew cause as to why the offender should not be committed. However, it may be anticipated that, as with cases under Part IV of the Family Law Act 1996, the new procedure for the issue of a warrant will be the most popular method of enforcement.

Unlike Part IV of the Family Law Act 1996, the 1997 Act does not prescribe the procedure to be followed when a defendant has been arrested and is brought before the court. This will be the subject of separate rules, but it is anticipated that the procedure will be similar to that adopted under Part IV of the Family Law Act 1996.

## Criminal penalty for breach of injunction

**10.13**  As an alternative to the civil contempt procedure, the 1997 Act provides that when the High Court or a county court has granted an injunction for the purpose of restraining a defendant from pursuing any course of conduct which amounts to harassment, and, without reasonable excuse, the defendant does anything which he is prohibited from doing by the injunction, he is guilty of an offence (s 3(6)). Such an offence attracts a penalty of up to five years' imprisonment or a fine or both, on conviction on indictment, or, on summary conviction, up to six months' imprisonment or a fine not exceeding the statutory maximum or both (s 3(9)).

However, a person cannot be convicted of an offence under sub-s (6) in respect of any conduct which has been punished as a contempt of court (s 3(8)). Similarly, where a person is convicted of an offence under sub-s (6), that conduct is not punishable as a contempt of court (s 3(7)).

A person seeking to punish breach of an injunction will therefore have to elect as to whether to deal with the matter by civil committal or to seek to bring about a criminal prosecution.

## Limitation

**10.14**  An action for harassment is, in effect, an action for personal injuries, and would normally be subject to a limitation period of three years. To avoid any problems which this might cause, s 6 of the 1992 Act amends s 11 of the Limitation Act 1980 by inserting a new sub-s (1A) which provides that s 11 (which contains the respective periods of limitation) does not apply to any action brought for damages under s 3 of the Protection from Harassment Act 1997.

It will therefore be possible to rely on events forming a course of conduct going back in time without limit.

# Comparison of the 1997 Act and Part IV of the Family Law Act 1996

**10.15**   As has been seen, the 1997 Act overlaps with Part IV of the Family Law Act 1996, and a victim of domestic violence may have to decide under which statute proceedings should be brought. The following considerations may be among those to be considered:

### (a) Availability of remedy

An applicant for an occupation order would not choose to bring proceedings under the 1997 Act because it provides no remedy comparable with those in Part IV of the Family Law Act 1996. The comparison is therefore limited to non-molestation orders.

Both statutes provide protection against harassment, the legal definition of which must be identical in both cases. Although the 1997 Act is intended to provide for conduct falling short of physical assault, there can be little doubt that physical assault amounts to harassment. There is nothing in the 1997 Act which makes it more difficult to establish harassment, save that it requires proof of a course of conduct, defined as conduct on at least two occasions.

### (b) Entitlement to apply

As was seen at para **2.23** et seq above, in order to apply for a non-molestation order under Part IV of the Family Law Act 1996, the applicant must be 'associated' with the other party, and there is a complicated list of who may be associated. There is no such requirement in respect of the 1997 Act; s 1 merely refers to 'a person' and 'another'. In this respect, therefore, there may be some advantage in the 1997 Act. Anyone may apply for an order against anyone else.

### (c) Nature of remedy

The first and most obvious advantage of the 1997 Act is that, if a victim could persuade the police to become involved, there might be a prosecution under either s 2 or s 4, which would relieve the victim of the responsibility of taking civil action. However, it may be open to doubt that the police would wish to be involved in most domestic disputes where a civil remedy would be available.

Apart from this, the civil orders which could be obtained under the two statutes would seem to be identical; in neither case is there any limitation on the time during which the order will remain in force.

Section 42(5) of the Family Law Act 1996 sets out guidelines which the court must observe when deciding whether or not to grant a non-molestation injunction. The 1997 Act contains no such guidelines so that, in theory, the court would be unconstrained.

### (d) Undertakings

As was seen at para **4.15** et seq above, Part IV of the Family Law Act 1996 contains provision for an application to be resolved by one party giving an undertaking, which is then as enforceable as an order of the court. This is, in fact, how the great majority of domestic violence applications have always been resolved. There is nothing in the 1997 Act which permits the court to accept an undertaking, and certainly nothing regarding its enforceability. It may be argued that there was nothing in the DVMPA to permit undertakings to be given; the court has an inherent jurisdiction to accept an undertaking, and the practice of the court evolved over a period of time and now reflected in, for example prescribed forms in the county court, clearly gives the court a discretion.

On the other hand, it may be said that there is nothing in the Act to support this, and it might be argued that, Parliament having gone to some lengths to prescribe the availability and enforceability of undertakings in Part IV of the Family Law Act 1996, it would not intentionally have left the question in doubt in the 1997 Act so soon afterwards.

If the latter argument were to be accepted (which is probably unlikely, but possible in theory), the court would have the choice of either granting or refusing an application, with no room for 'settlement' or compromise.

### (e) Enforcement

One possible advantage of a Part IV order is that a power of arrest may be attached, which might well speed the process of enforcement. However, the system of applying for a warrant for arrest is common to both statutes.

The fact that breach of an injunction granted under s 3 could be an offence under s 3(6) gives a potential applicant a possible additional remedy, which might in some respects compensate for the lack of a power of arrest.

### (f) Choice of court

Applications under Part IV may be brought in magistrates' courts or in a county court or the High Court, whereas protection under the 1997 Act is only available in a county court or in the High Court.

### (g) Legal aid

Nothing is yet known about the policy of the Legal Aid Board to applications under the 1997 Act. However, it would not be surprising if certificates were not readily granted for that purpose where an alternative remedy was available under Part IV.

### (h) Combined applications

There would seem to be no reason in principle why the provisions of both statutes should not be relied on in the same application, and why, except in matters proceeding in the PRFD, the court should not make an order, or orders, drawing on its jurisdiction under both statutes (provided, of course, that the orders did not duplicate each other).

# CHAPTER ELEVEN

# The Housing Act 1996

**11.1**   In the introduction to Chapter 10, it was noted that there are now two statutory provisions additional to Part IV of the Family Law Act 1996 which may provide partial protection for victims of domestic violence. One of those is the Protection from Harassment Act 1997 which was considered in Chapter 10. The other is contained in certain provisions of the Housing Act 1996. It must be said immediately that the important difference between the two statutes is that a victim of domestic violence has no direct access to the court under the Housing Act 1996. It is only the landlord, and specifically a local authority or social landlord, who can take action.

**11.2**   Section 145 of the Housing Act 1996 inserts a new Ground 2A into Sch 2 of the Housing Act 1988, and provides a new ground for the grant of a possession order. This ground applies where:

> 'The dwellinghouse was occupied (whether alone or with others) by a married couple or a couple living together as husband and wife and—
>
> (a)   one or both of the partners is a tenant of the dwellinghouse,
> (b)   one partner has left the dwellinghouse because of violence or threats of violence by the other towards—
> > (i)    that partner, or
> > (ii)   a member of the family of that partner who was residing with that partner immediately before the partner left, and
> (c)   the court is satisfied that the partner who has left is unlikely to return.'

**11.3**   As noted before, a victim of domestic violence has no direct remedy under this provision; it is only the landlord who can take the proceedings and this is further limited to secure tenancies, ie tenancies from a local housing authority.

There are identical provisions in respect of landlords qualifying as social landlords as defined in Part I of the Housing Act 1996 (ie housing associations) or a charitable housing trust. These are in the form of a new Ground 14A inserted by s 149 of the 1996 Act.

A tenancy granted by a private landlord would not qualify. Subject to those restrictions, the landlord is able, in effect, to take action for the benefit of a victim, and to obtain a possession order. It will be noted that the new Grounds are discretionary grounds for possession.

**11.4**    Sections 147 and 150 of the Housing Act 1996 introduce new s 83A and s 8A respectively into the Housing Act 1988 which, in effect, provide for notice to be given to the partner who has left the dwelling-house. This requirement may be dispensed with if the court considers it just and equitable to do so.

# CHAPTER TWELVE

# Transitional Provisions

**12.1** Part IV of the Family Law Act 1996 comes into force on 1 October 1997. By virtue of s 66(3) and Sch 10, it repeals in their entirety the DVMPA and MHA 1983, and ss 16 to 18 of the DPMCA. There will obviously be cases which overlap the old and the new law. Schedule 9 to the Act contains the transitional provisions and savings to govern this position.

Rule 9 of the Family Proceedings (Amendment No 3) Rules 1997 provides that subject to para 10(3), Sch 9 to the Family Law Act 1996 (as to which see below), rr 2 to 8 (which, in effect, govern the new procedure under Part IV of the Family Law Act 1996), shall not apply to proceedings commenced before Part IV came into force.

## Pending applications

**12.2** Paragraphs 7 and 8 of Sch 9 deal with the position where applications for orders or injunctions under ss 16 to 18 of the DPMCA, or ss 1 and 9 of the MHA 1983 are pending, ie have been issued and are undisposed of on the day on which the Act comes into force. At that time, those statutes were repealed. It is provided that nothing in the Act shall affect any such application; the court is therefore able to proceed to deal with the application on the basis of the old law.

**12.3** Paragraph 8 of Sch 9 provides that the same applies to pending applications under Sch 1 to the MHA 1983; this deals with applications for transfers of tenancies.

## Existing orders

**12.4** Paragraph 9 of Sch 9 deals with the position where there is in force immediately before the repeal of the statutory provisions referred to in para **12.2** above, an order made under one of those provisions, or, where an order is made after their repeal, in proceedings brought before such repeal. There are four points to be considered.

First, it is provided that nothing in the Act is to prevent such an existing order from remaining in force. It therefore continues to bind the parties notwithstanding the repeal of the Act by virtue of which it was made.

Secondly, the Act shall not affect the enforcement of an existing order.

Thirdly, application may be made to extend, vary or discharge an existing order, and nothing in the Act is to affect the power of the court to dispose of such an application under the old law. However, it is also provided that the court may, if it thinks it just and reasonable to do so, treat the application as an application for an order under the new legislation (para 10(3), Sch 9).

Finally, if an order is made under the 1996 Act, this discharges any existing order under the old law.

## Matrimonial home rights

**12.5**    Paragraph 10 of Sch 9 contains provisions to deal with the effect of matrimonial home rights in relation to rights of occupation, as they were called under the previous legislation. The effect of all this is that for the purpose of registration or enforcement, the terms are interchangeable. Interested readers are referred to Sch 9 itself, set out in Appendix I at p 165.

# APPENDIX I

# Family Law Act 1996
## (1996 c. 27)

ARRANGEMENT OF SECTIONS

PART IV
FAMILY HOMES AND DOMESTIC VIOLENCE

*An Act to make provision with respect to . . . rights of occupation of certain domestic premises; prevention of molestation; the inclusion in certain orders under the Children Act 1989 of provisions about the occupation of a dwelling-house; the transfer of tenancies between spouses and persons who have lived together as husband and wife; and for connected purposes.*

[4th July 1996]

*Rights to occupy matrimonial home*

## 30 Rights concerning matrimonial home where one spouse has no estate, etc.

(1) This section applies if—

    (a)   one spouse is entitled to occupy a dwelling-house by virtue of—
        (i)    a beneficial estate or interest or contract; or
        (ii)   any enactment giving that spouse the right to remain in occupation; and
    (b)   the other spouse is not so entitled.

(2) Subject to the provisions of this Part, the spouse not so entitled has the following rights ('matrimonial home rights')—

    (a)   if in occupation, a right not to be evicted or excluded from the dwelling-house or any part of it by the other spouse except with the leave of the court given by an order under section 33;
    (b)   if not in occupation, a right with the leave of the court so given to enter into and occupy the dwelling-house.

(3) If a spouse is entitled under this section to occupy a dwelling-house or any part of a dwelling-house, any payment or tender made or other thing done by that spouse in or towards satisfaction of any liability of the other spouse in respect of rent, mortgage payments or other outgoings affecting the dwelling-house shall, whether or not it is made or done in pursuance of an order under section 40, be as good as if made or done by the other spouse.

(4) A spouse's occupation by virtue of this section—

    (a)   is to be treated, for the purposes of the Rent (Agriculture) Act 1976 and the Rent Act 1977 (other than Part V and sections 103 to 106 of that Act), as occupation by the other spouse as the other spouse's residence, and
    (b)   if the spouse occupies the dwelling-house as that spouse's only or principal home, is to be treated, for the purposes of the Housing Act 1985 and Part I of the Housing Act 1988, as occupation by the other spouse as the other spouse's only or principal home.

(5) If a spouse ('the first spouse')—

    (a)   is entitled under this section to occupy a dwelling-house or any part of a dwelling-house, and
    (b)   makes any payment in or towards satisfaction of any liability of the other spouse ('the second spouse') in respect of mortgage payments affecting the dwelling-house,

the person to whom the payment is made may treat it as having been made by that other spouse, but the fact that that person has treated any such payment as having been so made does not affect any claim of the first spouse against the second spouse to an interest in the dwelling-house by virtue of the payment.

(6) If a spouse is entitled under this section to occupy a dwelling-house or part of a dwelling-house by reason of an interest of the other spouse under a trust, all the provisions of subsections (3) to (5) apply in relation to the trustees as they apply in relation to the other spouse.

(7) This section does not apply to a dwelling-house which has at no time been, and which was at no time intended by the spouses to be, a matrimonial home of theirs.

(8) A spouse's matrimonial home rights continue—

(a)  only so long as the marriage subsists, except to the extent that an order under section 33(5) otherwise provides; and

(b)  only so long as the other spouse is entitled as mentioned in subsection (1) to occupy the dwelling-house, except where provision is made by section 31 for those rights to be a charge on an estate or interest in the dwelling-house.

(9) It is hereby declared that a spouse—

(a)  who has an equitable interest in a dwelling-house or in its proceeds of sale, but

(b)  is not a spouse in whom there is vested (whether solely or as joint tenant) a legal estate in fee simple or a legal term of years absolute in the dwelling-house,

is to be treated, only for the purpose of determining whether he has matrimonial home rights, as not being entitled to occupy the dwelling-house by virtue of that interest.

### 31 Effect of matrimonial home rights as charge on dwelling-house

(1) Subsections (2) and (3) apply if, at any time during a marriage, one spouse is entitled to occupy a dwelling-house by virtue of a beneficial estate or interest.

(2) The other spouse's matrimonial home rights are a charge on the estate or interest.

(3) The charge created by subsection (2) has the same priority as if it were an equitable interest created at whichever is the latest of the following dates—

(a)  the date on which the spouse so entitled acquires the estate or interest;

(b)  the date of the marriage; and

(c)  1st January 1968 (the commencement date of the Matrimonial Homes Act 1967).

(4) Subsections (5) and (6) apply if, at any time when a spouse's matrimonial home rights are a charge on an interest of the other spouse under a trust, there are, apart from either of the spouses, no persons, living or unborn, who are or could become beneficiaries under the trust.

(5) The rights are a charge also on the estate or interest of the trustees for the other spouse.

(6) The charge created by subsection (5) has the same priority as if it were an equitable interest created (under powers overriding the trusts) on the date when it arises.

(7) In determining for the purposes of subsection (4) whether there are any persons who are not, but could become, beneficiaries under the trust, there is to be disregarded any potential exercise of a general power of appointment exercisable by either or both of the spouses alone (whether or not the exercise of it requires the consent of another person).

(8) Even though a spouse's matrimonial home rights are a charge on an estate or interest in the dwelling-house, those rights are brought to an end by—

(a)    the death of the other spouse, or

(b)    the termination (otherwise than by death) of the marriage,

unless the court directs otherwise by an order made under section 33(5).

(9) If—

(a)    a spouse's matrimonial home rights are a charge on an estate or interest in the dwelling-house, and

(b)    that estate or interest is surrendered to merge in some other estate or interest expectant on it in such circumstances that, but for the merger, the person taking the estate or interest would be bound by the charge,

the surrender has effect subject to the charge and the persons thereafter entitled to the other estate or interest are, for so long as the estate or interest surrendered would have endured if not so surrendered, to be treated for all purposes of this Part as deriving title to the other estate or interest under the other spouse or, as the case may be, under the trustees for the other spouse, by virtue of the surrender.

(10) If the title to the legal estate by virtue of which a spouse is entitled to occupy a dwelling-house (including any legal estate held by trustees for that spouse) is registered under the Land Registration Act 1925 or any enactment replaced by that Act—

(a)    registration of a land charge affecting the dwelling-house by virtue of this Part is to be effected by registering a notice under that Act; and

(b)    a spouse's matrimonial home rights are not an overriding interest within the meaning of that Act affecting the dwelling-house even though the spouse is in actual occupation of the dwelling-house.

(11) A spouse's matrimonial home rights (whether or not constituting a charge) do not entitle that spouse to lodge a caution under section 54 of the Land Registration Act 1925.

(12) If—

(a)    a spouse's matrimonial home rights are a charge on the estate of the other spouse or of trustees of the other spouse, and

(b)    that estate is the subject of a mortgage,

then if, after the date of the creation of the mortgage ('the first mortgage'), the charge is registered under section 2 of the Land Charges Act 1972, the charge is, for the purposes of section 94 of the Law of Property Act 1925 (which regulates the rights of mortgagees to make further advances ranking in priority to subsequent mortgages), to be deemed to be a mortgage subsequent in date to the first mortgage.

(13) It is hereby declared that a charge under subsection (2) or (5) is not registrable under subsection 10 or under section 2 of the Land Charges Act 1972 unless it is a charge on a legal estate.

## 32  Further provisions relating to matrimonial home rights

Schedule 4 re-enacts with consequential amendments and minor modifications provisions of the Matrimonial Homes Act 1983.

*Occupation orders*

## 33 Occupation orders where applicant has estate or interest etc. or has matrimonial home rights

(1) If—

    (a)    a person ('the person entitled')—

        (i)    is entitled to occupy a dwelling-house by virtue of a beneficial estate or interest or contract or by virtue of any enactment giving him the right to remain in occupation, or

        (ii)    has matrimonial home rights in relation to a dwelling-house, and

    (b)    the dwelling-house—

        (i)    is or at any time has been the home of the person entitled and of another person with whom he is associated, or

        (ii)    was at any time intended by the person entitled and any such other person to be their home,

the person entitled may apply to the court for an order containing any of the provisions specified in subsections (3), (4) and (5).

(2) If an agreement to marry is terminated, no application under this section may be made by virtue of section 62(3)(e) by reference to that agreement after the end of the period of three years beginning with the date on which it is terminated.

(3) An order under this section may—

    (a)    enforce the applicant's entitlement to remain in occupation as against the other person ('the respondent');

    (b)    require the respondent to permit the applicant to enter and remain in the dwelling-house or part of the dwelling-house;

    (c)    regulate the occupation of the dwelling-house by either or both parties;

    (d)    if the respondent is entitled as mentioned in subsection (1)(a)(i), prohibit, suspend or restrict the exercise by him of his right to occupy the dwelling-house;

    (e)    if the respondent has matrimonial home rights in relation to the dwelling-house and the applicant is the other spouse, restrict or terminate those rights;

    (f)    require the respondent to leave the dwelling-house or part of the dwelling-house; or

    (g)    exclude the respondent from a defined area in which the dwelling-house is included.

(4) An order under this section may declare that the applicant is entitled as mentioned in subsection (1)(a)(i) or has matrimonial home rights.

(5) If the applicant has matrimonial home rights and the respondent is the other spouse, an order under this section made during the marriage may provide that those rights are not brought to an end by—

    (a)    the death of the other spouse; or

    (b)    the termination (otherwise than by death) of the marriage.

(6) In deciding whether to exercise its powers under subsection (3) and (if so) in what manner, the court shall have regard to all the circumstances including—

(a)  the housing needs and housing resources of each of the parties and of any relevant child;
(b)  the financial resources of the parties;
(c)  the likely effect of any order, or of any decision by the court not to exercise its powers under subsection (3), on the health, safety or well-being of the parties and of any relevant child; and
(d)  the conduct of the parties in relation to each other and otherwise.

(7) If it appears to the court that the applicant or any relevant child is likely to suffer significant harm attributable to conduct of the respondent if an order under this section containing one or more of the provisions mentioned in subsection (3) is not made, the court shall make the order unless it appears to the court that—

(a)  the respondent or any relevant child is likely to suffer significant harm if the order is made; and
(b)  the harm likely to be suffered by the respondent or child in that event is as great as, or greater than, the harm attributable to conduct of the respondent which is likely to be suffered by the applicant or child if the order is not made.

(8) The court may exercise its powers under subsection (5) in any case where it considers that in all the circumstances it is just and reasonable to do so.

(9) An order under this section—

(a)  may not be made after the death of either of the parties mentioned in subsection (1); and
(b)  except in the case of an order made by virtue of subsection (5)(a), ceases to have effect on the death of either party.

(10) An order under this section may, in so far as it has continuing effect, be made for a specified period, until the occurrence of a specified event or until further order.

### 34  Effect of order under s 33 where rights are charge on dwelling-house

(1) If a spouse's matrimonial home rights are a charge on the estate or interest of the other spouse or of trustees for the other spouse—

(a)  any order under section 33 against the other spouse has, except so far as a contrary intention appears, the same effect against persons deriving title under the other spouse or under the trustees and affected by the charge, and
(b)  subsections 33(1), (3), (4) and (10) and 30(3) to (6) apply in relation to any person deriving title under the other spouse or under the trustees and affected by the charge as they apply in relation to the other spouse.

(2) The court may make an order under section 33 by virtue of subsection (1)(b) if it considers that in all the circumstances it is just and reasonable to do so.

### 35  One former spouse with no existing right to occupy

(1) This section applies if—

(a)  one former spouse is entitled to occupy a dwelling-house by virtue of a beneficial estate or interest or contract, or by virtue of any enactment giving him the right to remain in occupation;

(b)    the other former spouse is not so entitled; and

(c)    the dwelling-house was at any time their matrimonial home or was at any time intended by them to be their matrimonial home.

(2) The former spouse not so entitled may apply to the court for an order under this section against the other former spouse ('the respondent').

(3) If the applicant is in occupation, an order under this section must contain provision—

(a)    giving the applicant the right not to be evicted or excluded from the dwelling-house or any part of it by the respondent for the period specified in the order; and

(b)    prohibiting the respondent from evicting or excluding the applicant during that period.

(4) If the applicant is not in occupation, an order under this section must contain provision—

(a)    giving the applicant the right to enter into and occupy the dwelling-house for the period specified in the order; and

(b)    requiring the respondent to permit the exercise of that right.

(5) An order under this section may also—

(a)    regulate the occupation of the dwelling-house by either or both of the parties;

(b)    prohibit, suspend or restrict the exercise by the respondent of his right to occupy the dwelling-house;

(c)    require the respondent to leave the dwelling-house or part of the dwelling-house; or

(d)    exclude the respondent from a defined area in which the dwelling-house is included.

(6) In deciding whether to make an order under this section containing provision of the kind mentioned in subsection (3) or (4) and (if so) in what manner, the court shall have regard to all the circumstances including—

(a)    the housing needs and housing resources of each of the parties and of any relevant child;

(b)    the financial resources of each of the parties;

(c)    the likely effect of any order, or of any decision by the court not to exercise its powers under subsection (3) or (4), on the health, safety or well-being of the parties and of any relevant child;

(d)    the conduct of the parties in relation to each other and otherwise;

(e)    the length of time that has elapsed since the parties ceased to live together;

(f)    the length of time that has elapsed since the marriage was dissolved or annulled; and

(g)    the existence of any pending proceedings between the parties—

(i)    for an order under section 23A or 24 of the Matrimonial Causes Act 1973 (property adjustment orders in connection with divorce proceedings etc.);

(ii)   for an order under paragraph 1(2)(d) or (e) of Schedule 1 to the Children Act 1989 (orders for financial relief against parents); or

(iii)  relating to the legal or beneficial ownership of the dwelling-house.

(7) In deciding whether to exercise its power to include one or more of the provisions referred to in subsection (5) ('a subsection (5) provision') and (if so) in what manner, the court shall have regard to all the circumstances including the matters mentioned in subsection (6)(a) to (e).

(8) If the court decides to make an order under this section and it appears to it that, if the order does not include a subsection (5) provision, the applicant or any relevant child is likely to suffer significant harm attributable to conduct of the respondent, the court shall include the subsection (5) provision in the order unless it appears to the court that—

  (a)   the respondent or any relevant child is likely to suffer significant harm if the provision is included in the order; and
  (b)   the harm likely to be suffered by the respondent or child in that event is as great as or greater than the harm attributable to conduct of the respondent which is likely to be suffered by the applicant or child if the provision is not included.

(9) An order under this section—

  (a)   may not be made after the death of either of the former spouses; and
  (b)   ceases to have effect on the death of either of them.

(10) An order under this section must be limited so as to have effect for a specified period not exceeding six months, but may be extended on one or more occasions for a further specified period not exceeding six months.

(11) A former spouse who has an equitable interest in the dwelling-house or in the proceeds of sale of the dwelling-house but in whom there is not vested (whether solely or as joint tenant) a legal estate in fee simple or a legal term of years absolute in the dwelling-house is to be treated (but only for the purpose of determining whether he is eligible to apply under this section) as not being entitled to occupy the dwelling-house by virtue of that interest.

(12) Subsection (11) does not prejudice any right of such a former spouse to apply for an order under section 33.

(13) So long as an order under this section remains in force, subsections (3) to (6) of section 30 apply in relation to the applicant—

  (a)   as if he were the spouse entitled to occupy the dwelling-house by virtue of that section; and
  (b)   as if the respondent were the other spouse.

### 36 One cohabitant or former cohabitant with no existing right to occupy

(1) This section applies if—

  (a)   one cohabitant or former cohabitant is entitled to occupy a dwelling house by virtue of a beneficial estate or interest or contract or by virtue of any enactment giving him the right to remain in occupation;
  (b)   the other cohabitant or former cohabitant is not so entitled; and
  (c)   that dwelling-house is the home in which they live together as husband and wife or a home in which they at any time so lived together or intended so to live together.

(2) The cohabitant or former cohabitant not so entitled may apply to the court for an order under this section against the other cohabitant or former cohabitant ('the respondent').

(3) If the applicant is in occupation, an order under this section must contain provision—

    (a) giving the applicant the right not to be evicted or excluded from the dwelling-house or any part of it by the respondent for the period specified in the order, and

    (b) prohibiting the respondent from evicting or excluding the applicant during that period.

(4) If the applicant is not in occupation, an order under this section must contain provision—

    (a) giving the applicant the right to enter into and occupy the dwelling-house for the period specified in the order; and

    (b) requiring the respondent to permit the exercise of that right.

(5) An order under this section may also—

    (a) regulate the occupation of the dwelling-house by either or both of the parties;

    (b) prohibit, suspend or restrict the exercise by the respondent of his right to occupy the dwelling-house;

    (c) require the respondent to leave the dwelling-house or part of the dwelling-house; or

    (d) exclude the respondent from a defined area in which the dwelling-house is included.

(6) In deciding whether to make an order under this section containing provision of the kind mentioned in subsection (3) or (4) and (if so) in what manner, the court shall have regard to all the circumstances including—

    (a) the housing needs and housing resources of each of the parties and of any relevant child;

    (b) the financial resources of each of the parties;

    (c) the likely effect of any order, or of any decision by the court not to exercise its powers under subsection (3) or (4), on the health, safety or well-being of the parties and of any relevant child;

    (d) the conduct of the parties in relation to each other and otherwise;

    (e) the nature of the parties' relationship;

    (f) the length of time during which they have lived together as husband and wife;

    (g) whether there are or have been any children who are children of both parties or for whom both parties have or have had parental responsibility;

    (h) the length of time that has elapsed since the parties ceased to live together; and

    (i) the existence of any pending proceedings between the parties—

        (i) for an order under paragraph 1(2)(d) or (e) of Schedule 1 to the Children Act 1989 (orders for financial relief against parents), or

        (ii) relating to the legal or beneficial ownership of the dwelling-house.

(7) In deciding whether to exercise its powers to include one or more of the provisions referred to in subsection (5) ('a subsection (5) provision') and (if so) in what manner, the court shall have regard to all the circumstances including—

  (a)   the matters mentioned in subsection (6)(a) to (d); and

  (b)   the questions mentioned in subsection (8).

(8) The questions are—

  (a)   whether the applicant or any relevant child is likely to suffer significant harm attributable to conduct of the respondent if the subsection (5) provision is not included in the order; and

  (b)   whether the harm likely to be suffered by the respondent or child if the provision is included is as great as or greater than the harm attributable to conduct of the respondent which is likely to be suffered by the applicant or child if the provision is not included.

(9) An order under this section—

  (a)   may not be made after the death of either of the parties; and

  (b)   ceases to have effect on the death of either of them.

(10) An order under this section must be limited so as to have effect for a specified period not exceeding six months, but may be extended on one occasion for a further specified period not exceeding six months.

(11) A person who has an equitable interest in the dwelling-house or in the proceeds of sale of the dwelling-house but in whom there is not vested (whether solely or as joint tenant) a legal estate in fee simple or a legal term of years absolute in the dwelling-house is to be treated (but only for the purpose of determining whether he is eligible to apply under this section) as not being entitled to occupy the dwelling-house by virtue of that interest.

(12) Subsection (11) does not prejudice any right of such a person to apply for an order under section 33.

(13) So long as the order remains in force, subsections (3) to (6) of section 30 apply in relation to the applicant—

  (a)   as if he were a spouse entitled to occupy the dwelling-house by virtue of that section; and

  (b)   as if the respondent were the other spouse.

### 37 Neither spouse entitled to occupy

(1) This section applies if—

  (a)   one spouse or former spouse and the other spouse or former spouse occupy a dwelling-house which is or was the matrimonial home; but

  (b)   neither of them is entitled to remain in occupation—

      (i)   by virtue of a beneficial estate or interest or contract; or

      (ii)  by virtue of any enactment giving him the right to remain in occupation.

(2) Either of the parties may apply to the court for an order against the other under this section.

(3) An order under this section may—

  (a)   require the respondent to permit the applicant to enter and remain in the dwelling-house or part of the dwelling-house;

  (b)   regulate the occupation of the dwelling-house by either or both of the spouses;

(c) require the respondent to leave the dwelling-house or part of the dwelling-house; or

(d) exclude the respondent from a defined area in which the dwelling-house is included.

(4) Subsections (6) and (7) of section 33 apply to the exercise by the court of its powers under this section as they apply to the exercise by the court of its powers under subsection (3) of that section.

(5) An order under this section must be limited so as to have effect for a specified period not exceeding six months, but may be extended on one or more occasions for a further specified period not exceeding six months.

## 38 Neither cohabitant or former cohabitant entitled to occupy

(1) This section applies if—

(a) one cohabitant or former cohabitant and the other cohabitant or former cohabitant occupy a dwelling-house which is the home in which they live or lived together as husband and wife; but

(b) neither of them is entitled to remain in occupation—

    (i) by virtue of a beneficial estate or interest or contract; or

    (ii) by virtue of any enactment giving him the right to remain in occupation.

(2) Either of the parties may apply to the court for an order against the other under this section.

(3) An order under this section may—

(a) require the respondent to permit the applicant to enter and remain in the dwelling-house or part of the dwelling-house;

(b) regulate the occupation of the dwelling-house by either or both of the parties;

(c) require the respondent to leave the dwelling-house or part of the dwelling-house; or

(d) exclude the respondent from a defined area in which the dwelling-house is included.

(4) In deciding whether to exercise its powers to include one or more of the provisions referred to in subsection (3) ('a subsection (3) provision') and (if so) in what manner, the court shall have regard to all the circumstances including—

(a) the housing needs and housing resources of each of the parties and of any relevant child;

(b) the financial resources of each of the parties;

(c) the likely effect of any order, or of any decision by the court not to exercise its powers under subsection (3), on the health, safety or well-being of the parties and of any relevant child;

(d) the conduct of the parties in relation to each other and otherwise; and

(e) the questions mentioned in subsection (5).

(5) The questions are—

(a) whether the applicant or any relevant child is likely to suffer significant harm attributable to conduct of the respondent if the subsection (3) provision is not included in the order; and

(b)    whether the harm likely to be suffered by the respondent or child if the provision is included is as great as or greater than the harm attributable to conduct of the respondent which is likely to be suffered by the applicant or child if the provision is not included.

(6) An order under this section shall be limited so as to have effect for a specified period not exceeding six months, but may be extended on one occasion for a further specified period not exceeding six months.

## 39 Supplementary provisions

(1) In this Part an 'occupation order' means an order under section 33, 35, 36, 37 or 38.

(2) An application for an occupation order may be made in other family proceedings or without any other family proceedings being instituted.

(3) If—

(a)    an application for an occupation order is made under section 33, 35, 36, 37 or 38, and

(b)    the court considers that it has no power to make the order under the section concerned, but that it has power to make an order under one of the other sections,

the court may make an order under that other section.

(4) The fact that a person has applied for an occupation order under sections 35 to 38, or that an occupation order has been made, does not affect the right of any person to claim a legal or equitable interest in any property in any subsequent proceedings (including subsequent proceedings under this Part).

## 40 Additional provisions that may be included in certain occupation orders

(1) The court may on, or at any time after, making an occupation order under section 33, 35 or 36—

(a)    impose on either party obligations as to—

(i)    the repair and maintenance of the dwelling-house; or

(ii)    the discharge of rent, mortgage payments or other outgoings affecting the dwelling-house;

(b)    order a party occupying the dwelling-house or any part of it (including a party who is entitled to do so by virtue of a beneficial estate or interest or contract or by virtue of any enactment giving him the right to remain in occupation) to make periodical payments to the other party in respect of the accommodation, if the other party would (but for the order) be entitled to occupy the dwelling-house by virtue of a beneficial estate or interest or contract or by virtue of any such enactment;

(c)    grant either party possession or use of furniture or other contents of the dwelling-house;

(d)    order either party to take reasonable care of any furniture or other contents of the dwelling-house;

(e)    order either party to take reasonable steps to keep the dwelling-house and any furniture or other contents secure.

(2) In deciding whether and, if so, how to exercise its powers under this section, the court shall have regard to all the circumstances of the case including—

(a)    the financial needs and financial resources of the parties; and
(b)    the financial obligations which they have, or are likely to have in the foreseeable future, including financial obligations to each other and to any relevant child.

(3) An order under this section ceases to have effect when the occupation order to which it relates ceases to have effect.

### 41 Additional considerations if parties are cohabitants or former cohabitants

(1) This section applies if the parties are cohabitants or former cohabitants.

(2) Where the court is required to consider the nature of the parties' relationship, it is to have regard to the fact that they have not given each other the commitment involved in marriage.

*Non-molestation orders*

### 42 Non-molestation orders

(1) In this Part a 'non-molestation order' means an order containing either or both of the following provisions—

(a)    provision prohibiting a person ('the respondent') from molesting another person who is associated with the respondent;
(b)    provision prohibiting the respondent from molesting a relevant child.

(2) The court may make a non-molestation order—

(a)    if an application for the order has been made (whether in other family proceedings or without any other family proceedings being instituted) by a person who is associated with the respondent; or
(b)    if in any family proceedings to which the respondent is a party the court considers that the order should be made for the benefit of any other party to the proceedings or any relevant child even though no such application has been made.

(3) In subsection (2) 'family proceedings' includes proceedings in which the court has made an emergency protection order under section 44 of the Children Act 1989 which includes an exclusion requirement (as defined in section 44A(3) of that Act).

(4) Where an agreement to marry is terminated, no application under subsection (2)(a) may be made by virtue of section 62(3)(e) by reference to that agreement after the end of the period of three years beginning with the day on which it is terminated.

(5) In deciding whether to exercise its powers under this section and, if so, in what manner, the court shall have regard to all the circumstances including the need to secure the health, safety and well-being—

(a)    of the applicant or, in a case falling within subsection (2)(b), the person for whose benefit the order would be made; and

(b)   of any relevant child.

(6) A non-molestation order may be expressed so as to refer to molestation in general, to particular acts of molestation, or to both.

(7) A non-molestation order may be made for a specified period or until further order.

(8) A non-molestation order which is made in other family proceedings ceases to have effect if those proceedings are withdrawn or dismissed.

*Further provisions relating to occupation and non-molestation orders*

## 43  Leave of court required for applications by children under sixteen

(1) A child under the age of sixteen may not apply for an occupation order or a non-molestation order except with the leave of the court.

(2) The court may grant leave for the purposes of subsection (1) only if it is satisfied that the child has sufficient understanding to make the proposed application for the occupation order or non-molestation order.

## 44  Evidence of agreement to marry

(1) Subject to subsection (2) the court shall not make an order under section 33 or 42 by virtue of section 62(3)(e) unless there is produced to it evidence in writing of the existence of the agreement to marry.

(2) Subsection (1) does not apply if the court is satisfied that the agreement to marry was evidenced by—

(a)   the gift of an engagement ring by one party to the agreement to the other in contemplation of their marriage, or

(b)   a ceremony entered into by the parties in the presence of one or more other persons assembled for the purpose of witnessing the ceremony.

## 45  Ex parte orders

(1) The court may, in any case where it considers that it is just and convenient to do so, make an occupation order or a non-molestation order even though the respondent has not been given such notice of the proceedings as would otherwise be required by rules of court.

(2) In determining whether to exercise its powers under subsection (1), the court shall have regard to all the circumstances including—

(a)   any risk of significant harm to the applicant or a relevant child, attributable to conduct of the respondent, if the order is not made immediately;

(b)   whether it is likely that the applicant will be deterred or prevented from pursuing the application if an order is not made immediately; and

(c)   whether there is reason to believe that the respondent is aware of the proceedings but is deliberately evading service and that the applicant or a relevant child will be seriously prejudiced by the delay involved—

   (i)   where the court is a magistrates' court, in effecting service of proceedings; or

(ii) in any other case, in effecting substituted service.

(3) If the court makes an order by virtue of subsection (1) it must afford the respondent an opportunity to make representations relating to the order as soon as just and convenient at a full hearing.

(4) If, at a full hearing, the court makes an occupation order ('the full order'), then—

(a) for the purposes of calculating the maximum period for which the full order may be made to have effect, the relevant section is to apply as if the period for which the full order will have effect began on the date on which the initial order first had effect; and

(b) the provisions of section 36(10) or 38(6) as to the extension of orders are to apply as if the full order and the initial order were a single order.

(5) In this section—

'full hearing' means a hearing of which notice has been given to all the parties in accordance with rules of court;

'initial order' means an occupation order made by virtue of subsection (1); and

'relevant section' means section 33(10), 35(10), 36(10), 37(5) or 38(6).

## 46 Undertakings

(1) In any case where the court has power to make an occupation order or non-molestation order, the court may accept an undertaking from any party to the proceedings.

(2) No power of arrest may be attached to any undertaking given under subsection (1).

(3) The court shall not accept an undertaking under subsection (1) in any case where apart from this section a power of arrest would be attached to the order.

(4) An undertaking given to a court under subsection (1) is enforceable as if it were an order of the court.

(5) This section has effect without prejudice to the powers of the High Court and the county court apart from this section.

## 47 Arrest for breach of order

(1) In this section 'a relevant order' means an occupation order or a non-molestation order.

(2) If—

(a) the court makes a relevant order; and

(b) it appears to the court that the respondent has used or threatened violence against the applicant or a relevant child,

it shall attach a power of arrest to one or more provisions of the order unless the court is satisfied that in all the circumstances of the case the applicant or child will be adequately protected without such a power of arrest.

(3) Subsection (2) does not apply in any case where the relevant order is made by virtue of section 45(1), but in such a case the court may attach a power of arrest to one or more provisions of the order if it appears to it—

(a)   that the respondent has used or threatened violence against the applicant or a relevant child; and

(b)   that there is a risk of significant harm to the applicant or child, attributable to conduct of the respondent, if the power of arrest is not attached to those provisions immediately.

(4) If, by virtue of subsection (3), the court attaches a power of arrest to any provisions of a relevant order, it may provide that the power of arrest is to have effect for a shorter period than the other provisions of the order.

(5) Any period specified for the purposes of subsection (4) may be extended by the court (on one or more occasions) on an application to vary or discharge the relevant order.

(6) If, by virtue of subsection (2) or (3), a power of arrest is attached to certain provisions of an order, a constable may arrest without warrant a person whom he has reasonable cause for suspecting to be in breach of any such provision.

(7) If a power of arrest is attached under subsection (2) or (3) to certain provisions of the order and the respondent is arrested under subsection (6)—

(a)   he must be brought before the relevant judicial authority within the period of 24 hours beginning at the time of his arrest; and

(b)   if the matter is not then disposed of forthwith, the relevant judicial authority before whom he is brought may remand him.

In reckoning for the purposes of this subsection any period of 24 hours, no account is to be taken of Christmas Day, Good Friday or any Sunday.

(8) If the court has made a relevant order but—

(a)   has not attached a power of arrest under subsection (2) or (3) above to any provisions of the order, or

(b)   has attached that power only to certain provisions of the order,

then, if at any time the applicant considers that the respondent has failed to comply with the order, he may apply to the relevant judicial authority for the issue of a warrant for the arrest of the respondent.

(9) The relevant judicial authority shall not issue a warrant on an application under subsection (8) unless—

(a)   the application is substantiated on oath; and

(b)   the relevant judicial authority has reasonable grounds for believing that the respondent has failed to comply with the order.

(10) If a person is brought before a court by virtue of a warrant issued under subsection (9) and the court does not dispose of the matter forthwith, the court may remand him.

(11) Schedule 5 (which makes provision corresponding to that applying in magistrates' courts in civil cases under sections 128 and 129 of the Magistrates' Courts Act 1980) has effect in relation to the powers of the High Court and a county court to remand a person by virtue of this section.

(12) If a person remanded under this section is granted bail (whether in the High Court or a county court under Schedule 5 or in a magistrates' court under section 128 or 129 of the Magistrates' Courts Act 1980), he may be required by the relevant judicial

authority to comply, before release on bail or later, with such requirements as appear to that authority to be necessary to secure that he does not interfere with witnesses or otherwise obstruct the course of justice.

## 48 Remand for medical examination and report

(1) If the relevant judicial authority has reason to consider that a medical report will be required, any power to remand a person under section 47(7)(b) or (10) may be exercised for the purpose of enabling a medical examination and report to be made.

(2) If such a power is so exercised, the adjournment must not be for more than 4 weeks at a time unless the relevant judicial authority remands the accused in custody.

(3) If the relevant judicial authority so remands the accused, the adjournment must not be for more than 3 weeks at a time.

(4) If there is reason to suspect that a person who has been arrested—

    (a)    under section 47(6), or

    (b)    under a warrant issued on an application made under section 47(8),

is suffering from mental illness or severe mental impairment, the relevant judicial authority has the same power to make an order under section 35 of the Mental Health Act 1983 (remand for report on accused's mental condition) as the Crown Court has under section 35 of the Act of 1983 in the case of an accused person within the meaning of that section.

## 49 Variation and discharge of orders

(1) An occupation order or non-molestation order may be varied or discharged by the court on an application by—

    (a)    the respondent, or

    (b)    the person on whose application the order was made.

(2) In the case of a non-molestation order made by virtue of section 42(2)(b), the order may be varied or discharged by the court even though no such application has been made.

(3) If a spouse's matrimonial home rights are a charge on the estate or interest of the other spouse or of trustees for the other spouse, an order under section 33 against the other spouse may also be varied or discharged by the court on an application by any person deriving title under the other spouse or under the trustees and affected by the charge.

(4) If, by virtue of section 47(3), a power of arrest has been attached to certain provisions of an occupation order or non-molestation order, the court may vary or discharge the order under subsection (1) in so far as it confers a power of arrest (whether or not any application has been made to vary or discharge any other provision of the order).

*Enforcement powers of magistrates' courts*

## 50 Power of magistrates' court to suspend execution of committal order

(1) If, under section 63(3) of the Magistrates' Courts Act 1980, a magistrates' court has power to commit a person to custody for breach of a relevant requirement, the

court may by order direct that the execution of the order of committal is to be suspended for such period or on such terms and conditions as it may specify.

(2) In subsection (1) 'a relevant requirement' means—

(a)   an occupation order or non-molestation order;

(b)   an exclusion requirement included by virtue of section 38A of the Children Act 1989 in an interim care order made under section 38 of that Act; or

(c)   an exclusion requirement included by virtue of section 44A of the Children Act 1989 in an emergency protection order under section 44 of that Act.

## 51  Power of magistrates' court to order hospital admission or guardianship

(1) A magistrates' court shall have the same power to make a hospital order or guardianship order under section 37 of the Mental Health Act 1983 or an interim hospital order under section 38 of that Act in the case of a person suffering from mental illness or severe mental impairment who could otherwise be committed to custody for breach of a relevant requirement as a magistrates' court has under those sections in the case of a person convicted of an offence punishable on summary conviction with imprisonment.

(2) In subsection (1) 'a relevant requirement' has the meaning given by section 50(2).

*Interim care orders and emergency protection orders*

## 52  Amendments of Children Act 1989

Schedule 6 makes amendments of the provisions of the Children Act 1989 relating to interim care orders and emergency protection orders.

*Transfer of tenancies*

## 53  Transfer of certain tenancies

Schedule 7 makes provision in relation to the transfer of certain tenancies on divorce etc. or on separation of cohabitants.

*Dwelling-house subject to mortgage*

## 54  Dwelling-house subject to mortgage

(1) In determining for the purposes of this Part whether a person is entitled to occupy a dwelling-house by virtue of an estate or interest, any right to possession of the dwelling-house conferred on a mortgagee of the dwelling-house under or by virtue of his mortgage is to be disregarded.

(2) Subsection (1) applies whether or not the mortgagee is in possession.

(3) Where a person ('A') is entitled to occupy a dwelling-house by virtue of an estate or interest, a connected person does not by virtue of—

(a)   any matrimonial home rights conferred by section 30, or

(b)   any rights conferred by an order under section 35 or 36,

have any larger right against the mortgagee to occupy the dwelling-house than A has by virtue of his estate or interest and of any contract with the mortgagee.

(4) Subsection (3) does not apply, in the case of matrimonial home rights, if under section 31 those rights are a charge, affecting the mortgagee, on the estate or interest mortgaged.

(5) In this section 'connected person', in relation to any person, means that person's spouse, former spouse, cohabitant or former cohabitant.

## 55 Actions by mortgagees: joining connected persons as parties

(1) This section applies if a mortgagee of land which consists of or includes a dwelling-house brings an action in any court for the enforcement of his security.

(2) A connected person who is not already a party to the action is entitled to be made a party in the circumstances mentioned in subsection (3).

(3) The circumstances are that—

  (a)  the connected person is enabled by section 30(3) or (6) (or by section 30(3) or (6) as applied by section 35(13) or 36(13)), to meet the mortgagor's liabilities under the mortgage;
  (b)  he has applied to the court before the action is finally disposed of in that court; and
  (c)  the court sees no special reason against his being made a party to the action and is satisfied—

      (i)   that he may be expected to make such payments or do such other things in or towards satisfaction of the mortgagor's liabilities or obligations as might affect the outcome of the proceedings; or
      (ii)  that the expectation of it should be considered under section 36 of the Administration of Justice Act 1970.

(4) In this section 'connected person' has the same meaning as in section 54.

## 56 Actions by mortgagees: service of notice on certain persons

(1) This section applies if a mortgagee of land which consists, or substantially consists, of a dwelling-house brings an action for the enforcement of his security, and at the relevant time there is—

  (a)  in the case of unregistered land, a land charge of Class F registered against the person who is the estate owner at the relevant time or any person who, where the estate owner is a trustee, preceded him as trustee during the subsistence of the mortgage; or
  (b)  in the case of registered land, a subsisting registration of—

      (i)    a notice under section 31(10);
      (ii)   a notice under section 2(8) of the Matrimonial Homes Act 1983; or
      (iii)  a notice or caution under section 2(7) of the Matrimonial Homes Act 1967.

(2) If the person on whose behalf—

  (a)  the land charge is registered, or
  (b)  the notice or caution is entered,

is not a party to the action, the mortgagee must serve notice of the action on him.

(3) If—

    (a)   an official search has been made on behalf of the mortgagee which would disclose any land charge of Class F, notice or caution within subsection (1)(a) or (b),

    (b)   a certificate of the result of the search has been issued, and

    (c)   the action is commenced within the priority period,

the relevant time is the date of the certificate.

(4) In any other case the relevant time is the time when the action is commenced.

(5) The priority period is, for both registered and unregistered land, the period for which, in accordance with section 11(5) and (6) of the Land Charges Act 1972, a certificate on an official search operates in favour of a purchaser.

*Jurisdiction and procedure etc.*

## 57 Jurisdiction of courts

(1) For the purposes of this Act 'the court' means the High Court, a county court or a magistrates' court.

(2) Subsection (1) above is subject to the provision made by or under the following provisions of this section, to section 59 and to any express provision as to the jurisdiction of any court made by any other provision of this Part.

(3) The Lord Chancellor may by order specify proceedings under this Act which may only be commenced in—

    (a)   a specified level of court;

    (b)   a court which falls within a specified class of court; or

    (c)   a particular court determined in accordance with, or specified in, the order.

(4) The Lord Chancellor may by order specify circumstances in which specified proceedings under this Part may only be commenced in—

    (a)   a specified level of court;

    (b)   a court which falls within a specified class of court; or

    (c)   a particular court determined in accordance with, or specified in, the order.

(5) The Lord Chancellor may by order provide that in specified circumstances the whole, or any specified part of any specified proceedings under this Part shall be transferred to—

    (a)   a specified level of court;

    (b)   a court which falls within a specified class of court; or

    (c)   a particular court determined in accordance with, or specified in, the order.

(6) An order under subsection (5) may provide for the transfer to be made at any stage, or specified stage, of the proceedings and whether or not the proceedings, or any part of them, have already been transferred.

(7) An order under subsection (5) may make provision as the Lord Chancellor thinks appropriate for excluding specified proceedings from the operation of section 38 or 39 of the Matrimonial and Family Proceedings Act 1984 (transfer of family proceedings)

or any other enactment which would otherwise govern the transfer of those proceedings, or any part of them.

(8) For the purposes of subsections (3), (4) and (5), there are three levels of court—

(a) the High Court;
(b) any county court; and
(c) any magistrates' court.

(9) The Lord Chancellor may by order make provision for the principal registry of the Family Division of the High Court to be treated as if it were a county court for specified purposes of this Part, or of any provision made under this Part.

(10) Any order under subsection (9) may make such provision as the Lord Chancellor thinks expedient for the purpose of applying (with or without modifications) provisions which apply in relation to the procedure in county courts to the principal registry when it acts as if it were a county court.

(11) In this section 'specified' means specified by an order under this section.

## 58 Contempt proceedings

The powers of the court in relation to contempt of court arising out of a person's failure to comply with an order under this Part may be exercised by the relevant judicial authority.

## 59 Magistrates' courts

(1) A magistrates' court shall not be competent to entertain any application, or make any order, involving any disputed question as to a party's entitlement to occupy any property by virtue of a beneficial estate or interest or contract or by virtue of any enactment giving him the right to remain in occupation, unless it is unnecessary to determine the question in order to deal with the application or make the order.

(2) A magistrates' court may decline jurisdiction in any proceedings under this Part if it considers that the case can more conveniently be dealt with by another court.

(3) The powers of a magistrates' court under section 63(2) of the Magistrates' Courts Act 1980 to suspend or rescind orders shall not apply in relation to any order made under this Part.

## 60 Provision for third parties to act on behalf of victims of domestic violence

(1) Rules of court may provide for a prescribed person, or any person in a prescribed category, ('a representative') to act on behalf of another in relation to proceedings to which this Part applies.

(2) Rules made under this section may, in particular, authorise a representative to apply for an occupation order or for a non-molestation order for which the person on whose behalf the representative is acting could have applied.

(3) Rules made under this section may prescribe—

(a) conditions to be satisfied before a representative may make an application to the court on behalf of another; and

    (b)   considerations to be taken into account by the court in determining whether, and if so how, to exercise any of its powers under this Part when a representative is acting on behalf of another.

(4) Any rules made under this section may be made so as to have effect for a specified period and may make consequential or transitional provision with respect to the expiry of the specified period.

(5) Any such rules may be replaced by further rules made under this section.

## 61  Appeals

(1) An appeal shall lie to the High Court against—

    (a)   the making by a magistrates' court of any order under this Part, or
    (b)   any refusal by a magistrates' court to make such an order,

but no appeal shall lie against any exercise by a magistrates' court of the power conferred by section 59(2) of this Act.

(2) On an appeal under this section, the High Court may make such orders as may be necessary to give effect to its determination of the appeal.

(3) Where an order is made under subsection (2), the High Court may also make such incidental or consequential orders as appear to it to be just.

(4) Any order of the High Court made on an appeal under this section (other than one directing that an application be re-heard by a magistrates' court) shall, for the purposes—

    (a)   of the enforcement of the order, and
    (b)   of any power to vary, revive or discharge orders,

be treated as if it were an order of the magistrates' court from which the appeal was brought and not an order of the High Court.

(5) The Lord Chancellor may by order make provision as to the circumstances in which appeals may be made against decisions taken by courts on questions arising in connection with the transfer, or proposed transfer, of proceedings by virtue of any order under section 57(5).

(6) Except to the extent provided for in any order made under subsection (5), no appeal may be made against any decision of a kind mentioned in that subsection.

*General*

## 62  Meaning of 'cohabitants', 'relevant child' and 'associated persons'

(1) For the purposes of this Part—

    (a)   'cohabitants' are a man and a woman who, although not married to each other, are living together as husband and wife; and
    (b)   'former cohabitants' is to be read accordingly, but does not include cohabitants who have subsequently married each other.

(2) In this Part, 'relevant child', in relation to any proceedings under this Part, means—

    (a)   any child who is living with or might reasonably be expected to live with either party to the proceedings;

(b)  any child in relation to whom an order under the Adoption Act 1976 or the Children Act 1989 is in question in the proceedings; and

(c)  any other child whose interests the court considers relevant.

(3) For the purposes of this Part, a person is associated with another person if—

(a)  they are or have been married to each other;

(b)  they are cohabitants or former cohabitants;

(c)  they live or have lived in the same household, otherwise than merely by reason of one of them being the other's employee, tenant, lodger or boarder;

(d)  they are relatives;

(e)  they have agreed to marry one another (whether or not that agreement has been terminated);

(f)  in relation to any child, they are both persons falling within subsection (4); or

(g)  they are parties to the same family proceedings (other than proceedings under this Part).

(4) A person falls within this subsection in relation to a child if—

(a)  he is a parent of the child; or

(b)  he has or has had parental responsibility for the child.

(5) If a child has been adopted or has been freed for adoption by virtue of any of the enactments mentioned in section 16(1) of the Adoption Act 1976, two persons are also associated with each other for the purpose of this Part if—

(a)  one is a natural parent of the child or a parent of such a natural parent, and

(b)  the other is the child or any person—

   (i)  who had become a parent of the child by virtue of an adoption order or has applied for an adoption order, or

   (ii)  with whom the child has at any time been placed for adoption.

(6) A body corporate and another person are not, by virtue of subsection (3)(f) or (g), to be regarded for the purposes of this Part as associated with each other.

## 63  Interpretation of Part IV

(1) In this Part—

'adoption order' has the meaning given by section 72(1) of the Adoption Act 1976;

'associated', in relation to a person, is to be read with section 62(3) to (6);

'child' means a person under the age of eighteen years;

'cohabitant' and 'former cohabitant' have the meaning given by section 62(1);

'the court' is to be read with section 57;

'development' means physical, intellectual, emotional, social or behavioural development;

'dwelling-house' includes (subject to subsection (4))—

   (a)  any building or part of a building which is occupied as a dwelling,

   (b)  any caravan, house-boat or structure which is occupied as a dwelling,

   and any yard, garden, garage or outhouse belonging to it and occupied with it;

'family proceedings' means any proceedings—

   (a)  under the inherent jurisdiction of the High Court in relation to children; or

   (b)  under the enactments mentioned in subsection (2),

'harm'—

(a) in relation to a person who has reached the age of eighteen years, means ill-treatment or the impairment of health; and

(b) in relation to a child, means ill-treatment or the impairment of health or development;

'health' includes physical or mental health;

'ill-treatment' includes forms of ill-treatment which are not physical and, in relation to a child, includes sexual abuse;

'matrimonial home rights' has the meaning given by section 30;

'mortgage', 'mortgagor' and 'mortgagee' have the same meaning as in the Law of Property Act 1925;

'mortgage payments' includes any payments which, under the terms of the mortgage, the mortgagor is required to make to any person;

'non-molestation order' has the meaning given by section 42(1);

'occupation order' has the meaning given by section 39;

'parental responsibility' has the same meaning as in the Children Act 1989;

'relative', in relation to a person, means—

(a) the father, mother, stepfather, stepmother, son, daughter, stepson, stepdaughter, grandmother, grandfather, grandson or granddaughter of that person or of that person's spouse or former spouse, or

(b) the brother, sister, uncle, aunt, niece or nephew (whether of the full blood or of the half blood or by affinity) of that person or of that person's spouse or former spouse,

and includes, in relation to a person who is living or has lived with another person as husband or wife, any person who would fall within paragraph (a) or (b) if the parties were married to each other;

'relevant child', in relation to any proceedings under this Part, has the meaning given by section 62(2);

'the relevant judicial authority', in relation to any order under this Part, means—

(a) where the order was made by the High Court, a judge of that court;

(b) where the order was made by a county court, a judge or district judge of that or any other county court; or

(c) where the order was made by a magistrates' court, any magistrates' court.

(2) The enactments referred to in the definition of 'family proceedings' are—

(a) Part II;

(b) this Part;

(c) the Matrimonial Causes Act 1973;

(c) the Adoption Act 1976;

(e) the Domestic Proceedings and Magistrates' Court Act 1978;

(f) Part III of the Matrimonial and Family Proceedings Act 1984;

(g) Parts I, II and IV of the Children Act 1989;

(h) section 30 of the Human Fertilisation and Embryology Act 1990.

(3) Where the question of whether harm suffered by a child is significant turns on the child's health or development, his health or development shall be compared with that which could reasonably be expected of a similar child.

(4) For the purposes of sections 31, 32, 53 and 54 and such other provisions of this Part (if any) as may be prescribed, this Part is to have effect as if paragraph (b) of the definition of "dwelling-house" were omitted.

(5) It is hereby declared that this Part applies as between the parties to a marriage even though either of them is, or has at any time during the marriage been, married to more than one person.

## PART V
## SUPPLEMENTAL

### 64 Provision for separate representation for children

(1) The Lord Chancellor may by regulations provide for the separate representation of children in proceedings in England and Wales which relate to any matter in respect of which a question has arisen, or may arise, under—

    (a)   Part II;
    (b)   Part IV;
    (c)   the 1973 Act; or
    (d)   the Domestic Proceedings and Magistrates' Courts Act 1978.

(2) The regulations may provide for such representation only in specified circumstances.

### 65 Rules, regulations and orders

(1) Any power to make rules, orders or regulations which is conferred by this Act is exercisable by statutory instrument.

(2) Any statutory instrument made under this Act may—

    (a)   contain such incidental, supplemental, consequential and transitional provision as the Lord Chancellor considers appropriate; and
    (b)   make different provision for different purposes.

(3) Any statutory instrument containing an order, rules or regulations made under this Act, other than an order made under section 5(8) or 67(3), shall be subject to annulment by a resolution of either House of Parliament.

(4) No order shall be made under section 5(8) unless a draft of the order has been laid before, and approved by a resolution of, each House of Parliament.

(5) This section does not apply to rules of court made, or any power to make rules of court, for the purposes of this Act.

### 66 Consequential amendments, transitional provisions and repeals

(1) Schedule 8 makes minor and consequential amendments.

(2) Schedule 9 provides for the making of other modifications consequential on provisions of this Act, makes transitional provisions and provides for savings.

(3) Schedule 10 repeals certain enactments.

### 67 Short title, commencement and extent

(1) This Act may be cited as the Family Law Act 1996.

(2) Section 65 and this section come into force on the passing of this Act.

(3) The other provisions of this Act come into force on such day as the Lord Chancellor may by order appoint; and different days may be appointed for different purposes.

(4) This Act, other than section 17, extends only to England and Wales, except that—

  (a)  in Schedule 8—

     (i)   the amendments of section 38 of the Family Law Act 1986 extend also to Northern Ireland;

     (ii)  the amendments of the Judicial Proceedings (Regulation of Reports) Act 1926 extend also to Scotland; and

     (iii) the amendments of the Maintenance Orders Act 1950, the Civil Jurisdiction and Judgments Act 1982, the Finance Act 1985 and sections 42 and 51 of the Family Law Act 1986 extend also to both Northern Ireland and Scotland; and

  (b)  in Schedule 10, the repeal of section 2(1)(b) of the Domestic and Appellate Proceedings (Restriction of Publicity) Act 1968 extends also to Scotland.

## SCHEDULES

### SCHEDULE 4

### PROVISIONS SUPPLEMENTARY TO SECTIONS 30 AND 31

*Section 32*

*Interpretation*

**1**   (1) In this Schedule—

  (a)  any reference to a solicitor includes a reference to a licensed conveyancer or a recognised body, and

  (b)  any reference to a person's solicitor includes a reference to a licensed conveyancer or recognised body acting for that person.

(2) In sub-paragraph (1)—

'licensed conveyancer' has the meaning given by section 11(2) of the Administration of Justice Act 1985;

'recognised body' means a body corporate for the time being recognised under section 9 (incorporated practices) or section 32 (provision of conveyancing by recognised bodies) of that Act.

*Restriction on registration where spouse entitled to more than one charge*

**2**  Where one spouse is entitled by virtue of section 31 to a registrable charge in respect of each of two or more dwelling-houses, only one of the charges to which that spouse is so entitled shall be registered under section 31(10) or under section 2 of the Land Charges Act 1972 at any one time, and if any of those charges is registered under either of those provisions the Chief Land Registrar, on being satisfied that any other of them is so registered, shall cancel the registration of the charge first registered.

*Contract for sale of house affected by registered charge to include term requiring*
*cancellation of registration before completion*

**3** (1) Where one spouse is entitled by virtue of section 31 to a charge on an estate in a dwelling-house and the charge is registered under section 31(10) or section 2 of the Land Charges Act 1972, it shall be a term of any contract for the sale of that estate whereby the vendor agrees to give vacant possession of the dwelling-house on completion of the contract that the vendor will before such completion procure the cancellation of the registration of the charge at his expense.

(2) Sub-paragraph (1) shall not apply to any such contract made by a vendor who is entitled to sell the estate in the dwelling-house freed from any such charge.

(3) If, on the completion of such a contract as is referred to in sub-paragraph (1), there is delivered to the purchaser or his solicitor an application by the spouse entitled to the charge for the cancellation of the registration of that charge, the term of the contract for which sub-paragraph (1) provides shall be deemed to have been performed.

(4) This paragraph applies only if and so far as a contrary intention is not expressed in the contract.

(5) This paragraph shall apply to a contract for exchange as it applies to a contract for sale.

(6) This paragraph shall, with the necessary modifications, apply to a contract for the grant of a lease or underlease of a dwelling-house as it applies to a contract for the sale of an estate in a dwelling-house.

*Cancellation of registration after termination of marriage, etc.*

**4** (1) Where a spouse's matrimonial home rights are a charge on an estate in the dwelling-house and the charge is registered under section 31(10) or under section 2 of the Land Charges Act 1972, the Chief Land Registrar shall, subject to sub-paragraph (2), cancel the registration of the charge if he is satisfied—

   (a)   by the production of a certificate or other sufficient evidence, that either spouse is dead, or
   (b)   by the production of an official copy of a decree or order of a court, that the marriage in question has been terminated otherwise than by death, or
   (c)   by the production of an order of the court, that the spouse's matrimonial home rights constituting the charge have been terminated by the order.

(2) Where—

   (a)   the marriage in question has been terminated by the death of the spouse entitled to an estate in the dwelling-house or otherwise than by death, and
   (b)   an order affecting the charge of the spouse not so entitled had been made under section 35(5),

then if, after the making of the order, registration of the charge was renewed or the charge registered in pursuance of sub-paragraph (3), the Chief Land Registrar shall not cancel the registration of the charge in accordance with sub-paragraph (1) unless he is also satisfied that the order has ceased to have effect.

(3) Where such an order has been made, then, for the purposes of sub-paragraph (2), the spouse entitled to the charge affected by the order may—

(a)   if before the date of the order the charge was registered under section 31(10) or under section 2 of the Land Charges Act 1972, renew the registration of the charge, and

(b)   if before the said date the charge was not so registered, register the charge under section 31(10) or under section 2 of the Land Charges Act 1972.

(4) Renewal of the registration of a charge in pursuance of sub-paragraph (3) shall be effected in such manner as may be prescribed, and an application for such renewal or for registration of a charge in pursuance of that sub-paragraph shall contain such particulars of any order affecting the charge made under section 33(5) as may be prescribed.

(5) The renewal in pursuance of sub-paragraph (3) of the registration of a charge shall not affect the priority of the charge.

(6) In this paragraph 'prescribed' means prescribed by rules made under section 16 of the Land Charges Act 1972 or section 144 of the Land Registration Act 1925, as the circumstances of the case require.

### Release of matrimonial home rights

5   (1) A spouse entitled to matrimonial home rights may by a release in writing release those rights or release them as respects part only of the dwelling-house affected by them.

(2) Where a contract is made for the sale of an estate or interest in a dwelling-house, or for the grant of a lease or underlease of a dwelling-house, being (in either case) a dwelling-house affected by a charge registered under section 31(10) or under section 2 of the Land Charges Act 1972, then, without prejudice to sub-paragraph (1), the matrimonial home rights constituting the charge shall be deemed to have been released on the happening of whichever of the following events first occurs—

(a)   the delivery to the purchaser or lessee, as the case may be, or his solicitor on completion of the contract of an application by the spouse entitled to the charge for the cancellation of the registration of the charge; or

(b)   the lodging of such an application at Her Majesty's Land Registry.

### Postponement of priority of charge

6   A spouse entitled by virtue of section 31 to a charge on an estate or interest may agree in writing that any other charge on, or interest in, that estate or interest shall rank in priority to the charge to which that spouse is so entitled.

## SCHEDULE 5

## POWERS OF HIGH COURT AND COUNTY COURT TO REMAND

*Section 47(11)*

### Interpretation

1   In this Schedule 'the court' means the High Court or a county court and includes—

(a)   in relation to the High Court, a judge of that court, and

(b)   in relation to a county court, a judge or district judge of that court.

*Remand in custody or on bail*

**2** (1) Where a court has power to remand a person under section 47, the court may—

  (a)  remand him in custody, that is to say, commit him to custody to be brought before the court at the end of the period of remand or at such earlier time as the court may require, or

  (b)  remand him on bail—

    (i)  by taking from him a recognizance (with or without sureties) conditioned as provided in sub-paragraph (3), or

    (ii)  by fixing the amount of the recognizances with a view to their being taken subsequently in accordance with paragraph 4 and in the meantime committing the person to custody in accordance with paragraph (a).

(2) Where a person is brought before the court after remand, the court may further remand him.

(3) Where a person is remanded on bail under sub-paragraph (1), the court may direct that his recognizance be conditioned for his appearance—

  (a)  before that court at the end of the period of remand, or

  (b)  at every time and place to which during the course of the proceedings the hearing may from time to time be adjourned.

(4) Where a recognizance is conditioned for a person's appearance in accordance with sub-paragraph (1)(b), the fixing of any time for him next to appear shall be deemed to be a remand; but nothing in this sub-paragraph or sub-paragraph (3) shall deprive the court of power at any subsequent hearing to remand him afresh.

(5) Subject to paragraph 3, the court shall not remand a person under this paragraph for a period exceeding 8 clear days, except that—

  (a)  if the court remands him on bail, it may remand him for a longer period if he and the other party consent, and

  (b)  if the court adjourns a case under section 48(1), the court may remand him for the period of the adjournment.

(6) Where the court has power under this paragraph to remand a person in custody it may, if the remand for a period not exceeding 3 clear days, commit him to the custody of a constable.

*Further remand*

**3** (1) If the court is satisfied that any person who has been remanded under paragraph 2 is unable by reason of illness or accident to appear or be brought before the court at the expiration of the period for which he was remanded, the court may, in his absence, remand him for a further time; and paragraph 2(5) shall not apply.

(2) Notwithstanding anything in paragraph 2(1), the power of the court under sub-paragraph (1) to remand a person on bail for a further time may be exercised by enlarging his recognizance and those of any sureties for him to a later time.

(3) Where a person remanded on bail under paragraph 2 is bound to appear before the court at any time and the court has no power to remand him under sub-paragraph (1), the court may in his absence enlarge his recognizance and those of any sureties for him

to a later time; and the enlargement of his recognizance shall be deemed to be a further remand.

*Postponement of taking of recognizance*

**4**   Where under paragraph 2(1)(b)(ii) the court fixes the amount in which the principal and his sureties, if any, are to be bound, the recognizance may thereafter be taken by such person as may be prescribed by rules of court, and the same consequences shall follow as if it had been entered into before the court.

## SCHEDULE 6

## AMENDMENTS OF CHILDREN ACT 1989

*Section 52*

**1**   After section 38 of the Children Act 1989 insert—

### '38A   Power to include exclusion requirement in interim care order

(1) Where—

(a)   on being satisfied that there are reasonable grounds for believing that the circumstances with respect to a child are as mentioned in section 31(2)(a) and (b)(i), the court makes an interim care order with respect to a child, and

(b)   the conditions mentioned in subsection (2) are satisfied,

the court may include an exclusion requirement in the interim care order.

(2) The conditions are—

(a)   that there is reasonable cause to believe that, if a person ("the relevant person") is excluded from a dwelling-house in which the child lives, the child will cease to suffer, or cease to be likely to suffer, significant harm, and

(b)   that another person living in the dwelling-house (whether a parent of the child or some other person)—

(i)   is able and willing to give to the child the care which it would be reasonable to expect a parent to give him, and

(ii)   consents to the inclusion of the exclusion requirement.

(3) For the purposes of this section an exclusion requirement is any one or more of the following—

(a)   a provision requiring the relevant person to leave a dwelling-house in which he is living with the child,

(b)   a provision prohibiting the relevant person from entering a dwelling-house in which the child lives, and

(c)   a provision excluding the relevant person from a defined area in which a dwelling-house in which the child lives is situated.

(4) The court may provide that the exclusion requirement is to have effect for a shorter period than the other provisions of the interim care order.

(5) Where the court makes an interim care order containing an exclusion requirement, the court may attach a power of arrest to the exclusion requirement.

(6) Where the court attaches a power of arrest to an exclusion requirement of an interim care order, it may provide that the power of arrest is to have effect for a shorter period than the exclusion requirement.

(7) Any period specified for the purposes of subsection (4) or (6) may be extended by the court (on one or more occasions) on an application to vary or discharge the interim care order.

(8) Where a power of arrest is attached to an exclusion requirement of an interim care order by virtue of subsection (5), a constable may arrest without warrant any person whom he has reasonable cause to believe to be in breach of the requirement.

(9) Sections 47(7), (11) and (12) and 48 of, and Schedule 5 to, the Family Law Act 1996 shall have effect in relation to a person arrested under subsection (8) of this section as they have effect in relation to a person arrested under section 47(6) of that Act.

(10) If, while an interim care order containing an exclusion requirement is in force, the local authority have removed the child from the dwelling-house from which the relevant person is excluded to other accommodation for a continuous period of more than 24 hours, the interim care order shall cease to have effect in so far as it imposes the exclusion requirement.

### 38B Undertakings relating to interim care orders

(1) In any case where the court has power to include an exclusion requirement in an interim care order, the court may accept an undertaking from the relevant person.

(2) No power of arrest may be attached to any undertaking given under sub-section (1).

(3) An undertaking given to a court under subsection (1)—

(a) shall be enforceable as if it were an order of the court, and
(b) shall cease to have effect if, while it is in force, the local authority have removed the child from the dwelling-house from which the relevant person is excluded to other accommodation for a continuous period of more than 24 hours.

(4) This section has effect without prejudice to the powers of the High Court and county court apart from this section.

(5) In this section "exclusion requirement" and "relevant person" have the same meaning as in section 38A.'

2   In section 39 of the Children Act 1989 (discharge and variation etc. of care orders and supervision orders) after subsection (3) insert—

'(3A) On the application of a person who is not entitled to apply for the order to be discharged, but who is a person to whom an exclusion requirement contained in the order applies, an interim care order may be varied or discharged by the court in so far as it imposes the exclusion requirement.

(3B) Where a power of arrest has been attached to an exclusion requirement of an interim care order, the court may, on the application of any person entitled to apply for the discharge of the order so far as it imposes the exclusion requirement, vary or discharge the order in so far as it confers a power of arrest (whether or not any application has been made to vary or discharge any other provision of the order).'

**3**    After section 44 of the Children Act 1989 insert—

### '44A  Power to include exclusion requirement in emergency protection order

(1) Where—

  (a)   on being satisfied as mentioned in section 44(1)(a), (b) or (c), the court makes an emergency protection order with respect to a child, and

  (b)   the conditions mentioned in subsection (2) are satisfied,

the court may include an exclusion requirement in the emergency protection order.

(2) The conditions are—

  (a)   that there is reasonable cause to believe that, if a person ("the relevant person") is excluded from a dwelling-house in which the child lives, then—

    (i)    in the case of an order made on the ground mentioned in section 44(1)(a), the child will not be likely to suffer significant harm, even though the child is not removed as mentioned in section 44(1)(a)(i) or does not remain as mentioned in section 44(1)(a)(ii), or

    (ii)   in the case of an order made on the ground mentioned in paragraph (b) or (c) of section 44(1), the enquiries referred to in that paragraph will cease to be frustrated, and

  (b)   that another person living in the dwelling-house (whether a parent of the child or some other person)—

    (i)    is able and willing to give to the child the care which it would be reasonable to expect a parent to give him, and

    (ii)   consents to the inclusion of the exclusion requirement.

(3) For the purposes of this section an exclusion requirement is any one or more of the following—

  (a)   a provision requiring the relevant person to leave a dwelling-house in which he is living with the child,

  (b)   a provision prohibiting the relevant person from entering a dwelling-house in which the child lives, and

  (c)   a provision excluding the relevant person from a defined area in which a dwelling-house in which the child lives is situated.

(4) The court may provide that the exclusion requirement is to have effect for a shorter period than the other provisions of the order.

(5) Where the court makes an emergency protection order containing an exclusion requirement, the court may attach a power of arrest to the exclusion requirement.

(6) Where the court attaches a power of arrest to an exclusion requirement of an emergency protection order, it may provide that the power of arrest is to have effect for a shorter period than the exclusion requirement.

(7) Any period specified for the purposes of subsection (4) or (6) may be extended by the court (on one or more occasions) on an application to vary or discharge the emergency protection order.

(8) Where a power of arrest is attached to an exclusion requirement of an emergency protection order by virtue of subsection (5), a constable may arrest without warrant any person whom he has reasonable cause to believe to be in breach of the requirement.

(9) Sections 47(7), (11) and (12) and 48 of, and Schedule 5 to, the Family Law Act 1996 shall have effect in relation to a person arrested under subsection (8) of this section as they have effect in relation to a person arrested under section 47(6) of that Act.

(10) If, while an emergency protection order containing an exclusion requirement is in force, the applicant has removed the child from the dwelling-house from which the relevant person is excluded to other accommodation for a continuous period of more than 24 hours, the order shall cease to have effect in so far as it imposes the exclusion requirement.

### 44B Undertakings relating to emergency protection orders

(1) In any case where the court has power to include an exclusion requirement in an emergency protection order, the court may accept an undertaking from the relevant person.

(2) No power of arrest may be attached to any undertaking given under subsection (1).

(3) An undertaking given to a court under subsection (1)—

   (a)   shall be enforceable as if it were an order of the court, and

   (b)   shall cease to have effect if, while it is in force, the applicant has removed the child from the dwelling-house from which the relevant person is excluded to other accommodation for a continuous period of more than 24 hours.

(4) This section has effect without prejudice to the powers of the High Court and county court apart from this section.

(5) In this section "exclusion requirement" and "relevant person" have the same meaning as in section 44A.'

4   In section 45 of the Children Act 1989 (duration of emergency protection orders and other supplemental provisions), after subsection (8) insert—

'(8A) On the application of a person who is not entitled to apply for the order to be discharged, but who is a person to whom an exclusion requirement contained in the order applies, an emergency protection order may be varied or discharged by the court in so far as it imposes the exclusion requirement.

(8B) Where a power of arrest has been attached to an exclusion requirement of an emergency protection order, the court may, on the application of any person entitled to apply for the discharge of the order so far as it imposes the exclusion requirement, vary or discharge the order in so far as it confers a power of arrest (whether or not any application has been made to vary or discharge any other provision of the order).'

**5**    In section 105(1) of the Children Act 1989 (interpretation), after the definition of "domestic premises", insert—

"dwelling-house" includes—

(a)  any building or part of a building which is occupied as a dwelling;
(b)  any caravan, house-boat or structure which is occupied as a dwelling;

and any yard, garden garage or outhouse belonging to it and occupied with it;".

## SCHEDULE 7

### TRANSFER OF CERTAIN TENANCIES ON DIVORCE ETC OR ON SEPARATION OF COHABITANTS

### PART I
### GENERAL

*Section 53*

*Interpretation*

**1**    In this Schedule—

'cohabitant', except in paragraph 3, includes (where the context requires) former cohabitant,
'the court' does not include a magistrates' court,
'landlord' includes—

(a)  any person from time to time deriving title under the original landlord; and
(b)  in relation to any dwelling-house, any person other than the tenant who is, or (but for Part VII of the Rent Act 1977 or Part II of the Rent (Agriculture) Act 1976) would be, entitled to possession of the dwelling-house;

'Part II order' means an order under Part II of this Schedule;
'a relevant tenancy' means—

(a)  a protected tenancy or statutory tenancy within the meaning of the Rent Act 1977;
(b)  a statutory tenancy within the meaning of the Rent (Agriculture) Act 1976;
(c)  a secure tenancy within the meaning of section 79 of the Housing Act 1985; or
(d)  an assured tenancy or assured agricultural occupancy within the meaning of Part I of the Housing Act 1988;

'spouse', except in paragraph 2, includes (where the context requires) former spouse; and
'tenancy' includes sub-tenancy.

*Cases in which court may make order*

**2**    (1) This paragraph applies if one spouse is entitled, either in his own right or jointly with the other spouse, to occupy a dwelling-house by virtue of a relevant tenancy.

(2) At any time when it has power to make a property adjustment order under section 23A (divorce or separation) or 24 (nullity) of the Matrimonial Causes Act 1973 with respect to the marriage, the court may make a Part II order.

**3** (1) This paragraph applies if one cohabitant is entitled, either in his own right or jointly with the other cohabitant, to occupy a dwelling-house by virtue of a relevant tenancy.

(2) If the cohabitants cease to live together as husband and wife, the court may make a Part II order.

**4** The court shall not make a Part II order unless the dwelling-house is or was—

 (a) in the case of spouses, a matrimonial home; or
 (b) in the case of cohabitants, a home in which they lived together as husband and wife.

*Matters to which the court must have regard*

**5** In determining whether to exercise its powers under Part II of this Schedule and, if so, in what manner, the court shall have regard to all the circumstances of the case including—

 (a) the circumstances in which the tenancy was granted to either or both of the spouses or cohabitants or, as the case requires, the circumstances in which either or both of them became tenant under the tenancy;
 (b) the matters mentioned in section 33(6)(a), (b) and (c) and, where the parties are cohabitants and only one of them is entitled to occupy the dwelling-house by virtue of the relevant tenancy, the further matters mentioned in section 36(6)(e), (f), (g) and (h); and
 (c) the suitability of the parties as tenants.

## PART II
### ORDERS THAT MAY BE MADE

*References to entitlement to occupy*

**6** References in this Part of this Schedule to a spouse or a cohabitant being entitled to occupy a dwelling-house by virtue of a relevant tenancy apply whether that entitlement is in his own right or jointly with the other spouse or cohabitant.

*Protected, secure or assured tenancy or assured agricultural occupancy*

**7** (1) If a spouse or cohabitant is entitled to occupy the dwelling-house by virtue of a protected tenancy within the meaning of the Rent Act 1977, a secure tenancy within the meaning of the Housing Act 1985 or an assured tenancy or assured agricultural occupancy within the meaning of Part I of the Housing Act 1988, the court may by order direct that, as from such date as may be specified in the order, there shall, by virtue of the order and without further assurance, be transferred to, and vested in, the other spouse or cohabitant—

 (a) the estate or interest which the spouse or cohabitant so entitled had in the dwelling-house immediately before that date by virtue of the lease or agreement creating the tenancy and any assignment of that lease or agreement, with all rights, privileges and appurtenances attaching to that estate or interest but subject to all covenants, obligations, liabilities and incumbrances to which it is subject; and

(b) where the spouse or cohabitant so entitled is an assignee of such lease or agreement, the liability of that spouse or cohabitant under any covenant of indemnity by the assignee express or implied in the assignment of the lease or agreement to that spouse or cohabitant.

(2) If an order is made under this paragraph, any liability or obligation to which the spouse or cohabitant so entitled is subject under any covenant having reference to the dwelling-house in the lease or agreement, being a liability or obligation falling due to be discharged or performed on or after the date so specified, shall not be enforceable against that spouse or cohabitant.

(3) If the spouse so entitled is a successor within the meaning of Part IV of the Housing Act 1985, his former spouse or former cohabitant (or, if a separation order is in force, his spouse) shall be deemed also to be a successor within the meaning of that Part.

(4) If the spouse or cohabitant so entitled is for the purpose of section 17 of the Housing Act 1988 a successor in relation to the tenancy or occupancy, his former spouse or former cohabitant (or, if a separation order is in force, his spouse) is to be deemed to be a successor in relation to the tenancy or occupation for the purposes of that section.

(5) If the transfer under sub-paragraph (1) is of an assured agricultural occupancy, then, for the purposes of Chapter III of Part I of the Housing Act 1988—

(a) the agricultural worker condition is fulfilled with respect to the dwelling-house while the spouse or cohabitant to whom the assured agricultural occupancy is transferred continues to be the occupier under that occupancy, and

(b) that condition shall be treated as so fulfilled by virtue of the same paragraph of Schedule 3 to the Housing Act 1988 as was applicable before the transfer.

(6) In this paragraph, references to a separation order being in force include references to there being a judicial separation in force.

*Statutory tenancy within the meaning of the Rent Act 1977*

**8** (1) This paragraph applies if the spouse or cohabitant is entitled to occupy the dwelling-house by virtue of a statutory tenancy within the meaning of the Rent Act 1977.

(2) The court may by order direct that, as from the date specified in the order—

(a) that spouse or cohabitant is to cease to be entitled to occupy the dwelling-house; and

(b) the other spouse or cohabitant is to be deemed to be the tenant or, as the case may be, the sole tenant under that statutory tenancy.

(3) The question whether the provisions of paragraphs 1 to 3, or (as the case may be) paragraphs 5 to 7 of Schedule 1 to the Rent Act 1977, as to the succession by the surviving spouse of a deceased tenant, or by a member of the deceased tenant's family, to the right to retain possession are capable of having effect in the event of the death of the person deemed by an order under this paragraph to be the tenant or sole tenant under the statutory tenancy is to be determined according as those provisions have or have not already had effect in relation to the statutory tenancy.

*Statutory tenancy within the meaning of the Rent (Agriculture) Act 1976*

**9**   (1) This paragraph applies if the spouse or cohabitant is entitled to occupy the dwelling-house by virtue of a statutory tenancy within the meaning of the Rent (Agriculture) Act 1976.

(2) The court may by order direct that, as from such date as may be specified in the order—

(a)   that spouse or cohabitant is to cease to be entitled to occupy the dwelling-house; and

(b)   the other spouse or cohabitant is to be deemed to be the tenant or, as the case may be, the sole tenant under that statutory tenancy.

(3) A spouse or cohabitant who is deemed under this paragraph to be the tenant under a statutory tenancy is (within the meaning of that Act) a statutory tenant in his own right, or a statutory tenant by succession, according as the other spouse or cohabitant was a statutory tenant in his own right or a statutory tenant by succession.

## PART III
## SUPPLEMENTARY PROVISIONS

*Compensation*

**10**   (1) If the court makes a Part II order, it may by the order direct the making of a payment by the spouse or cohabitant to whom the tenancy is transferred ('the transferee') to the other spouse or cohabitant ('the transferor').

(2) Without prejudice to that, the court may, on making an order by virtue of sub-paragraph (1) for the payment of a sum—

(a)   direct that payment of that sum or any part of it is to be deferred until a specified date or until the occurrence of a specified event, or

(b)   direct that that sum or any part of it is to be paid by instalments.

(3) Where an order has been made by virtue of sub-paragraph (1), the court may, on the application of the transferee or the transferor—

(a)   exercise its powers under sub-paragraph (2), or

(b)   vary any direction previously given under that sub-paragraph,

at any time before the sum whose payment is required by the order is paid in full.

(4) In deciding whether to exercise its powers under this paragraph and, if so, in what manner, the court shall have regard to all the circumstances including—

(a)   the financial loss that would otherwise be suffered by the transferor as a result of the order;

(b)   the financial needs and financial resources of the parties; and

(c)   the financial obligations which the parties have, or are likely to have in the foreseeable future, including financial obligations to each other and to any relevant child.

(5) The court shall not give any direction under sub-paragraph (2) unless it appears to it that immediate payment of the sum required by the order would cause the transferee financial hardship which is greater than any financial hardship that would be caused to the transferor if the direction were given.

*Liabilities and obligations in respect of the dwelling-house*

**11** (1) If the court makes a Part II order, it may by the order direct that both spouses or cohabitants are to be jointly and severally liable to discharge or perform any or all of the liabilities and obligations in respect of the dwelling-house (whether arising under the tenancy or otherwise) which—

(a) have at the date of the order fallen due to be discharged or performed by one only of them; or

(b) but for the direction, would before the date specified as the date on which the order is to take effect fall due to be discharged or performed by one only of them.

(2) If the court gives such a direction, it may further direct that either spouse or cohabitant is to be liable to indemnify the other in whole or in part against any payment made or expenses incurred by the other in discharging or performing any such liability or obligation.

*Date when order made between spouses is to take effect*

**12** (1) In the case of a decree of nullity of marriage, the date specified in a Part II order as the date on which the order is to take effect must not be earlier than the date on which the decree is made absolute.

(2) In the case of divorce proceedings or separation proceedings, the date specified in a Part II order as the date on which the order is to take effect is to be determined as if the court were making a property adjustment order under section 23A of the Matrimonial Causes Act 1973 (regard being had to the restrictions imposed by section 23B of that Act).

*Remarriage of either spouse*

**13** (1) If after the making of a divorce order or the grant of a decree annulling a marriage either spouse remarries, that spouse is not entitled to apply, by reference to the making of that order or the grant of that decree, for a Part II order.

(2) For the avoidance of doubt it is hereby declared that the reference in sub-paragraph (1) to remarriage includes a reference to a marriage which is by law void or voidable.

*Rules of court*

**14** (1) Rules of court shall be made requiring the court, before it makes an order under this Schedule, to give the landlord of the dwelling-house to which the order will relate an opportunity of being heard.

(2) Rules of court may provide that an application for a Part II order by reference to an order or decree may not, without the leave of the court by which that order was made or decree was granted, be made after the expiration of such period from the order or grant as may be prescribed by the rules.

*Saving for other provisions of Act*

**15** (1) If a spouse is entitled to occupy a dwelling-house by virtue of a tenancy, this Schedule does not affect the operation of sections 30 and 31 in relation to the other spouse's matrimonial home rights.

(2) If a spouse or cohabitant is entitled to occupy a dwelling-house by virtue of a tenancy, the court's powers to make orders under this Schedule are additional to those conferred by sections 33, 35 and 36.

## SCHEDULE 8

## MINOR AND CONSEQUENTIAL AMENDMENTS

*Section 66(1)*

## PART III
### AMENDMENTS CONNECTED WITH PART IV

*The Land Registration Act 1925 (c. 21)*

**45**   In section 64 of the Land Registration Act 1925 (certificates to be produced and noted on dealings) in subsection (5) for 'section 2(8) of the Matrimonial Homes Act 1983' substitute 'section 31(10) of the Family Law Act 1996 and for 'rights of occupation' substitute 'matrimonial home rights'.

*The Land Charges Act 1972 (c. 61)*

**46**   In section 1(6A) of the Land Charges Act 1972 (cases where county court has jurisdiction to vacate registration) in paragraph (d)—

(a)   after 'section 1 of the Matrimonial Homes Act 1983' insert 'or section 33 of the Family Law Act 1996'; and

(b)   for 'that section' substitute 'either of those sections'.

**47**   In section 2(7) of that Act (Class F land charge) for 'Matrimonial Homes Act 1983' substitute 'Part IV of the Family Law Act 1996'.

*The Land Compensation Act 1973 (c. 34)*

**48**   (1) Section 29A of the Land Compensation Act 1973 (spouses having statutory rights of occupation) is amended as follows.

(2) In subsection (1), for 'rights of occupation (within the meaning of the Matrimonial Homes Act 1983)' substitute 'matrimonial home rights (within the meaning of Part IV of the Family Law Act 1996)'.

(3) In subsection (2)(a), for 'rights of occupation' substitute 'matrimonial home rights'.

*The Magistrates' Courts Act 1980 (c. 43)*

**49**   In section 65(1) of the Magistrates' Courts Act 1980 (meaning of family proceedings) after paragraph (o) insert—

'(p)   Part IV of the Family Law Act 1996;'.

*The Contempt of Court Act 1981 (c. 49)*

**50**   In Schedule 3 to the Contempt of Court Act 1981 (application of Magistrates' Courts Act 1980 to civil contempt proceedings), in paragraph 3 for the words from '"or, having been arrested" onwards substitute—

"'or, having been arrested under section 47 of the Family Law Act 1996 in connection with the matter of the complaint, is at large after being remanded under subsection (7)(b) or (10) of that section.'"

*The Supreme Court Act 1981 (c. 54)*

**51**  In Schedule 1 to the Supreme Court Act 1981 (distribution of business in High Court), in paragraph 3 (Family Division)—

    (a)   in paragraph (d), after 'matrimonial proceedings' insert 'or proceedings under Part IV of the Family Law Act 1996', and

    (b)   in paragraph (f)(i), for 'Domestic Violence and Matrimonial Proceedings Act 1976' substitute 'Part IV of the Family Law Act 1996'.

*The Matrimonial and Family Proceedings Act 1984 (c. 42)*

**52**  For section 22 of the Matrimonial and Family Proceedings Act 1984 substitute—

### '22  Powers of court in relation to certain tenancies of dwelling-houses

(1) This section applies if—

    (a)   an application is made by a party to a marriage for an order for financial relief; and

    (b)   one of the parties is entitled, either in his own right or jointly with the other party, to occupy a dwelling-house situated in England or Wales by virtue of a tenancy which is a relevant tenancy within the meaning of Schedule 7 to the Family Law Act 1996 (certain statutory tenancies).

(2) The court may make in relation to that dwelling-house any order which it could make under Part II of that Schedule if—

    (a)   a divorce order,

    (b)   a separation order, or

    (c)   a decree of nullity of marriage,

had been made or granted in England and Wales in respect of the marriage.

(3) The provisions of paragraphs 10, 11 and 14(1) in Part III of that Schedule apply in relation to any order under this section as they apply to any order under Part II of that Schedule.'

*The Housing Act 1985 (c. 68)*

**53**  (1) Section 85 of the Housing Act 1985 (extended discretion of court in certain proceedings for possession) is amended as follows.

(2) In subsection (5)—

    (a)   in paragraph (a), for 'rights of occupation under the Matrimonial Homes Act 1983' substitute 'matrimonial home rights under Part IV of the Family Law Act 1996'; and

    (b)   for 'those rights of occupation' substitute 'those matrimonial home rights'.

(3) After subsection (5) insert—

'(5A) If proceedings are brought for possession of a dwelling-house which is let under a secure tenancy and—

  (a)  an order is in force under section 35 of the Family Law Act 1996 conferring rights on the former spouse of the tenant or an order is in force under section 36 of that Act conferring rights on a cohabitant or former cohabitant (within the meaning of that Act) of the tenant,

  (b)  the former spouse, cohabitant or former cohabitant is then in occupation of the dwelling-house, and

  (c)  the tenancy is terminated as a result of those proceedings,

the former spouse, cohabitant or former cohabitant shall, so long as he or she remains in occupation, have the same rights in relation to, or in connection with, any adjournment, stay, suspension or postponement in pursuance of this section as he or she would have if the rights conferred by the order referred to in paragraph (a) were not affected by the termination of the tenancy.'

**54**  In section 99B of that Act (persons qualifying for compensation for improvements) in subsection (2) for paragraph (f) substitute—

'(f)  a spouse, former spouse, cohabitant or former cohabitant of the improving tenant to whom the tenancy has been transferred by an order made under Schedule 1 to the Matrimonial Homes Act 1983 or Schedule 7 to the Family Law Act 1996.'

**55**  In section 101 of that Act (rent not to be increased on account of tenant's improvements) in subsection (3) for paragraph (d) substitute—

'(d)  a spouse, former spouse, cohabitant or former cohabitant of the tenant to whom the tenancy has been transferred by an order made under Schedule 1 to the Matrimonial Homes Act 1983 or Schedule 7 to the Family Law Act 1996.'

**56**  In section 171B of that Act (extent of preserved right to buy: qualifying persons and dwelling-houses) in subsection (4)(b)(ii) after 'Schedule 1 to the Matrimonial Homes Act 1983' insert 'or Schedule 7 to the Family Law Act 1996'.

*The Insolvency Act 1986 (c. 45)*

**57**  (1) Section 336 of the Insolvency Act 1986 (rights of occupation etc of bankrupt's spouse) is amended as follows.

(2) In subsection (1), for 'rights of occupation under the Matrimonial Homes Act 1983' substitute 'matrimonial home rights under Part IV of the Family Law Act 1996'.

(3) In subsection (2)—

  (a)  for 'rights of occupation under the Act of 1983' substitute 'matrimonial home rights under the Act of 1996', and

  (b)  in paragraph (b), for 'under section 1 of that Act' substitute 'under section 33 of that Act'.

(4) In subsection (4), for 'section 1 of the Act of 1983' substitute 'section 33 of the Act of 1996'.

**58**  (1) Section 337 of that Act is amended as follows.

(2) In subsection (2), for 'rights of occupation under the Matrimonial Homes Act 1983' substitute 'matrimonial home rights under Part IV of the Family Law Act 1996'.

(3) For subsection (3) substitute—

'(3) The Act of 1996 has effect, with the necessary modifications, as if—

(a)    the rights conferred by paragraph (a) of subsection (2) were matrimonial home rights under that Act,

(b)    any application for such leave as is mentioned in that paragraph were an application for an order under section 33 of that Act, and

(c)    any charge under paragraph (b) of that subsection on the estate or interest of the trustee were a charge under that Act on the estate or interest of a spouse.'

(4) In subsections (4) and (5) for 'section 1 of the Act of 1983' substitute 'section 33 of the Act of 1996'.

*The Housing Act 1988 (c. 50)*

**59**    (1) Section 9 of the Housing Act 1988 (extended discretion of court in possession claims) is amended as follows.

(2) In subsection (5)—

(a)    in paragraph (a), for 'rights of occupation under the Matrimonial Homes Act 1983' substitute 'matrimonial home rights under Part IV of the Family Law Act 1996', and

(b)    for 'those rights of occupation' substitute 'those matrimonial home rights'.

(3) After subsection (5) insert—

'(5A) In any case where—

(a)    at a time when proceedings are brought for possession of a dwelling-house let on an assured tenancy—

(i)    an order is in force under section 35 of the Family Law Act 1996 conferring rights on the former spouse of the tenant, or

(ii)    an order is in force under section 36 of that Act conferring rights on a cohabitant or former cohabitant (within the meaning of that Act) of the tenant,

(b)    that cohabitant, former cohabitant or former spouse is then in occupation of the dwelling-house, and

(c)    the assured tenancy is terminated as a result of those proceedings,

the cohabitant, former cohabitant or former spouse shall have the same rights in relation to, or in connection with, any such adjournment as is referred to in subsection (1) above or any such stay, suspension or postponement as is referred to in subsection (2) above as he or she would have if the rights conferred by the order referred to in paragraph (a) above were not affected by the termination of the tenancy.'

*The Children Act 1989 (c. 41)*

**60**    (1) In section 8(4) of the Children Act 1989 (meaning of 'family proceedings' for purposes of that Act), omit paragraphs (c) and (f) and after paragraph (g) insert—

'(h)    the Family Law Act 1996'.

(2) In Schedule 11 to that Act, in paragraph 6(a) (amendment of the Domestic Proceedings and Magistrates' Courts Act 1978), for 'sections 16(5)(c) and' substitute 'section'.

*The Courts and Legal Services Act 1990 (c. 41)*

**61** In section 58 of the Courts and Legal Services Act 1990 (conditional fee agreements) in subsection (10), omit paragraphs (b) and (e) and immediately before the 'or' following paragraph (g) insert—

'(gg) Part IV of the Family Law Act 1996'.

## SCHEDULE 9

## MODIFICATIONS, SAVING AND TRANSITIONAL

*Section 66(2)*

### Interpretation

**7** In paragraphs 8 to 15 'the 1983 Act' means the Matrimonial Homes Act 1983.

### Pending applications for orders relating to occupation and molestation

**8** (1) In this paragraph and paragraph 10 below 'the existing enactments' means—

    (a) the Domestic Violence and Matrimonial Proceedings Act 1976;

    (b) sections 16 to 18 of the Domestic Proceedings and Magistrates' Courts Act 1978; and

    (c) sections 1 and 9 of the 1983 Act.

(2) Nothing in Part IV, Part III of Schedule 8 or Schedule 10 affects any application for an order or injunction under any of the existing enactments which is pending immediately before the commencement of the repeal of that enactment.

### Pending applications under Schedule 1 to the Matrimonial Homes Act 1983

**9** Nothing in Part IV, Part III of Schedule 8 or Schedule 10 affects any application for an order under Schedule 1 to the 1983 Act which is pending immediately before the commencement of the repeal of that Schedule.

### Existing orders relating to occupation and molestation

**10** (1) In this paragraph 'an existing order' means any order or injunction under any of the existing enactments which—

    (a) is in force immediately before the commencement of the repeal of that enactment; or

    (b) was made or granted after that commencement in proceedings brought before that commencement.

(2) Subject to sub-paragraphs (3) and (4), nothing in Part IV, Part III of Schedule 8 or Schedule 10—

    (a) prevents an existing order from remaining in force; or

    (b) affects the enforcement of an existing order.

(3) Nothing in Part IV, Part III of Schedule 8 or Schedule 10 affects any application to extend, vary or discharge an existing order, but the court may, if it thinks it just and reasonable to do so, treat the application as an application for an order under Part IV.

(4) The making of an order under Part IV between parties with respect to whom an existing order is in force discharges the existing order.

### *Matrimonial home rights*

**11**  (1) Any reference (however expressed) in any enactment, instrument or document (whether passed or made before or after the passing of this Act) to rights of occupation under, or within the meaning of, the 1983 Act shall be construed, so far as is required for continuing the effect of the instrument or document, as being or as the case requires including a reference to matrimonial home rights under, or within the meaning of Part IV.

(2) Any reference (however expressed) in this Act or in any other enactment, instrument or document (including any enactment amended by Schedule 8) to matrimonial home rights under, or within the meaning of, Part IV shall be construed as including, in relation to times, circumstances and purposes before the commencement of sections 30 to 32, a reference to rights of occupation under, or within the meaning of, the 1983 Act.

**12**  (1) Any references (however expressed) in any enactment, instrument or document (whether passed or made before or after the passing of this Act) to registration under section 2(8) of the 1983 Act shall, in relation to any time after the commencement of sections 30 to 32, be construed as being or as the case requires including a reference to registration under section 31(10).

(2) Any reference (however expressed) in this Act or in any other enactment, instrument or document (including any enactment amended by Schedule 8) to registration under section 31(10) shall be construed as including a reference to—

    (a)    registration under section 2(7) of the Matrimonial Homes Act 1967 or section 2(8) of the 1983 Act, and

    (b)    registration by caution duly lodged under section 2(7) of the Matrimonial Homes Act 1967 before 14th February 1983 (the date of the commencement of section 4(2) of the Matrimonial Homes and Property Act 1981).

**13**  In sections 30 and 31 and Schedule 4—

    (a)    any reference to an order made under section 33 shall be construed as including a reference to an order made under section 1 of the 1983 Act, and

    (b)    any reference to an order made under section 33(5) shall be construed as including a reference to an order made under section 1 of the 1983 Act by virtue of section 2(4) of that Act.

**14**  Neither section 31(11) nor the repeal by the Matrimonial Homes and Property Act 1981 of the words 'or caution' in section 2(7) of the Matrimonial Homes Act 1967, affects any caution duly lodged as respects any estate or interest before 14th February 1983.

**15**  Nothing in this Schedule is to be taken to prejudice the operation of sections 16 and 17 of the Interpretation Act 1978 (which relate to the effect of repeals).

## SCHEDULE 10

### Repeals

| Chapter | Short title | Extent of repeal |
|---------|-------------|------------------|
| 1968 c. 63. | The Domestic and Appellate Proceedings (Restriction of Publicity) Act 1968. | Section 2(1)(b). |
| 1973 c. 18. | The Matrimonial Causes Act 1973. | Sections 1 to 7.<br>In section 8(1)(b), the words 'or before the decree nisi is made absolute'.<br>Sections 9 and 10.<br>Sections 17 and 18.<br>Section 20.<br>Section 22.<br>In section 24A(3), the words 'divorce or'.<br>In section 25(2)(h), the words 'in the case of proceedings for divorce or nullity of marriage,'.<br>In section 28(1), the words from 'in', in the first place where it occurs, to 'nullity of marriage' in the first place where those words occur.<br>In section 29(2), the words from 'may begin' to 'but'.<br>In section 30, the words 'divorce' and 'or judicial separation'.<br>In section 31, in subsection (2)(a), the words 'order for maintenance pending suit and any'.<br>In section 41, in subsection (1) the words 'divorce or' and 'or a decree of judicial separation' and in subsection (2) the words 'divorce or' and 'or that the decree of judicial separation is not to be granted.'<br>Section 49.<br>In section 52(2)(b), the words 'to orders for maintenance pending suit and', 'respectively' and 'section 22 and'.<br>In Schedule 1, paragraph 8. |
| 1973 c. 45. | The Domicile and Matrimonial Proceedings Act 1973. | In section 5, in subsection (1), the words 'subject to section 6(3) and (4) of this Act' and, in paragraph (a), 'divorce, |

| Chapter | Short title | Extent of repeal |
|---------|-------------|------------------|
| | | judicial separation or' and sub-section (2). Section 6(3) and (4). In Schedule 1, in paragraph 11, in sub-paragraph (2)(a), in sub-paragraph (2)(c), in the first place where they occur, and in sub-paragraph (3)(b) and (c), the words 'in connection with the stayed proceedings'. |
| 1976 c. 50. | The Domestic Violence and Matrimonial Proceedings Act 1976. | The whole Act. |
| 1978 c. 22. | The Domestic Proceedings and Magistrates' Courts Act 1978. | In section 1, paragraphs (c) and (d) and the word 'or' preceding paragraph (c). In section 7(1), the words 'neither party having deserted the other'. Sections 16 to 18. Section 28(2). Section 63(3). In Schedule 2, paragraphs 38 and 53. |
| 1980 c. 43. | The Magistrates' Courts Act 1980. | In Schedule 7, paragraph 159. |
| 1981 c. 54. | The Supreme Court Act 1981. | In section 18(1)(d), the words 'divorce or'. |
| 1982 c. 53. | The Administration of Justice Act 1982. | Section 16. |
| 1983 c. 19. | The Matrimonial Homes Act 1983. | The whole Act. |
| 1984 c. 42. | The Matrimonial and Family Proceedings Act 1984. | Section 1. In section 21(f) the words 'except subsection (2)(e) and subsection (4)'. In section 27, the definition of 'secured periodical payments order'. In Schedule 1, paragraph 10. |
| 1985 c. 61. | The Administration of Justice Act 1985. | In section 34(2), paragraph (f) and the word 'and' immediately preceding it. |

| Chapter | Short title | Extent of repeal |
|---|---|---|
| | | In Schedule 2, in paragraph 37, paragraph (e) and the word 'and' immediately preceding it. |
| 1985 c. 71. | The Housing (Consequential Provisions) Act 1985. | In Schedule 2, paragraph 56. |
| 1986 c. 53. | The Building Societies Act 1986. | In Schedule 21, paragraph 9(f). |
| 1986 c. 55. | The Family Law Act 1986. | In Schedule 1, paragraph 27. |
| 1988 c. 34. | The Legal Aid Act 1988. | In section 16(9), the word 'and' at the end of paragraph (a). |
| 1988 c. 50. | The Housing Act 1988. | In Schedule 17, paragraphs 33 and 34. |
| 1989 c. 41. | The Children Act 1989. | Section 8(4)(c) and (f). In Schedule 11, paragraph 6(b). In Schedule 13, paragraphs 33(1) and 65(1). |
| 1990 c. 41. | The Courts and Legal Services Act 1990. | Section 58(10)(b) and (e). In Schedule 18, paragraph 21. |
| 1995 c. 42. | The Private International Law (Miscellaneous Provisions) Act 1995. | In the Schedule, paragraph 3. |

# Protection from Harassment Act 1997
## (1997 c. 40)

### ARRANGEMENT OF SECTIONS

*England and Wales*

*An Act to make provision for protecting persons from harassment and similar conduct*
[21st March 1997]

*England and Wales*

## 1 Prohibition of harassment

(1) A person must not pursue a course of conduct—

  (a)   which amounts to harassment of another, and
  (b)   which he knows or ought to know amounts to harassment of the other.

(2) For the purposes of this section, the person whose course of conduct is in question ought to know that it amounts to harassment of another if a reasonable person in possession of the same information would think the course of conduct amounted to harassment of the other.

(3) Subsection (1) does not apply to a course of conduct if the person who pursued it shows—

  (a)   that it was pursued for the purpose of preventing or detecting crime,
  (b)   that it was pursued under any enactment or rule of law or to comply with any condition or requirement imposed by any person under any enactment, or

    (c)    that in the particular circumstances the pursuit of the course of conduct was reasonable.

## 2 Offence of harassment

(1) A person who pursues a course of conduct in breach of section 1 is guilty of an offence.

(2) A person guilty of an offence under this section is liable on summary conviction to imprisonment for a term not exceeding six months, or a fine not exceeding level 5 on the standard scale, or both.

(3) In section 24(2) of the Police and Criminal Evidence Act 1984 (arrestable offences), after paragraph (m) there is inserted—

    '(n)    an offence under section 2 of the Protection from Harassment Act 1997 (harassment).'.

## 3 Civil remedy

(1) An actual or apprehended breach of section 1 may be the subject of a claim in civil proceedings by the person who is or may be the victim of the course of conduct in question.

(2) On such a claim, damages may be awarded for (among other things) any anxiety caused by the harassment and any financial loss resulting from the harassment.

(3) Where—

    (a)    in such proceedings the High Court or a county court grants an injunction for the purpose of restraining the defendant from pursuing any conduct which amounts to harassment, and

    (b)    the plaintiff considers that the defendant has done anything which he is prohibited from doing by the injunction,

the plaintiff may apply for the issue of a warrant for the arrest of the defendant.

(4) An application under subsection (3) may be made—

    (a)    where the injunction was granted by the High Court, to a judge of that court, and

    (b)    where the injunction was granted by a county court, to a judge or district judge of that or any other county court.

(5) The judge or district judge to whom an application under subsection (3) is made may only issue a warrant if—

    (a)    the application is substantiated on oath, and

    (b)    the judge or district judge has reasonable grounds for believing that the defendant has done anything which he is prohibited from doing by the injunction.

(6) Where—

    (a)    the High Court or a county court grants an injunction for the purpose mentioned in subsection (3)(a), and

(b)   without reasonable excuse the defendant does anything which he is prohibited from doing by the injunction,

he is guilty of an offence.

(7) Where a person is convicted of an offence under subsection (6) in respect of any conduct, that conduct is not punishable as a contempt of court.

(8) A person cannot be convicted of an offence under subsection (6) in respect of any conduct which has been punished as a contempt of court.

(9) A person guilty of an offence under subsection (6) is liable—

(a)   on conviction on indictment, to imprisonment for a term not exceeding five years, or a fine, or both, or

(b)   on summary conviction, to imprisonment for a term not exceeding six months, or a fine not exceeding the statutory maximum, or both.

## 4 Putting people in fear of violence

(1) A person whose course of conduct causes another to fear, on at least two occasions, that violence will be used against him is guilty of an offence if he knows or ought to know that his course of conduct will cause the other so to fear on each of those occasions.

(2) For the purposes of this section, the person whose course of conduct is in question ought to know that it will cause another to fear that violence will be used against him on any occasion if a reasonable person in possession of the same information would think the course of conduct would cause the other so to fear on that occasion.

(3) It is a defence for a person charged with an offence under this section to show that—

(a)   his course of conduct was pursued for the purpose of preventing or detecting crime,

(b)   his course of conduct was pursued under any enactment or rule of law or to comply with any condition or requirement imposed by any person under any enactment, or

(c)   the pursuit of his course of conduct was reasonable for the protection of himself or another or for the protection of his or another's property.

(4) A person guilty of an offence under this section is liable—

(a)   on conviction on indictment, to imprisonment for a term not exceeding five years, or a fine, or both, or

(b)   on summary conviction, to imprisonment for a term not exceeding six months, or a fine not exceeding the statutory maximum, or both.

(5) If on the trial on indictment of a person charged with an offence under this section the jury find him not guilty of the offence charged, they may find him guilty of an offence under section 2.

(6) The Crown Court has the same powers and duties in relation to a person who is by virtue of subsection (5) convicted before it of an offence under section 2 as a magistrates' court would have on convicting him of the offence.

## 5  Restraining orders

(1) A court sentencing or otherwise dealing with a person ('the defendant') convicted of an offence under section 2 or 4 may (as well as sentencing him or dealing with him in any other way) make an order under this section.

(2) The order may, for the purpose of protecting the victim of the offence, or any other person mentioned in the order, from further conduct which—

- (a)  amounts to harassment, or
- (b)  will cause a fear of violence,

prohibit the defendant from doing anything described in the order.

(3) The order may have effect for a specified period or until further order.

(4) The prosecutor, the defendant or any other person mentioned in the order may apply to the court which made the order for it to be varied or discharged by a further order.

(5) If without reasonable excuse the defendant does anything which he is prohibited from doing by an order under this section, he is guilty of an offence.

(6) A person guilty of an offence under this section is liable—

- (a)  on conviction on indictment, to imprisonment for a term not exceeding five years, or a fine, or both, or
- (b)  on summary conviction, to imprisonment for a term not exceeding six months, or a fine not exceeding the statutory maximum, or both.

## 6  Limitation

In section 11 of the Limitation Act 1980 (special time limit for actions in respect of personal injuries), after subsection (1) there is inserted—

'(1A) This section does not apply to any action brought for damages under section 3 of the Protection from Harassment Act 1997.'

## 7  Interpretation of this group of sections

(1) This section applies for the interpretation of sections 1 to 5.

(2) References to harassing a person include alarming the person or causing the person distress.

(3) A 'course of conduct' must involve conduct on at least two occasions.

(4) 'Conduct' includes speech.

*General*

## 12  National security, etc.

(1) If the Secretary of State certifies that in his opinion anything done by a specified person on a specified occasion related to—

- (a)  national security,
- (b)  the economic well-being of the United Kingdom, or
- (c)  the prevention or detection of serious crime,

and was done on behalf of the Crown, the certificate is conclusive evidence that this Act does not apply to any conduct of that person on that occasion.

(2) In subsection (1), 'specified' means specified in the certificate in question.

(3) A document purporting to be a certificate under subsection (1) is to be received in evidence and, unless the contrary is proved, be treated as being such a certificate.

## 13 Corresponding provision for Northern Ireland

An Order in Council made under paragraph 1(1)(b) of Schedule 1 to the Northern Ireland Act 1974 which contains a statement that it is made only for purposes corresponding to those of sections 1 to 7 and 12 of this Act—

   (a)   shall not be subject to sub-paragraphs (4) and (5) of paragraph 1 of that Schedule (affirmative resolution of both Houses of Parliament), but

   (b)   shall be subject to annulment in pursuance of a resolution of either House of Parliament.

## 14 Extent

(1) Sections 1 to 7 extend to England and Wales only.

(2) Sections 8 to 11 extend to Scotland only.

(3) This Act (except section 13) does not extend to Northern Ireland.

## 15 Commencement

(1) Sections 1, 2, 4, 5 and 7 to 12 are to come into force on such day as the Secretary of State may by order made by statutory instrument appoint.

(2) Sections 3 and 6 are to come into force on such day as the Lord Chancellor may by order made by statutory instrument appoint.

(3) Different days may be appointed under this section fo different purposes.

## 16 Short title

This Act may be cited as the Protection from Harassment Act 1997.

# APPENDIX II

## STATUTORY INSTRUMENTS

# Family Proceedings (Amendment No 3) Rules 1997 (SI 1997/1893)

## 1   Citation, commencement and interpretation

(1) These Rules may be cited as the Family Proceedings (Amendment No 3) Rules 1997 and shall come into force on 1st October 1997.

(2) In these Rules, a rule referred to by number means the rule so numbered in the Family Proceedings Rules 1991 and a reference to Appendix 1 is a reference to Appendix 1 to those Rules.

**2** For rules 3.8, 3.9 and 3.10, there shall be substituted the following—

### '3.8   Applications under Part IV of the Family Law Act 1996 (Family Homes and Domestic Violence)

(1) An application for an occupation order or a non-molestation order under Part IV of the Family Law Act 1996 shall be made in Form FL401.

(2) An application for an occupation order or a non-molestation order made by a child under the age of sixteen shall be made in Form FL401 but shall be treated, in the first instance, as an application to the High Court for leave.

(3) An application for an occupation order or a non-molestation order which is made in other proceedings which are pending shall be made in Form FL401.

(4) An application in Form FL401 shall be supported by a statement which is signed by the applicant and is sworn to be true.

(5) Where an application is made without giving notice, the sworn statement shall state the reasons why notice was not given.

(6) An application made on notice (together with the sworn statement and a notice in Form FL402) shall be served by the applicant on the respondent personally not less than 2 days before the date on which the application will be heard.

(7) The court may abridge the period specified in paragaph (6).

(8) Where the applicant is acting in person, service of the application shall be effected by the court if the applicant so requests.
   This does not affect the court's power to order substituted service.

(9) Where an application for an occupation order or a non-molestation order is pending, the court shall consider (on the application of either party or of its own motion) whether to exercise its powers to transfer the hearing of that application to another court and shall make an order for transfer in Form FL417 if it seems necessary or expedient to do so.

(10) Rule 9.2A shall not apply to an application for an occupation order or a non-molestation order under Part IV of the Family Law Act 1996.

(11) A copy of an application for an occupation order under section 33, 35 or 36 of the Family Law Act 1996 shall be served by the applicant by first-class post on the mortgagee or, as the case may be, the landlord of the dwelling-house in question, with a notice in Form FL416 informing him of his right to make representations in writing or at any hearing.

(12) Where the application is for the transfer of a tenancy, notice of the application shall be served by the applicant on the other cohabitant or spouse and on the landlord (as those terms are defined by paragraph 1 of Schedule 7 to the Family Law Act 1996) and any person so served shall be entitled to be heard on the application.

(13) Rules 2.62(4) to (6) and 2.63 (investigation, requests for further information) shall apply, with the necessary modifications, to

  (a)  an application for an occupation order under section 3, 35 or 36 of the Family Law Act 1996, and
  (b)  an application for the transfer of a tenancy,

as they apply to an application for ancillary relief.

(14) Rule 3.6(7) to (9) (Married Women's Property Act 1882) shall apply, with the necessary modifications, to an application for the transfer of a tenancy, as they apply to an application under rule 3.6.

(15) The applicant shall file a statement in Form FL415 after he has served the application.

### 3.9  Hearing of applications under Part IV of the Family Law Act 1996

(1) An application for an occupation order or a non-molestation order under Part IV of the Family Law Act 1996 shall be dealt with in chambers unless the court otherwise directs.

(2) Where an order is made on an application made ex parte, a copy of the order together with a copy of the application and of the sworn statement in support shall be served by the applicant on the respondent personally.

(3) Where the application is for an occupation order under section 33, 35 or 36 of the Family Law Act 1996, a copy of any order made on the application shall be served by the applicant by first-class post on the mortgagee or, as the case may be, the landlord of the dwelling-house in question.

(4) A copy of an order made on an application heard inter partes shall be served by the applicant on the respondent personally.

(5) Where the applicant is acting in person, service of a copy of any order made on the hearing of the application shall be effected by the court if the applicant so requests.

(6) The following forms shall be used in connection with hearings of applications under Part IV of the Family Law Act 1996—

  (a)  a record of the hearing shall be made on Form FL405, and

(b)   any order made on the hearing shall be issued in Form FL404.

(7) The court may direct that a further hearing be held in order to consider any representations made by a mortgagee or a landlord.

(8) An application to vary, extend or discharge an order made under Part IV of the Family Law Act 1996 shall be made in Form FL403 and this rule shall apply to the hearing of such an application.

### 3.9A   Enforcement of orders made on applications under Part IV of the Family Law Act 1996

(1) Where a power of arrest is attached to one or more of the provisions ("the relevant provisions") of an order made under Part IV of the Family Law Act 1996—

(a)   the relevant provisions shall be set out in Form FL406 and the form shall not include any provisions of the order to which the power of arrest was not attached; and

(b)   a copy of the form shall be delivered to the officer for the time being in charge of any police station for the applicant's address or of such other police station as the court may specify.

The copy of the form delivered under sub-paragraph (b) shall be accompanied by a statement showing that the respondent has been served with the order or informed of its terms (whether by being present when the order was made or by telephone or otherwise).

(2) Where an order is made varying or discharging the relevant provisions, the proper officer shall—

(a)   immediately inform the officer who received a copy of the form under paragraph (1) and, if the applicant's address has changed, the officer for the time being in charge of the police station for the new address; and

(b)   deliver a copy of the order to any officer so informed.

(3) An application for the issue of a warrant for the arrest of the respondent shall be made in Form FL407 and the warrant shall be issued in Form FL408.

(4) The court before whom a person is brought following his arrest may—

(a)   determine whether the facts, and the circumstances which led to the arrest, amounted to disobedience of the order, or

(b)   adjourn the proceedings and, where such an order is made, the arrested person may be released and—

(i)    be dealt with within 14 days of the day on which he was arrested; and

(ii)   be given not less than 2 days' notice of the adjourned hearing.

Nothing in this paragraph shall prevent the issue of a notice under CCR Order 29, rule 1(4) if the arrested person is not dealt with within the period mentioned in sub-paragraph (b)(i) above.

(5) The following provisions shall apply, with the necessary modifications, to the enforcement of orders made on applications under Part IV of the Family Law Act 1996—

(a)    RSC Order 52, rule 7 (power to suspend execution of committal order);
(b)    (in a case where an application for an order of committal is made to the High Court) RSC Order 52, rule 2 (application for leave);
(c)    CCR Order 29, rule 1 (committal for breach of order);
(d)    CCR Order 29, rule 1A (undertakings);
(e)    CCR Order 29, rule 3 (discharge of person in custody);

and CCR Order 29, rule 1 shall have effect, as if for paragraph (3), there were substituted the following—

"(3) At the time when the order is drawn up, the proper officer shall—

(a)    where the order made is (or includes) a non-molestation order and
(b)    where the order made is an occupation order and the court so directs,

issue a copy of the order, indorsed with or incorporating a notice as to the consequences of disobedience, for service in accordance with paragraph (2).".

(6) The court may adjourn consideration of the penalty to be imposed for contempts found proved and such consideration may be restored if the respondent does not comply with any conditions specified by the court.

(7) Where the court makes a hospital order in Form FL413 or a guardianship order in Form FL414 under the Mental Health Act 1983, the proper officer shall

(a)    send to the hospital any information which will be of assistance in dealing with the patient;
(b)    inform the applicant when the respondent is being transferred to hospital.

(8) Where a transfer direction given by the Secretary of State under section 48 of the Mental Health Act 1983 is in force in respect of a person remanded in custody by the court under Schedule 5 to the Family Law Act 1996, the proper officer shall notify—

(a)    the governor of the prison to which that person was remanded; and
(b)    the hospital where he is detained,

of any committal hearing which that person is required to attend and the proper officer shall give notice in writing to the hospital where that person is detained of any further remand under paragraph 3 of Schedule 5 to the Family Law Act 1996.

(9) An order for the remand of the respondent shall be in Form FL409.

(10) In paragraph (4) "arrest" means arrest under a power of arrest attached to an order or under a warrant of arrest.

### 3.10    Applications under Part IV of the Family Law Act 1996: bail

(1) An application for bail made by a person arrested under a power of arrest or a warrant of arrest may be made either orally or in writing.

(2) Where an application is made in writing, it shall contain the following particulars—

   (a)   the full name of the person making the application;

   (b)   the address of the place where the person making the application is detained at the time when the application is made;

   (c)   the address where the person making the application would reside if he were to be granted bail;

   (d)   the amount of the recognizance in which he would agree to be bound; and

   (e)   the grounds on which the application is made and, where a previous application has been refused, full particulars of any change in circumstances which has occurred since that refusal.

(3) An application made in writing shall be signed by the person making the application or by a person duly authorised by him in that behalf or, where the person making the application is a minor or is for any reason incapable of acting, by a guardian ad litem acting on his behalf and a copy shall be served by the person making the application on the applicant for the Part IV order.

(4) The persons prescribed for the purposes of paragraph 4 of Schedule 5 to the Family Law Act 1996 (postponement of taking of recognizance) are

   (a)   a district judge,

   (b)   a justice of the peace,

   (c)   a justices' clerk,

   (d)   a police officer of the rank of inspector or above or in charge of a police station, and

   (e)   (where the person making the application is in his custody) the governor or keeper of a prison.

(5) The person having custody of the person making the application shall—

   (a)   on receipt of a certificate signed by or on behaf of the district judge stating that the recognizance of any sureties required have been taken, or on being otherwise satisfied that all such recognizances have been taken; and

   (b)   on being satisfied that the person making the application has entered into his recognizance,

release the person making the application.

(6) The following forms shall be used:

   (a)   the recognizance of the person making the application shall be in Form FL410 and that of a surety in Form FL411;

   (b)   a bail notice in Form FL412 shall be given to the respondent where he is remanded on bail.'.

**3** (1) Rule 4.24 shall stand as paragraph (1) of that rule and shall be amended by inserting, as sub-paragraph (b), the following—

'(b) section 38A(2)(b)(ii) or 44A(2)(b)(ii), or'.

(2) After rule 4.24(1), there shall be inserted the following—

'(2) Any written consent given for the purposes of subsection (2) of section 38A or section 44A, shall include a statement that the person giving consent—

   (a)   is able and willing to give to the child the care which it would be reasonable to expect a parent to give him; and

(b)  understands that the giving of consent could lead to the exclusion of the relevant person from the dwelling-house in which the child lives.'.

**4** After rule 4.24, there shall be inserted the following new rule—

### '4.24A    Exclusion requirements: interim care orders and emergency protection orders

(1) This rule applies where the court includes an exclusion requirement in an interim care order or an emergency protection order.

(2) The applicant for an interim care order or emergency protection order shall

(a)  prepare a separate statement of the evidence in support of the application for an exclusion requirement;

(b)  serve the statement personally on the relevant person with a copy of the order containing the exclusion requirement (and of any power of arrest which is attached to it);

(c)  inform the relevant person of his right to apply to vary or discharge the exclusion requirement.

(3) Where a power of arrest is attached to an exclusion requirement in an interim care order or an emergency protection order, a copy of the order shall be delivered to the officer for the time being in charge of the police station for the area in which the dwelling-house in which the child lives is situated (or of such other station as the court may specify) together with a statement showing that the relevant person has been served with the order or informed of its terms (whether by being present when the order was made or by telephone or otherwise).

(4) Rules 3.9(5), 3.9A (except paragraphs (1) and (3)) and 3.10 shall apply, with the necessary modifications, for the service, variation, discharge and enforcement of any exclusion requirement to which a power of arrest is attached as they apply to an order made on an application under Part IV of the Family Law Act 1996.

(5) The relevant person shall serve the parties to the proceedings with any application which he makes for the variation or discharge of the exclusion requirement.

(6) Where an exclusion requirement ceases to have effect whether—

(a)  as a result of the removal of a child under section 38A(10) or 44A(10),

(b)  because of the discharge of the interim care order or emergency protection order, or

(c)  otherwise,

the applicant shall inform—

(i)  the relevant person,

(ii)  the parties to the proceedings,

(iii)  any officer to whom a copy of the order was delivered under paragraph (3), and

(iv)  (where necessary) the court.

(7) Where the court includes an exclusion requirement in an interim care order or an emergency protection order of its own motion, paragraph (2) shall apply with the omission of any reference to the statement of the evidence.'.

**5** After Rule 7.2(3) there shall be inserted the following new paragraph—

'(3A) Where an order or warrant for the arrest or committal of any person has been made or issued in proceedings under Part IV of the Family Law Act 1996 pending in the principal registry which are treated as pending in a county court, the order or warrant may, if the court so directs, be executed by the tipstaff within any county court district.'.

**6** Rule 8.1(2)(b) shall be amended by substituting for ', 3.6 or 3.8', 'or 3.6'.

**7** After rule 8.1, there shall be inserted the following new rule—

**'8.1A    Appeals from orders made under Part IV of the Family Law Act 1996**

(1) This rule applies to all appeals from orders made under Part IV of the Family Law Act 1996 and on such an appeal—

    (a)   paragraphs (2), (3), (4), (5), (7) and (8) of rule 4.22,

    (b)   paragraphs (5) and (6) of rule 8.1, and

    (c)   paragraphs (4)(e) and (6) of rule 8.2,

shall apply subject to the following provisions of this rule and with the necessary modifications.

(2) The justices' clerk of the magistrates' court from which an appeal is brought shall be served with the documents mentioned in rule 4.22(2).

(3) Where an appeal lies to the High Court, the documents required to be filed by rule 4.22(2) shall be filed in the registry of the High Court which is nearest to the magistrates' court from which the appeal is brought.

(4) Where the appeal is brought against the making of a hospital order or a guardianship order under the Mental Health Act 1983, a copy of any written evidence considered by the magistrates' court under section 37(1)(a) of the 1983 Act shall be sent by the justices' clerk to the registry of the High Court in which the documents relating to the appeal are filed in accordance with paragraph (3).

(5) A district judge may dismiss an appeal to which this rule applies for want of prosecution and may deal with any question of costs arising out of the dismissal or withdrawal of an appeal.

(6) Any order or decision granting or varying an order (or refusing to do so) in proceedings in which an application is made in accordance with rule 3.8 for

    (a)   an occupation order as described in section 33(4) of the Family Law Act 1996,

    (b)   an occupation order containing any of the provisions specified in section 33(3) where the applicant or the respondent has matrimonial home rights, or

    (c)   a transfer of tenancy,

shall be treated as a final order for the purposes of CCR Order 37, rule 6 and, on an appeal from such an order, the judge may exercise his own discretion in substitution for that of the district judge and the provisions of CCR Order 37, rule 6 shall apply.'.

**8** In Appendix 1—

(a) at the end of the list of forms, there shall be inserted the list of forms set out in Schedule 1 to these Rules; and

(b) the forms set out in Schedule 2 to these Rules shall be inserted at the end of Appendix 1.

**9** Subject to paragraph 10(3) of Schedule 9 to the Family Law Act 1996, rules 2 to 8 shall not apply to proceedings commenced before Part IV of that Act came into force.

## 10   Miscellaneous amendments

After rule 2.9(6) there shall be inserted the following new paragraph—

'(6A) Paragraph (6) shall not apply in cases where—

(a) the petition alleges two years' separation coupled with the respondent's consent to a decree being granted; and

(b) none of the other facts mentioned in section 1(2) of the Act of 1973 is alleged

unless the petitioner produces to the court a written statement containing the respondent's consent to the grant of a decree.'.

**11** Rule 2.29 shall be amended by substituting, for the words 'CCR Order 20, rule 18' in both places where they occur, the words 'CCR Order 20, rule 13'.

**12** Rule 2.36(4) shall be amended by inserting, after the words 'evidence filed under rule 2.24(3)', the words '(except the statement of arrangements)'.

**13** After rule 2.40(2) there shall be inserted the following new paragraph—

'(3) A cause shall be treated as pending for the purposes of this rule for a period of one year after the last hearing or judicial intervention in the cause and rule 1.2(2) shall not apply.'.

**14** Rule 3.13(5) shall be amended by substituting, for the words 'in Form M26', the words 'in Form M30'.

**15** Rule 4.27(1) shall be amended by substituting, for the words 'in Form C37', the words 'in writing'.

**16** Rule 6.2(1) shall be amended by inserting, at the end, the words 'and issued out of the principal registry'.

**17** (1) Rule 7.2(3) shall be amended by inserting, after the words 'divorce county court', the words 'or a county court' and by substituting, for the words 'a judge', the words 'the court'.

(2) Rule 7.2(4) shall be amended by inserting, after the words 'Royal Courts of Justice', the words 'or the principal registry'.

**18** Rule 7.20(3) shall be amended by substituting, for the words 'under section 2(2)', the words 'under section 21(2)'.

**19** After rule 9.2A(6) there shall be inserted the following new paragraph—

'(6A) In exercising its powers under paragraph (6) the court may order the next friend or guardian ad litem to take such part in the proceedings as the court may direct.'.

**20** Form M18 shall be omitted from Appendix 1.

# Family Proceedings Courts (Matrimonial Proceedings etc) (Amendment) Rules 1997 (SI 1997/1894)

## 1   Citation, commencement and interpretation

(1) These Rules may be cited as the Family Proceedings Courts (Matrimonial Proceedings etc) (Amendment) Rules 1997 and shall come into force on 1st October 1997.

(2) The Family Proceedings Courts (Matrimonial Proceedings etc) Rules 1991 shall be amended in accordance with the following provisions of these Rules and, in those provisions, any reference to a rule by number alone shall be construed as a reference to the rule so numbered in the said Rules of 1991.

**2** The heading to Part II shall be amended by inserting at the end 'AND PROCEEDINGS UNDER PART IV OF THE FAMILY LAW ACT 1996'.

**3** Rule 2(1) shall be amended—

(a) by inserting, in the definition of 'application' after the words 'the Act', the words 'or, as the case may be, the Family Law Act 1996';

(b) by omitting, in the definition of 'court', the words '(save where section 16(5) of the Act applies)';

(c) by omitting the definition of 'family protection order'; and

(d) by substituting, for the definition of 'form', the following—

'"form" means a form in Schedule 1 to these Rules and, where a form is referred to by number, means the form so numbered in that Schedule, with such variation as the circumstances of the particular case may require;'.

**4** Rule 2(2) shall be amended by inserting at the end 'or, as the case may be, in the Family Law Act 1996'.

**5** Rule 3(1) shall be amended by substituting, for the words 'Subject to paragraphs (3) and (4),', the words 'Subject to paragraph (3) and rule 3A,'.

**6** Rule 3(1)(b) shall be amended by omitting the words 'save where section 16(6) of the Act applies,' and 'and, in the case of an application under section 16, at least one day,'.

**7** Rule 3(2)(a) shall be amended by omitting the words 'which in the case of an application under section 16 shall be no later than 14 days after receipt of the application'.

**8** Rule 3(2)(c) and (4) shall be omitted.

**9** After rule 3, there shall be inserted the following new rule—

### '3A   Applications under Part IV of the Family Law Act 1996

(1) An application for an occupation order or a non-molestation order under Part IV of the Family Law Act 1996 (Family Homes and Domestic Violence) shall be made in Form FL401.

(2) An application for an occupation order or a non-molestation order which is made in other proceedings which are pending shall be made in Form FL401.

(3) An application in Form FL401 shall be supported—

   (a)   by a statement which is signed and is declared to be true; or
   (b)   with the leave of the court, by oral evidence.

(4) An application in Form FL401 may, with the leave of the justices' clerk or of the court, be made ex parte, in which case

   (a)   the applicant shall file with the justices' clerk or the court the application at the time when the application is made or as directed by the justices' clerk; and
   (b)   the evidence in support of the application shall state the reasons why the application is made ex parte.

(5) An application made on notice (together with any statement supporting it and a notice in Form FL402) shall be served by the applicant on the respondent personally not less than 2 business days prior to the date on which the application will be heard.

(6) The court or the justices' clerk may abridge the period specified in paragraph (5).

(7) Where the applicant is acting in person, service of the application may, with the leave of the justices' clerk, be effected in accordance with rule 4.

(8) Where an application for an occupation order or a non-molestation order is pending, the court shall consider (on the application of either party or of its own motion) whether to exercise its powers to transfer the hearing of that application to another court and the justices' clerk or the court shall make an order for transfer in Form FL417 if it seems necessary or expedient to do so.

(9) Where an order for transfer is made, the justices' clerk shall send a copy of the order—

   (a)   to the parties, and
   (b)   to the family proceedings court or to the county court to which the proceedings are to be transferred.

(10) A copy of an application for an occupation order under section 33, 35 or 36 of the Family Law Act 1996 shall be served by the applicant by first-class post on the mortgagee or, as the case may be, the landlord of the dwelling-house in question, with a notice in Form FL416 informing him of his right to make representations in writing or at any hearing.

(11) The applicant shall file a statement in Form FL415 after he has served the application.

(12) Rule 33A of the Family Proceedings Courts (Children Act 1989) Rules 1991(a) (disclosure of addresses) shall apply for the purpose of preventing the

disclosure of addresses where an application is made in Form FL401 as it applies for that purpose in proceedings under the Children Act 1989.'.

**10** Rule 4(4) shall be amended by omitting the words 'Save where section 16(6) of the Act applies,'.

**11** Rules 7(4), 7(5)(a), 9(1), 10(1), 12(3), 12(4), 13(1), 14 and 16(2) shall be amended by omitting the words 'under the Act'.

**12** Rule 8(2) shall be amended by omitting the words 'Without prejudice to section 16(6) of the Act, and'.

**13** Rule 11 shall be amended by substituting, for the words 'proceedings under the Act', the words 'any proceedings'.

**14** After rule 12, there shall be inserted the following new rules—

### '12A   Hearing of applications under Part IV of the Family Law Act 1996

(1) This rule applies to the hearing of applications under the Part IV of the Family Law Act 1996 and the following forms shall be used in connection with such hearings:

    (a)   a record of the hearing shall be made on Form FL405, and
    (b)   any order made on the hearing shall be issued in Form FL404.

(2) Where an order is made on an application made ex parte, a copy of the order together with a copy of the application and of any statement supporting it shall be served by the applicant on the respondent personally.

(3) Where the applicant is acting in person, service of a copy of an order made on an application made ex parte shall be effected by the justices' clerk if the applicant so requests.

(4) Where the application is for an occupation order under section 33, 35 or 36 of the Family Law Act 1996, a copy of any order made on the application shall be served by the applicant by first-class post on the mortgagee or, as the case may be, the landlord of the dwelling-house in question.

(5) A copy of an order made on an application heard inter partes shall be served by the applicant on the respondent personally.

(6) Where the applicant is acting in person, service of a copy of the order made on an application heard inter partes may, with the leave of the justices' clerk, be effected in accordance with rule 4.

(7) The court may direct that a further hearing be held in order to consider any representations made by a mortgagee or a landlord.

### 12B   Applications to vary etc orders made under Part IV of the Family Law Act 1996

An application to vary, extend or discharge an order made under Part IV of the Family Law Act 1996 shall be made in Form FL403 and rules 12 and 12A shall apply to the hearing of such an application.'.

**15** For rules 20 and 21, there shall be substituted the following—

### '20   Enforcement of orders made on applications under Part IV of the Family Law Act 1996

(1) Where a power of arrest is attached to one or more of the provisions ("the relevant provisions") of an order made under Part IV of the Family Law Act 1996—

    (a)   the relevant provisions shall be set out in Form FL406 and the form shall not include any provisions of the order to which the power of arrest was not attached; and

    (b)   a copy of the form shall be delivered to the officer for the time being in charge of any police station for the applicant's address or of such other police station as the court may specify.

The copy of the form delivered under sub-paragraph (b) shall be accompanied by a statement showing that the respondent has been served with the order or informed of its terms (whether by being present when the order was made or by telephone or otherwise).

(2) Where an order is made varying or discharging the relevant provisions, the justices' clerk shall—

    (a)   immediately inform the officer who received a copy of the form under paragraph (1) and, if the applicant's address has changed, the officer for the time being in charge of the police station for the new address; and

    (b)   deliver a copy of the order to any officer so informed.

(3) An application for the issue of a warrant for the arrest of the respondent shall be made in Form FL407 and the warrant shall be issued in Form FL408 and delivered by the justices' clerk to the officer for the time being in charge of any police station for the respondent's address or of such other police station as the court may specify.

(4) The court before whom a person is brought following his arrest may—

    (a)   determine whether the facts, and the circumstances which led to the arrest, amounted to disobedience of the order, or

    (b)   adjourn the proceedings and, where such an order is made, the arrested person may be released and

        (i)   be dealt with within 14 days of the day on which he was arrested; and

        (ii)  be given not less than 2 business days' notice of the adjourned hearing.

Nothing in this paragraph shall prevent the issue of a notice under paragraph (8) if the arrested person is not dealt with within the period mentioned in sub-paragraph (b)(i) above.

(5) Paragraphs (6) to (13) shall apply for the enforcement of orders made on applications under Part IV of the Family Law Act 1996 by committal order.

(6) Subject to paragraphs (11) and (12), an order shall not be enforced by committal order unless

    (a)   a copy of the order in Form FL404 has been served personally on the respondent; and

(b)  where the order requires the respondent to do an act, the copy has been so served before the expiration of the time within which he was required to do the act and was accompanied by a copy of any order, made between the date of the order and the date of service, fixing that time.

(7) At the time when the order is drawn up, the justices' clerk shall—

(a)  where the order made is (or includes) a non-molestation order, and
(b)  where the order made is an occupation order and the court so directs,

issue a copy of the order, indorsed with or incorporating a notice as to the consequences of disobedience, for service in accordance with paragraph (6).

(8) If the respondent fails to obey the order, the justices' clerk shall, at the request of the applicant, issue a notice in Form FL418 warning the respondent that an application will be made for him to be committed and, subject to paragraph (12), the notice shall be served on him personally.

(9) The request for issue of the notice under paragraph (8) shall be treated as a complaint and shall

(a)  identify the provisions of the order or undertaking which it is alleged have been disobeyed or broken;
(b)  list the ways in which it is alleged that the order or undertaking has been disobeyed or broken;
(c)  be supported by a statement which is signed and is declared to be true and which states the grounds on which the application is made,

and, unless service is dispensed with under paragraph (12), a copy of the statement shall be served with the notice.

(10) If an order in Form FL419 (a committal order) is made, it shall include provision for the issue of a warrant of committal in Form FL420 and, unless the court otherwise orders—

(a)  a copy of the order shall be served personally on the person to be committed either before or at the time of the execution of the warrant; or
(b)  the order for the issue of the warrant may be served on the person to be committed at any time within 36 hours after the execution of the warrant.

(11) An order requiring a person to abstain from doing an act may be enforced by committal order notwithstanding that a copy of the order has not been served personally if the court is satisfied that, pending such service, the respondent had notice thereof either—

(a)  by being present when the order was made;
(b)  by being notified of the terms of the order whether by telephone or otherwise.

(12) The court may dispense with service of a copy of the order under paragraph (6) or a notice under paragraph (8) if the court thinks it just to do so.

(13) Where service of a notice to show cause is dispensed with under paragraph (12) and a committal order is made, the court may of its own motion fix a date and time when the person to be committed is to be brought before the court.

(14) Paragraphs (6) to (10), (12) and (13) shall apply to the enforcement of undertakings with the necessary modifications and as if

(a)    for paragraph (6) there were substituted the following—
"(6) A copy of Form FL422 recording the undertaking shall be delivered by the justices' clerk to the party giving the undertaking

(a)    by handing a copy of the document to him before he leaves the court building; or
(b)    where his place of residence is known, by posting a copy to him at his place of residence; or
(c)    through his solicitor,

and, where delivery cannot be effected in this way, the justices' clerk shall deliver a copy of the document to the party for whose benefit the undertaking is given and that party shall cause it to be served personally as soon as is practicable.";
(b)    in paragraph (12), the words from "a copy" to "paragraph (6) or" were omitted.

(15) Where a person in custody under a warrant or order, desires to apply to the court for his discharge, he shall make his application in writing attested by the governor of the prison showing that he has purged or is desirous of purging his contempt and the justices' clerk shall, not less than one day before the application is heard, serve notice of it on the party (if any) at whose instance the warrant or order was issued.

(16) The court by whom an order of committal is made may by order direct that the execution of the order of committal shall be suspended for such period or on such terms or conditions as it may specify.

(17) Where execution of an order of committal is suspended by an order under paragraph (16), the applicant for the order of committal must, unless the court otherwise directs, serve on the person against whom it was made a notice informing him of the making and terms of the order under that paragraph.

(18) The court may adjourn consideration of the penalty to be imposed for contempts found proved and such consideration may be restored if the respondent does not comply with any conditions specified by the court.

(19) Where the court makes a hospital order in Form FL413 or a guardianship order in Form FL414 under the Mental Health Act 1983(a), the justices' clerk shall—

(a)    send to the hospital any information which will be of assistance in dealing with the patient;
(b)    inform the applicant when the respondent is being transferred to hospital.

(20) Where a transfer direction given by the Secretary of State under section 48 of the Mental Health Act 1983 is in force in respect of a person remanded in custody by the court, the justices' clerk shall notify—

(a)    the governor of the prison to which that person was remanded; and

(b)   the hospital where he is detained,

of any committal hearing which that person is required to attend and the justices' clerk shall give notice in writing to the hospital where that person is detained of any further remand.

(21) An order for the remand of the respondent shall be in Form FL409 and an order discharging the respondent from custody shall be in Form FL421.

(22) In paragraph (4) "arrest" means arrest under a power of arrest attached to an order or under a warrant of arrest.

### 21   Applications under Part IV of the Family Law Act 1996: bail

(1) An application for bail made by a person arrested under a power of arrest or a warrant of arrest may be made either orally or in writing.

(2) Where an application is made in writing, it shall contain the following particulars—

(a)   the full name of the person making the application;
(b)   the address of the place where the person making the application is detained at the time when the application is made;
(c)   the address where the person making the application would reside if he were to be granted bail;
(d)   the amount of the recognizance in which he would agree to be bound; and
(e)   the grounds on which the application is made and, where a previous application has been refused, full particulars of any change in circumstances which has occurred since that refusal.

(3) An application made in writing shall be signed by the person making the application or by a person duly authorised by him in that behalf or, where the person making the application is a minor or is for any reason incapable of acting, by a guardian ad litem acting on his behalf and a copy shall be served by the person making the application on the applicant for the Part IV order.

(4) The following forms shall be used:

(a)   the recognizance of the person making the application shall be in Form FL410 and that of a surety in Form FL411;
(b)   a bail notice in Form FL412 shall be given to the respondent where he is remanded on bail.'.

**16** For rule 24 there shall be substituted the following—

### '24   Setting aside on failure of service

Where an application has been sent to a respondent in accordance with rule 4(1) and, after an order has been made on the application, it appears to the court that the application did not come to the knowledge of the respondent in due time, the court may of its own motion set aside the order and may give such directions as it thinks fit for the rehearing of the application.'.

**17** For rule 25 there shall be substituted the following—

**'25   Proceedings with respect to which a single justice may discharge the functions of a court**

The following proceedings are prescribed as proceedings with respect to which a single justice may discharge the functions of a court, that is to say, proceedings—

(a)   in which an application is made ex parte for an occupation order or a non-molestation order under Part IV of the Family Law Act 1996;

(b)   in accordance with rules 3, 3A(2), (6) and (8), 4, 6 (except paragraph (2)), 7 to 14 and 20(4).'.

**18** In Schedule 1—

(a)   forms MAT 8, 10, 11, 12 and 13 shall be omitted; and

(b)   at the end there shall be inserted the list of forms in Schedule 1 to these Rules and the forms in Schedule 2 to these Rules.

**19** Subject to paragraph 10(3) of Schedule 9 to the Family Law Act 1996, rules 2 to 15, 17 and 18 shall not apply to proceedings commenced before Part IV of that Act came into force.

# Family Law Act 1996 (Part IV) (Allocation of Proceedings) Order 1997 (SI 1997/1896)

1—(1) This Order may be cited as the Family Law Act 1996 (Part IV) (Allocation of Proceedings) Order 1997 and shall come into force on 1st October 1997.

(2) In this Order, unless the context otherwise requires—

'county court' means a county court of one of the classes specified in article 2;

'family proceedings' has the meaning assigned by section 63 and includes proceedings which are family business within the meaning of section 32 of the Matrimonial and Family Proceedings Act 1984;

'family proceedings court' has the meaning assigned by article 3;

'the Act' means the Family Law Act 1996 and a section, Part or Schedule referred to by number alone means the section, Part or Schedule so numbered in that Act.

## 2 Classes of county court

The classes of county court specified for the purposes of this Order are—

(a) divorce county courts, being those courts designated for the time being as divorce county courts by an order under section 33 of the Matrimonial and Family Proceedings Act 1984;

(b) family hearing centres, being those courts set out in Schedule 1 to the Children (Allocation of Proceedings) Order 1991; and

(c) care centres, being those courts set out in column (ii) of Schedule 2 to that Order.

## 3 Classes of magistrates' court

The classes of magistrates' court specified for the purpose of this order are family proceedings courts, being those courts constituted in accordance with section 67 of the Magistrates' Courts Act 1980.

## 4 Commencement of proceedings

(1) Subject to section 59, paragraph 1 of Schedule 7 and the provisions of this article, proceedings under Part IV may be commenced in a county court or in a family proceedings court.

(2) An application—

(a) under Part IV brought by an applicant who is under the age of eighteen; and

(b) for the grant of leave under section 43 (Leave of court required for applications by children under sixteen),

shall be commenced in the High Court.

(3) Where family proceedings are pending in a county court or a family proceedings court, an application under Part IV may be made in those proceedings.

## 5 Application to extend, vary or discharge order

(1) Proceedings under Part IV—

- (a)   to extend, vary or discharge an order, or
- (b)   the determination of which may have the effect of varying or discharging an order, shall be made to the court which made the order.

(2) A court may transfer proceedings made in accordance with paragraph (1) to any other court in accordance with the provisions of articles 6 to 14.

## TRANSFER OF PROCEEDINGS

## 6 Disapplication of enactments about transfer

Sections 38 and 39 of the Matrimonial and Family Proceedings Act 1984 shall not apply to proceedings under Part IV.

## 7 Transfer from one family proceedings court to another

A family proceedings court ("the transferring court") shall (on application or of its own motion) transfer proceedings under Part IV to another family proceedings court ("the receiving court") where—

- (a)   the transferring court considers that it would be appropriate for those proceedings to be heard together with other family proceedings which are pending in the receiving court; and
- (b)   the receiving court, by its justices' clerk (as defined by rule 1(2) of the Family Proceedings Courts (Children Act 1989) Rules 1991), consents to the transfer.

## 8 Transfer from family proceedings court to county court

(1) A family proceedings court may, on application or of its own motion, transfer proceedings under Part IV to a county court where it considers that—

- (a)   it would be appropriate for those proceedings to be heard together with other family proceedings which are pending in that court; or
- (b)   the proceedings involve—
  - (i)     a conflict with the law of another jurisdiction;
  - (ii)    some novel and difficult point of law;
  - (iii)   some question of general public interest; or
- (c)   the proceedings are exceptionally complex.

(2) A family proceedings court must transfer proceedings under Part IV to a county court where—

- (a)   a child under the age of eighteen is the respondent to the application or wishes to become a party to the proceedings; or
- (b)   a party to the proceedings is a person who, by reason of mental disorder within the meaning of the Mental Health Act 1983, is incapable of managing and administering his property and affairs.

(3) Except where transfer is ordered under paragraph (1)(a), the proceedings shall be transferred to the nearest county court.

## 9 Transfer from family proceedings court to High Court

A family proceedings court may, on application or of its own motion, transfer proceedings under Part IV to the High Court where it considers that it would be appropriate for those proceedings to be heard together with other family proceedings, which are pending in that Court.

## 10 Transfer from one county court to another

A county court may, on application or of its own motion, transfer proceedings under Part IV to another county court where—

(a) it considers that it would be appropriate for those proceedings to be heard together with other family proceedings which are pending in that court;

(b) the proceedings involve the determination of a question of a kind mentioned in section 59(1) and the property in question is situated in the district of another county court; or

(c) it seems necessary or expedient so to do.

## 11 Transfer from county court to family proceedings court

A county court may, on application or of its own motion, transfer proceedings under Part IV to a family proceedings court where—

(a) it considers that it would be appropriate for those proceedings to be heard together with other family proceedings which are pending in that court; or

(b) it considers that the criterion

    (i) in article 8(1)(a) no longer applies because the proceedings with which the transferred proceedings were to be heard have been determined;

    (b) in article 8(1)(b) or (c) does not apply.

## 12 Transfer from county court to High Court

A county court may, on application or of its own motion, transfer proceedings under Part IV to the High Court where it considers that the proceedings are appropriate for determination in the High Court.

## 13 Transfer from High Court to family proceedings court

The High Court may, on application or of its own motion, transfer proceedings under Part IV to a family proceedings court where it considers that it would be appropriate for those proceedings to be heard together with other family proceedings which are pending in that court.

## 14 Transfer from High Court to county court

The High Court may, on application or of its own motion, transfer proceedings under Part IV to a county court where it considers that—

(a) it would be appropriate for those proceedings to be heard together with other family proceedings which are pending in that court;

(b) the proceedings are appropriate for determination in a county court; or

(c) it is appropriate for an application made by a child under the age of eighteen to be heard in a county court.

### 15  Disposal following arrest

Where a person is brought before—

    (a)   a relevant judicial authority in accordance with section 47(7)(a), or

    (b)   a court by virtue of a warrant issued under section 47(9),

and the matter is not disposed of forthwith, the matter may be transferred to be disposed of by the relevant judicial authority or court which issued the warrant or, as the case may be, which attached the power to arrest under section 47(2) or (3), if different.

## MISCELLANEOUS

### 16  Principal Registry of the Family Division

(1) The principal registry of the Family Division of the High Court shall be treated, for the purposes of this Order, as if it were a divorce county court, a family hearing centre and a care centre.

(2) Without prejudice to article 10, the principal registry may transfer an order made in proceedings which are pending in the principal registry to the High Court for enforcement.

### 17  Lambeth, Shoreditch and Woolwich County Courts

Proceedings under Part IV may be commenced in, transferred to and tried in Lambeth, Shoreditch or Woolwich County Court.

### 18  Contravention of provisions of this Order

Where proceedings are commenced or transferred in contravention of a provision of this Order, the contravention shall not have the effect of making the proceedings invalid.

# APPENDIX III

## FORMS

## Application for:
## a non-molestation order
## an occupation order

*Family Law Act 1996 (Part IV)*

**The court**

To be completed by the court

Date issued

Case number

### 1  About you (the applicant)

State your title (Mr, Mrs etc), full name, address,
telephone number and date of birth (if under 18):

State your solicitor's name, address, reference,
telephone, FAX and DX numbers:

### 2  About the respondent

State the respondent's name, address and date of
birth (if known):

### 3  The Order(s) for which you are applying

This application is for:

☐   a non-molestation order

☐   an occupation order

☐   Tick this box if you wish the court to hear your
application without notice being given to the
respondent. The reasons relied on for an
application being heard without notice must be
stated in the statement in support.

## 4　Your relationship to the respondent (the person to be served with this application)

Your relationship to the respondent is:
*Please tick only one of the following*

1 ☐　Married

2 ☐　Were married

3 ☐　Cohabiting

4 ☐　Were cohabiting

5 ☐　Both of you live or have lived in the same household

6 ☐　Relative
　　　State how related:

7 ☐　Agreed to marry.
　　　Give the date the agreement was made. If the agreement has ended, state when.

8 ☐　Both of you are parents of or have parental responsibility for a child

9 ☐　One of you is a parent of a child and the other has parental responsibility for that child

10 ☐ One of you is the natural parent or
grandparent of a child adopted or freed for
adoption, and the other is:
   (i)  the adoptive parent
or (ii)  a person who has applied for an
       adoption order for the child
or (iii)  a person with whom the child has
       been placed for adoption
or (iv)  the child who has been adopted or
       freed for adoption.
State whether (i), (ii), (iii) or (iv):

11 ☐ Both of you are parties to the same family
proceedings (see also Section 11 below).

## 5    Application for a non-molestation order

If you wish to apply for a non-molestation order,
state briefly in this section the order you want.

Give full details in support of your application in
your sworn evidence

## 6    Application for an occupation order

*If you do not wish to apply for an occupation
order, please go to section 9 of this form.*

(A)  State the address of the dwelling-house to which
your application relates:

(B)  State whether it is occupied by you or the
respondent now or in the past, or whether it was
intended to be occupied by you or the respondent:

(C) State whether you are entitled to occupy the dwelling-house:    ☐ Yes    ☐ No

If yes, explain why:

(D) State whether the respondent is entitled to occupy the dwelling-house:    ☐ Yes    ☐ No

If yes, explain why:

**On the basis of your answer to (C) and (D) above, tick one of the boxes 1 to 5 below to show the category into which you fit**

1 ☐    a spouse who has matrimonial home rights in the dwelling-house, or a person who is entitled to occupy it by virtue of a beneficial estate or interest or contract or by virtue of any enactment giving him or her the right to remain in occupation.

If you tick box 1, state whether there is a dispute or pending proceedings between you and the respondent about your right to occupy the dwelling-house.

2 ☐    a former spouse with no existing right to occupy, where the respondent spouse is entitled.

3 ☐    a cohabitant or former cohabitant with no existing right to occupy, where the respondent cohabitant or former cohabitant is so entitled.

4 ☐    a spouse or former spouse who is not entitled to occupy, where the respondent spouse or former spouse is also not entitled.

5 ☐    a cohabitant or former cohabitant who is not entitled to occupy, where the respondent cohabitant or former cohabitant is also not entitled.

**Matrimonial Home Rights**

If you do have matrimonial home rights please:
State whether the title to the land is registered or
unregistered (if known):

If registered, state the Land Registry title number (if
known):

**If you wish to apply for an occupation order,
state briefly here the order you want.** Give full
details in support of your application in your sworn
evidence.

## 7 Application for additional order(s) about the dwelling-house

If you want to apply for any of the orders listed in
the notes to this section, state what order you would
like the court to make:

## 8 Mortgage and rent

Is the dwelling-house subject to a mortgage?

☐ Yes ☐ No

If yes, please provide the name and address of the
mortgagee:

Is the dwelling-house rented?

☐ Yes ☐ No

If yes, please provide the name and address of the
landlord:

**9 At the court**

State whether you will need an interpreter at court
(parties are responsible for providing their own):
If so, specify the language.

If you need disabled facilities at court please tell the
court in advance

**10 Other information**

State the name and date of birth of any child living
with or staying with, or likely to live with or stay
with, you or the respondent:

State the name of any other person living in the
same household as you and the respondent, and say
why they live there:

**11 Other Proceedings and Orders**

If there are any other current family proceedings or
orders in force involving you and the respondent,
state the type of proceedings or orders, the court
and the case number. This includes any application
for an occupation order or non-molestation order
against you by the respondent.

**This application is to be served upon the respondent**

Signed             Date

# Application for a non-molestation order or occupation order
## Notes for Guidance

## Section 1

***If you are under 18, someone over 18 must help you make this application.*** *That person, who might be one of your parents, is called a 'next friend'.*

***If you are under 16 you need permission to make this application.*** *You must apply to the High Court for permission, using this form. If the High Court gives you permission to make this application, it will then either hear the application itself or transfer it to a county court.*

***If you do not wish your address to be made known to the respondent,*** *leave the space on the form blank and complete Confidential Address Form C8. The court can give you this form.*

## Section 3

*An urgent order made by the court before notice of the application is served on the respondent is called an ex-parte order. In deciding whether to make an ex-parte order the court will consider all the circumstances of the case, including:*

■ *any risk of significant harm to the applicant or a relevant child, attributable to conduct of the respondent, if the order is not made immediately.*

■ *whether it is likely that the applicant will be deterred or prevented from pursuing the application if an order is not made immediately*

■ *whether there is reason to believe that the respondent is aware of the proceedings but is deliberately evading service and that the applicant or a relevant child will be seriously prejudiced by the delay involved.*

*If the court makes an ex-parte order, it must give the respondent an opportunity to make representations about the order as soon as just and convenient at a full hearing.*

*'Harm' in relation to a person who has reached the age of 18 means ill-treatment or the impairment of health, and in relation to a child means ill-treatment or the impairment of health and development. 'Ill-treatment' includes forms of ill-treatment which are not physical and, in relation to a child, includes sexual abuse. The court will require evidence of any harm which you allege in support of your application. This evidence should be included in the statement accompanying this application.*

## Section 4

*For you to be able to apply for an order you must be related to the respondent in one of the ways listed in this section of the form. If you are not related in one of these ways you should seek legal advice.*

***Cohabitants*** *are a man and a woman who, although not married to each other, are living or have lived together as husband and wife. People who have cohabited, but have then married will not fall within this category, but will fall within the category of married people.*

***Those who live or have lived in the same household*** *do not include people who share the same household because one of them is the other's employee, tenant, lodger or boarder.*

***You will only be able to apply as a relative of the respondent if you are:***

*(A) the father, mother, stepfather, stepmother, son, daughter, stepson, stepdaughter, grandmother, grandfather, grandson or granddaughter of the respondent or of the respondent's spouse or former spouse.*

*(B) the brother, sister, uncle, aunt, niece or nephew (whether of the full blood or of the half blood or by marriage) of the respondent or of the respondent's spouse or former spouse.*

*This includes, in relation to a person who is living or has lived with another person as husband and wife, any person who would fall within (A) or (B) if the parties were married to each other (for example, your cohabitee's father or brother).*

***Agreements to marry:*** *You will fall within this category only if you make this application within three years of the termination of the agreement. The court will require the following evidence of the agreement:*

*evidence in writing*

***or*** *the gift of an engagement ring in contemplation of marriage*

***or*** *evidence that a ceremony has been entered into in the presence of one or more other persons assembled for the purpose of witnessing it.*

***Parents and parental responsibility:*** *You will fall within this category if*

*both you and the respondent are either the parents of a child or have parental responsibility for that child*

***or*** *if one of you is the parent and the other has parental responsibility.*

## Section 4 (continued)

*Under the Children Act 1989, parental responsibility is held automatically by a child's mother, and by the child's father if he and the mother were married to each other at the time of the child's birth or have married subsequently. Where this is not the case, parental responsibility can be acquired by the father in accordance with the provisions of the Children Act 1989.*

## Section 5

*A non-molestation order can forbid the respondent to molest you or a relevant child. Molestation can include, for example, violence, threats, pestering and other forms of harassment. The court can forbid particular acts of the respondent, molestation in general, or both.*

## Section 6

**If you wish to apply for an occupation order but you are uncertain about your answer to any of the questions in this part of the application form, you should seek legal advice.**

**(A)**   *A dwelling-house includes any building or part of a building which is occupied as a dwelling: any caravan, houseboat or structure which is occupied as a dwelling: and any yard, garden, garage or outhouse belonging to it and occupied with it.*

**(C) & (D)** *The following questions give examples to help you to decide if you or the respondent, or both of you, are entitled to occupy the dwelling-house:*

*(a)   Are you the sole legal owner of the dwelling-house?*

*(b)   Are you and the respondent joint legal owners of the dwelling-house?*

*(c)   Is the respondent the sole legal owner of the dwelling-house?*

*(d)   Do you rent the dwelling-house as sole tenant?*

*(e)   Do you and the respondent rent the dwelling-house as joint tenants?*

*(f)   Does the respondent rent the dwelling-house as sole tenant?*

*If you answer* ■ **Yes** *to (a), (b), (d) or (e) you are likely to be entitled to occupy the dwelling-house*

■ **Yes** *to (c) or (f) you may not be entitled (unless, for example, you are a spouse and have matrimonial home rights – see the notes under 'Matrimonial Home Rights' below)*

■ **Yes** *to (b), (c), (e) or (f), the respondent is likely to be entitled to occupy the dwelling-house.*

■ **Yes** *to (a) or (d) the respondent may not be entitled (unless, for example, he is a spouse and has matrimonial home rights).*

**Box 1** *For example, if you are sole owner, joint owner, or if you rent the property. If you are not a spouse, former spouse, cohabitant or former cohabitant of the respondent, you will only be able to apply for an occupation order if you fall within this category.*

*If you answer* **Yes** *to this question, it will not be possible for a magistrates' court to deal with the application, unless the court decides that it is unnecessary for it to decide this question in order to deal with the application or make an order. If the court decides that it cannot deal with the application, it will transfer the application to a county court.*

**Box 2** *For example, if the respondent was married to you and is sole owner or rents the property.*

**Box 3** *For example, if the respondent is or was cohabiting with you and is sole owner or rents the property.*

**Matrimonial Home Rights**

*Where one spouse is entitled to occupy the dwelling-house by virtue of a beneficial estate or interest or contract or by virtue of any enactment giving him or her the right to remain in occupation, and the other spouse is not so entitled, the spouse who is not entitled has matrimonial home rights. These are a right, if the spouse is in occupation, not to be evicted or excluded from the dwelling-house except with the leave of the court and, if the spouse is not in occupation, the right with the leave of the court to enter into and occupy the dwelling-house.*

*Matrimonial home rights do not exist if the dwelling-house has never been, and was never intended to be, the matrimonial home of the two spouses. If the marriage has come to an end, matrimonial home rights will also have ceased, unless a court order has been made during the marriage for the rights to continue after the end of the marriage.*

**Occupation Orders** *The possible orders are:*

**If you have ticked box 1 above,** *an order under section 33 of the Act may:*

■ *enforce the applicant's entitlement to remain in occupation as against the respondent.*

## Section 6 (continued)

- require the respondent to permit the applicant to enter and remain in the dwelling-house or part of it
- regulate the occupation of the dwelling-house by either or both parties
- if the respondent is also entitled to occupy, the order may prohibit, suspend or restrict the exercise by him, of that right
- restrict or terminate any matrimonial home rights of the respondent
- require the respondent to leave the dwelling-house or part of it
- exclude the respondent from a defined area around the dwelling-house
- declare that the applicant is entitled to occupy the dwelling-house or has matrimonial home rights in it
- provide that matrimonial home rights of the applicant are not brought to an end by the death of the other spouse or termination of the marriage.

**If you have ticked box 2 or box 3 above,** an order under section 35 or 36 of the Act may:

- give the applicant the right not to be evicted or excluded from the dwelling-house or any part of it by the respondent for a specified period
- prohibit the respondent from evicting or excluding the applicant during that period
- give the applicant the right to enter and occupy the dwelling-house for a specified period
- require the respondent to permit the exercise of that right
- regulate the occupation of the dwelling-house by either or both of the parties
- prohibit, suspend or restrict the exercise by the respondent of his right to occupy
- require the respondent to leave the dwelling-house or part of it
- exclude the respondent from a defined area around the dwelling-house.

**If you have ticked box 4 or box 5 above,** an order under section 37 or 38 of the Act may:

- require the respondent to permit the applicant to enter and remain in the dwelling-house or part of it
- regulate the occupation of the dwelling-house by either or both of the parties
- require the respondents to leave the dwelling-house or part of it
- exclude the respondent from a defined area around the dwelling-house.

*You should provide any evidence which you have on the following matters in your evidence in support of this application. If necessary, further statements may be submitted after the application has been issued.*

**If you have ticked box 1, 4 or 5 above,** the court will need any available evidence of the following:

- the housing needs and resources of you, the respondent and any relevant child
- the financial resources of you and the respondent
- the likely effect of any order, or of any decision not to make an order, on the health, safety and well-being of you, the respondent and any relevant child
- the conduct of you and the respondent in relation to each other and otherwise.

**If you have ticked box 2 above,** the court will need any available evidence of:

- the housing needs and resources of you, the respondent and relevant child
- the financial resources of you and the respondent
- the likely effect of any order, or of any decision not to make an order on the health, safety and well-being of you, the respondent and any relevant child
- the conduct of you and the respondent in relation to each other and otherwise
- the length of time that has elapsed since you and the respondent ceased to live together
- the length of time that has elapsed since the marriage was dissolved or annulled
- the existence of any pending proceedings between you and the respondent:

  under section 23A of the Matrimonial Causes Act 1973 (property adjustment orders in connection with divorce proceedings etc.)

  **or** under Schedule 1 para 1(2)(d) or (e) of the Children Act 1989 (orders for financial relief against parents)

  **or** relating to the legal or beneficial ownership of the dwelling-house.

**If you have ticked box 3 above,** the court will need any available evidence of:

- the housing needs and resources of you, the respondent and any relevant child
- the financial resources of you and the respondent

## Section 6 (continued)

- the likely effect of any order, or of any decision not to make an order, on the health, safety and well-being of you, the respondent and any relevant child
- the conduct of you and the respondent in relation to each other and otherwise
- the nature of you and the respondent's relationship
- the length of time during which you have lived together as husband and wife
- whether you and the respondent have had any children, or have both had parental responsibility for any children
- the length of time which has elapsed since you and the respondent ceased to live together
- the existence of any pending proceedings between you and the respondent under Schedule 1 para 1(2)(d) or (e) of the Children Act 1989 or relating to the legal or beneficial ownership of the dwelling-house.

## Section 7

*Under section 40 of the Act the court may make the following additional orders when making an occupation order:*

- impose on either party obligations as to the repair and maintenance of the dwelling-house
- impose on either party obligations as to the payment of rent, mortgage or other outgoings affecting it

- order a party occupying the dwelling-house to make periodical payments to the other party in respect of the accommodation, if the other party would (but for the order) be entitled to occupy it
- grant either party possession or use of furniture or other contents
- order either party to take reasonable care of any furniture or other contents
- order either party to take reasonable steps to keep the dwelling-house and any furniture or other contents secure.

## Section 8

*If the dwelling-house is rented or subject to a mortgage, the landlord or mortgagee must be served with notice of the proceedings in Form FL416. He or she will then be able to make representations to the court regarding the rent or mortgage.*

## Section 10

*A person living in the same household may, for example, be a member of the family or a tenant or employee of you or the respondent.*

In the

Case Number

| | | | |
|---|---|---|---|
| [Order] | [Direction] | Sheet | of |
| | Family Law Act 1996 | | |

In the

Case Number

---

[Order]    [Direction]                    Sheet    of

Family Law Act 1996

---

Ordered by    [Mr] [Mrs] Justice
              [His] [Her] Honour Judge
              [Deputy] District Judge [of the Family Division]
              Justice[s] of the Peace
              [Assistant] Recorder
              Clerk of the Court

on

# Orders under Family Law Act 1996 Part IV

*(General heading followed by Notice A **or** Notice B and numbered options as appropriate)*

*Notice A – order includes non-molestation order – penal notice mandatory*

**Important Notice to the Respondent [name]**

**This order gives you instructions which you must follow. You should read it all carefully. If you do not understand anything in this order you should go to a solicitor, Legal Advice Centre or Citizens Advice Bureau. You have a right to ask the court to change or cancel the order but you must obey it unless the court does change or cancel it.**

**You must obey the instructions contained in this order. If you do not, you will be guilty of contempt of court, and you may be sent to prison.**

*Notice B – order does not include non-molestation order – \*penal notice discretionary*

**Important Notice to the Respondent [name]**

**This order gives you instructions which you must follow. You should read it all carefully. If you do not understand anything in this order you should go to a solicitor, Legal Advice Centre or Citizens Advice Bureau. You have a right to ask the court to change or cancel the order but you must obey it unless the court does change or cancel it.**

**You must obey the instructions contained in this order. \*[If you do not, you will be guilty of contempt of court, and you may be sent to prison.]**

## Occupation orders under s33 of the Family Law Act 1996

1.   The court declares that the applicant [name] is entitled to occupy [*address of home or intended home*] as [*his/her*] home. **OR**

2.   The court declares that the applicant [name] has matrimonial home rights in [*address of home or intended home*]. **AND/OR**

3.   The court declares that the applicant [name]'s matrimonial home rights shall not end when the respondent [name] dies or their marriage is dissolved and shall continue until ....................................... or further order.

**It is ordered that:**

4.   The respondent [name] shall allow the applicant [name] to occupy [*address of home or intended home*] **OR**

5.   The respondent [name] shall allow the applicant [name] to occupy part of [*address of home or intended home*] namely: [*specify part*]

6.   The respondent [name] shall not obstruct, harass or interfere with the applicant [name]'s peaceful occupation of [*address of home or intended home*]

7.   The respondent [name] shall not occupy [*address of home or intended home*] **OR**

8.   The respondent [name] shall not occupy [*address of home or intended home*] from [*specify date*] until [*specify date*] **OR**

9.   The respondent [name] shall not occupy [*specify part of address of home or intended home*] **AND/OR**

10.   The respondent [name] shall not occupy [*address or part of address*] between [*specify date or times*]

11.   The respondent [name] shall leave [*address or part of address*] [forthwith] [within _____ [*hours/days*] of service on [*him/her*] of this order.] **AND/OR**

12.   Having left [*address or part of address*], the respondent [name] shall not return to, enter or attempt to enter [or go within [*specify distance*] of] it.

## Occupation orders under ss35 & 36 of the Family Law Act 1996

**It is ordered that**

13.   The applicant [name] has the right to occupy [*address of home or intended home*] and the respondent [name] shall allow the applicant [name] to do so. **OR**

14.   The respondent [name] shall not evict or exclude the applicant [name] from [*address of home or intended home*] or any part of it namely [*specify part*]. **AND/OR**

15.   The respondent [name] shall not occupy [*address of home or intended home*]. **OR**

16.   The respondent [name] shall not occupy [*address of home or intended home*] from [*specify date*] until [*specify date*] **OR**

17.   The respondent [name] shall not occupy [*specify part of address of home or intended home*] **OR**

18. The respondent [name] shall leave [*address or part of address*] [forthwith] [within _____ [*hours/days*] of service on [*him/her*] of this order.] **AND/OR**

19. Having left [*address or part of address*], the respondent [name] shall not return to, enter or attempt to enter [or go within [*specify distance*] of] it.

## Occupation orders under ss37 & 38 of the Family Law Act 1996

**It is ordered that**

20. The respondent [name] shall allow the applicant [name] to occupy [*address of home or intended home*] or part of it namely: [*specify*]. **AND/OR**

21. [One or both of the provisions in paragraphs 6 & 10 above may be inserted] **AND/OR**

22. The respondent [name] shall leave [*address or part of address*] [forthwith] [within _____ [*hours/days*] of service on [*him/her*] of this order]. **AND/OR**

23. Having left [*address or part of address*], the respondent [name] may not return to, enter or attempt to enter [or go within [*specify distance*] of] it.

## Additional provisions which may be included in occupation orders made under ss33, 35 or 36 of the Family Law Act 1996

**It is ordered that**

24. The [*applicant [name]*] [*respondent [name]*] shall maintain and repair [*address of home or intended home*] **AND/OR**

25. The [*applicant [name]*] [*respondent [name]*] shall pay the rent for [*address of home or intended home*]. **OR**

26. The [*applicant [name]*] [*respondent [name]*] shall pay the mortgage payments on [*address of home or intended home*]. **OR**

27. The [*applicant [name]*] [*respondent [name]*] shall pay the following for [*address of home or intended home*]: [*specify outgoings as bullet points*].

28. The [*party in occupation*] shall pay to the [*other party*] £ each [*week, month, etc*] for [*address of home etc*].

29. The [*party in occupation*] shall keep and use the [*furniture*] [*contents*] [*specify if necessary*] of [*address of home or intended home*] and the [*applicant [name]*] [*respondent [name]*] shall return to the [*party in occupation*] the [*furniture*] [*contents*] [*specify if necessary*] [*no later than [date/time]*].

30. The [*party in occupation*] shall take reasonable care of the [*furniture*] [*contents*] [*specify if necessary*] of [*address of home or intended home*].

31. The [*party in occupation*] shall take all reasonable steps to keep secure [*address of home or intended home*] and the furniture or other contents [*specify if necessary*].

## Duration

### Occupation orders under ss33 of the Family Law Act 1996

32.    This order shall last until [*specify event or date*]  **OR**

33.    This order shall last until a further order is made.

### Occupation orders under ss35 & 37 of the Family Law Act 1996

34.    This order shall last until [*state date which must not be more than 6 months from the date of this order*].

35.    The occupation order made on [*state date*] is extended until [*state date which must not be more than 6 months from the date of this extension*].

### Occupation orders under ss36 & 38 of the Family Law Act 1996

36.    This order shall last until [*state date which must not be more than 6 months from the date of this order*].

37.    The occupation order made on [*state date*] is extended until [*state date which must not be more than 6 months from the date of this extension*] and must end on that date.

## Non-molestation orders

**It is ordered that**

38.    The respondent [name] is forbidden to use or threaten violence against the applicant [name] [and must not instruct, encourage or in any way suggest that any other person should do so].  **AND/OR**

39.    The respondent [name] is forbidden to intimidate, harass or pester [*or [specify]*] the applicant [name] [and must not instruct, encourage or in any way suggest that any other person should do so].  **AND/OR**

40.    The respondent [name] is forbidden to use or threaten violence against the relevant child(ren) [name(s) and date(s) of birth] [and must not instruct, encourage or in any way suggest that any other person should so so].  **AND/OR**

41.    The respondent [name] is forbidden to intimidate, harass or pester [*or [specify]*] [the relevant child(ren) [name(s) and date(s) of birth] [and must not instruct, encourage or in any way suggest that any other person should do so].

# INDEX

**References are to paragraph numbers.**